Kinship and Rituals among the Meo of Northern India

French Studies in South Asian Culture and Society

Louis Dumont
A South Indian Subcaste
Social Organization and Religion of the Pramalai Kallar

Madeleine Biardeau
Hinduism
The Anthropology of a Civilzation

Olivier Guillaume (editor and compiler)
Graeco-Bactrian and Indian Coins from Afghanistan
Analysis of Reasonings in Archaeology

Jean Deloche
Transport and Communications in India Prior to Steam Locomotion
Volume 1 Land Transport
Volume 2 Water Transport

Gerard Heuze
Workers of Another World
Miners, the Countryside and Coalfields in Dhanbad

Phillippe Sagant
The Dozing Shaman
The Limbus of Eastern Nepal

Charles Malamoud
Cooking the World
Ritual and Thought in Ancient India

Jacques Pouchepadass
Champaran and Gandhi
Planters, Peasants and Gandhian Politics

French Studies in South Asian Culture and Society

Kinship and Rituals among the Meo of Northern India
Locating Sibling Relationship

RAYMOND JAMOUS

Translated from the French
by
NORA SCOTT

OXFORD
UNIVERSITY PRESS

YMCA Library Building, Jai Singh Road, New Delhi 110 001

Oxford University Press is a department of the University of Oxford.
It furthers the University's objective of excellence in research, scholarship,
and education by publishing worldwide in

Oxford New York
Auckland Bangkok Buenos Aires Cape Town Chennai
Dar es Salaam Delhi Hong Kong Istanbul Karachi Kolkata
Kuala Lumpur Madrid Melbourne Mexico City Mumbai Nairobi
Sao Paulo Shanghai Taipei Tokyo Toronto

Oxford is a registered trademark of Oxford University Press
in the UK and in certain other countries

Published in India
By Oxford University Press, New Delhi

© Oxford University Press 2003

The moral rights of the author have been asserted
Database right Oxford University Press (maker)
First published 2003

All rights reserved. No part of this publication may be reproduced,
stored in a retrieval system, or transmitted, in any form or by any means,
without the prior permission in writing of Oxford University Press,
or as expressly permitted by law, or under terms agreed with the appropriate
reprographics rights organization. Enquiries concerning reproduction
outside the scope of the above should be sent to the Rights Department,
Oxford University Press, at the address above

You must not circulate this book in any other binding or cover and you must
impose this same condition on any acquirer

ISBN 0 19 566459 0

Typeset in Times by Eleven Arts, Keshav Puram, Delhi 110 035
Printed by Roopak Printers, Delhi 110 032
Published by Manzar Khan, Oxford University Press
YMCA Library Building, Jai Singh Road, New Delhi 110 001

In memory of my mother who taught me tradition

Do you have any sisters, Pierre?
No, I am a bachelor.

Lucette Savier, *Abecedaire*

French Studies in South Asian Culture and Society

The above series of books was conceived in the early 1980s in the course of discussions between Mr Clemens Heller, administrateur adjoint, Maison des Sciences de l'Homme (MSH), Paris, and myself. (I was member-secretary of the Indian Council of Social Science Research). It was widely acknowledged at that time that Indian social scientists were inadequately familiar with the work of their colleagues in France because not many of us were proficient in French. Their work was important not only because of its empirical content but also, indeed more significantly, because much of it was characterized by theoretical orientations that set it apart from Anglo-American and Indian scholarship.

Mr Heller offered to arrange and pay for the translations. Mr Ravi Dayal, former executive head of the Oxford University Press in India, undertook to publish the translated works aided by subsidies from MSH. Pursuantly, an editorial committee was set up with Jean-Claude Galey, Rajni Kothari, Charles Malamoud, Jacques Pouchepadass, Romila Thapar, and me as members.

The first book chosen for inclusion in the series was Louis Dumont's classic monographic study of a South Indian community that had remained untranslated since its publication in 1957. It was released in 1986 under the title of *A South Indian Subcaste: Social Organization and Religion of the Pramalai Kallar*. Subsequently, works by the following authors were published:

Genevieve Bouchon: 'Regent of the Sea': *Cannanore's Response to Portuguese Expansion, 1507–1528*

Madeleine Biardeau: *Hinduism: The Anthropology of a Civilization*

Olivier Guillaume: *Graeco-Bactrian and Indian Coins from Afghanistan: Analysis of Reasonings in Archaeology*

Jean Deloche: *Transport and Communication in India prior to Steam Locomotion. Vol. 1: Land Transport. Vol. 2: Water Transport*

Gérard Heuzé: *Workers of Another World: Miners, the Countryside and Coalfields in Dhanbad*

Phillipe Sagant: *The Dozing Shaman: The Limbus of Eastern Nepal*

Charles Malamoud: *Cooking the World: Ritual and Thought in Ancient India*

Jacques Pouchepadass: *Champaran and Gandhi: Planters, Peasants and Gandhian Politics*

About ten years ago Raymond Jamous's monograph on kinship and ritual with special reference to the brother–sister relationship among the Meos was taken up for translation. This took much longer than expected due to a number of reasons. Meanwhile, the programme priorities of both MSH and OUP have changed. Regrettably therefore the present volume will not be followed by any more studies: the series is now closed.

Many persons have contributed significantly to this project over the years. I would like to mention in particular: Mr François Descouyette and Mr Vincent Grimaud, successive cultural counsellors at the French embassy in Delhi during the 1980s; Professor Maurice Aymard and Dr Jean-Luc Racine at MSH; and Mr Manzar Khan at OUP. Without the support and collaboration of Dr Jean-Claude Galey the series would never have materialized. Personally, I would have liked to see the series continue but that cannot be. I do, however, wish to dedicate the set of works that comprise it to the memory of Clemens Heller, a great and generous friend of Indian social scientists.

March 2003
T.N. Madan

Emeritus Professor
Institute of Economic Growth

Acknowledgements

The present book stems from ethnographic fieldwork conducted among the Meo in October 1982–July 1983 and December 1985. The work, carried out on the framework of ongoing Franco-Indian exchanges, was funded, on the Indian side, by the Indian Council for Social Science Research and the University Grants Commission, and, on the French side, by the Maison des Sciences de l'Homme, Paris. The ERASME group of the Centre National de la Recherche Scientifique helped finance the study. I would like to thank these institutions and particularly the late Clemens Heller, who encouraged me throughout the process.

In Delhi, the friendship of T.N. Madan was a constant support during the time in the field. Our dialogues were fruitful and stimulating. I would also like to thank him for his great help concerning the translation and publication of this book. We have fond memories of his hospitality, together with that of his wife, Uma, and their children. I would also like to thank Imtiaz Ahmed, Karuna Chanana, and Gene Smith for their friendly advice.

The warm-hearted welcome and friendship of the Meo of Bisru village, as also of those in the other villages touched us deeply. I think that this sense of hospitality will appear clearly in the introduction to this book, devoted in large part to our integration into the Meo community. It was thanks to my 'brother' Abdulaziz, who was my assistant during this time, that my wife and I were able to work in the best possible conditions. To him, to my 'brother' Suleikha, who presented me with the land on which to build our house, to my 'sister' Nur Jahan, who consecrated the house, and to all my Meo kin, I would like to express my heartfelt gratitude.

My wife, Marie-Josée Pineau-Jamous was an active participant in the fieldwork and in all the stages of the present volume. In the course of long and often spirited discussions, we confronted our ideas and advanced together in the complex analysis of Meo kinship and rites. She is in a way the co-author of this book.

I would like to express particular gratitude to the late Louis Dumont, whose work lies at the root of the present study. He read different drafts of the manuscript and was kind enough to share his profound knowledge of India. Our long discussions on kinship will remain unforgettable moments for me.

Charles Malamoud's remarkable studies of the Sanskrit texts have renewed the anthropological perspective on the analysis of rites. I have taken my inspiration largely from them. He greeted my research with warm and friendly curiosity. I cannot measure the debt I owe him. Thanks also to Mark Augé for his constant support.

It was thanks to Henri Stern's enthusiasm for Rajasthan that I discovered the richness of this region. His friendship has been unfailing. Marie-Louise Reiniche gave me the opportunity to present the different aspects of my research at a seminar at the École des Hautes Études en Sciences Sociales, before an audience of Indianists. Her encouragement, the many comparisons she drew with south India were enlightening and enabled me to make significant improvements. Jean-François Guermonprez and Dominique Casajus reread different sections of this work and their pertinent remarks were a help. It was a real pleasure working with Nora Scott for the translation. I want to thank her for the excellent work she has done.

Lastly, a special word for my son Aram. At the age of ten, not only did he adapt to the daily routine of the Meo but he also found the small gestures, words, and attitudes which created a sort of 'magical' relationship between him and the people of Bisru village. I would like to thank him together with his 'brothers', Rafik, Zakir, and Zahid, and his 'sisters', Zarina, Tahira, and Anisa, whose vivaciousness illuminated our home. I also owe to my son the original computer-generated diagrams in the book.

RAYMOND JAMOUS

Contents

Illustrations and tables	xii
Introduction	1
1. The Meo: A caste and a faith	17
2. Meo kinship vocabulary	38
3. Kinship and territory	80
4. The marriage alliance	106
5. Marriage ceremonies: Ritual prestations	124
6. The Meo kinship System: A comparative view	177
Bibliography	189
Glossary	192
Index	195

Illustrations and tables

Photographs

1. Building the anthropologist's house — 3
2. Girls pay a visit to their 'paternal uncle', the anthropologist, to play with their 'brother' — 3
3. My 'brother', Suleikha, who gave me the land for my house, and his two sons — 4
4. My 'brother' and assistant Abdulaziz (in the middle) with his two nephews — 4
5. A 'brother's' daughter at the anthropologist's, before going back to her husband's village — 4
6. My 'paternal uncle' — 5
7. My 'paternal uncle's' wife setting out for a day in the fields — 8
8. Id-Ga, mosque reserved for Muslim festivals — 27
9. Tomb of a saint (*pir*) — 31
10. Group of houses belonging to close kinsmen, with grain silo and outdoor kitchen — 92
11. An old-fashioned house (wattle and thatch) — 92
12. A *tharu*, lineage house in the village of Bisru — 92
13. Men smoking a *hookah* — 97
14. *Cak pūjā*: New pots are carried back to the house — 128
15. Recording the *nota* gifts — 129
16. Giving the *bhāṭ* — 130
17. Distributing the *guṛ* to the children — 131
18. The groom receives the departure gifts or *salam* — 132
19. The candidates for circumcision are adorned like bridegrooms and receive the *salam* gifts — 133
20. The women sing before the departure of the *barāt* — 133
21. The *gorva* fee paid to the eldest member of the *barāt* — 135
22. The ceremonial food prepared by the barbers for a Meo wedding — 135
23. The ceremonial food given to the *barāt* by the groom's family — 136

24.	The groom surrounded by furniture and other objects which make up the dowry (*dān-dahej*)	138
25.	A short bargaining session over the jewellery and money in the dowry (the groom's side always demands more than is given)	138
26.	Wife's 'sisters' mock and pinch the groom	139
27.	The bride laments	139
28.	Detail of the gifts from the wife's 'sisters'	140
29.	The *samdhan*, after the *samdhī pūjā* performed on the anthropologist	159
30.	The *samdhan* hides and mocks her *samdhī* while her husband looks on amused	160

Figures

1.1	Map of Bisru village	21
2.1	Chain of brother–sister relations in Meerut (S. Vatuk)	40
2.2	Kinship terms for parents' generation	44
2.3	Affinity and kinship terms by marriage for ego's (male) generation	45
2.4	Affinity and kinship terms by marriage for ego's (female) generation	45
2.5	Relationship marriage creates between two brothers-in-law/sisters-in-law	48
2.6	Chains of two brother–sister pairs linked by a marriage	49
2.7	Chain of metasibling reciprocal terms	50
2.8	Chain of same-sex siblings/affines	51
2.9	Reciprocal terms in the siblings/affines chain	53
2.10	Properties of hierarchical opposition in the basic cell	55
2.11	Different sets of opposition	56
2.12	Sister–brother vector	59
2.13	Brother–sister vector	59
2.14	Global configuration of brother–sister chains	60
2.15	Brother–brother chain	61
2.16	Sister–sister chain	61
2.17	Metasiblings chain of relations and generation −1	64
2.18	Same-sex chain of siblings and generation −1	65

2.19	Metasiblings chain of relations and generation +1	67
2.20	Same-sex chain of relations and generation +1	68
2.21	Brother–sister and generation –2, +2	69
2.22	Same-sex siblings and generation –2, +2	70
2.23	Different uses of *bhāī* and *bahin*	71
2.24	Brother-in-law and brothers–sisters	74
3.1	Sketch map of the Mewat region, empirical division	83
3.2	Subdivision of the Chirklot clan	85
3.3	Composition of Bisseriya *thamba* with the central village Bisru surrounded by nine satellite villages	87
3.4	Structure of a typical *got-palya* village	90
4.1	Permission and prohibition of intermarriage between clans	112
4.2	Alliance between *thamba*	114
4.3	Preferential marriage in diachrony	116
4.4	Marriage alliance and kinship terminology	120
5.1	Gifts given by the father and the brother	147
5.2	Complementarity between ritual services and ceremonial prestations	153
5.3	Synchronic sequence of ritual services and ceremonial prestations	154
5.4	Asymmetrical relations between the two brother–sister chains	156
5.5	Metasiblingship chain in diachrony	156
5.6	Reciprocal terms in affinity	158
5.7	Diachronic sequence of ritual roles	162
5.8	Successive marriages and ritual roles	162
5.9	Paternal aunt with her niece	164
5.10	Marriage configurations	165

Tables

3.1	Allocation of villages to clans	81
3.2	Summary of the territorial, residential, and agnatic segmentations	93
5.1	Gifts given at two *sagāī*	143
5.2	Gifts exchanged between the two sides at marriage	145

Introduction

THE ANTHROPOLOGIST IN THE FIELD

After my field research in the Moroccan Rif,[1] I wanted to study another Muslim community, located this time outside the Arab world, one with very different institutions and traditions. Having chosen India, and after visiting several different Muslim groups, I decided to carry out an ethnographic study in the north, among the Meo, who have been Muslims for several centuries. The Meo live among Hindus of different castes and are themselves high-ranking Rājpūts. Several observers speak of a mixture of Hinduism and Islam in their representations as well as their rituals.

Although I set out to study a community having a highly original relationship with Islam, I was soon led not to give up this plan but to approach it from what was for me an altogether unexpected angle—through a detailed study of kinship as it relates to life-cycle rites. Kinship, in the Rif, comes second to politics and religion, and my informants would have found it preposterous to regard me as a relative. Among the Meo, on the other hand, some 250,000 members of the community are all related, and it was essential to study their system of kinship if I wanted to understand the internal organization of the group. All this I learned through being integrated into the kinship system. Indeed, they could not imagine communicating with me if I was not one of the community and if I did not take part in the daily and ritual activities of their kinship relations.

First contacts, my first *bhāī*

I left for Delhi with my wife, also an anthropologist, and our ten-year-old son. As soon as we arrived, I looked up Abdulaziz, a Meo man who had gone to university and held a doctorate in geography. He showed us around several villages in his home area, Mewat. Over the course of our conversations, we began to gain some familiarity with the Meo culture and its traditions, and our relations rapidly took a friendly turn.

One day as we were talking, he asked if he could consider me as a *bhāī*, a 'brother' (later on we will see the importance of this term; as a first approximation, we will note simply that Hindi makes no distinction between 'brother' and 'cousin', and among the Meo, this term is very inclusive). I said yes, but I wondered what he actually meant by this gesture. In my previous research in Morocco, as well as in Lebanon, where I grew up, I was accustomed to interpreting my informants' words at several levels. Here again I thought that this kin term merely translated friendship, but I decided to wait until I was more familiar with the Meo culture to look for other meanings behind this request.

As it turned out, I was wrong about everything. For Abdulaziz, there was nothing behind this term—I had become his *bhāī*, his 'brother'. And it would not be long before I realized it. Thanks to him, we were most warmly received in his home village, Bisru. We decided to make this our headquarters and so set out to look for a house. We were shown one in the *baniyā* merchant-caste quarter. My Meo companions followed the visit; however, they urged us not to accept this dwelling and adopted a wooden attitude I had never seen before. At my prompting, my Meo 'brother' explained the reason for their reticence: 'If you want to know the Meo, you must live with them. If you live with the *baniyā*, the Meo will consider you and your family as *baniyā*.' I replied that I wanted to live with them, but there was no place available. An elderly Meo man, who had recently added a *banglā* (male section of the house) to his stable, offered to convert it into lodgings for my family. Once again I noticed that my Meo companions were ill at ease. My 'brother' Abdulaziz gave me to understand that the old man and his family had fallen out with most of the other families in the quarter. If I accepted his offer of housing, I would be siding with him and marginalizing myself with respect to the other Meo in the quarter; no one would come to our house for tea or to talk with me. I followed his advice and politely declined the offer. Then Dr Abdulaziz's real brother, Suleikha, made me the following proposition: 'Why not build? I can let you have a piece of land across from my house.' The lot stood in the middle of one of the Meo quarters. Touched by this offer, I accepted, thinking that they would build me a simple mud-brick house known as *kaccâ*, which would not be very expensive.

Building our house: My first '*bahin*'

Until we could move into the village, a temporary solution was found—we lived in a state-owned guest house some ten kilometres from the village and each day came to visit the building site and spend the day among the Meo. Construction dragged on, however, because my 'brothers' had decided to build a hard-walled house, called *pakkā*, which was better suited to their social position in the village. One day I saw that the door frame had been set, and was about to step over the threshold when an unfamiliar woman barred my way. At my surprise, everyone broke out laughing. My 'brother' came up to me and said, 'This is your "sister", your *bahin*. She has tied the sacred thread (*kangnā*) to the top of the frame so that your new house may always prosper; you must give her *neg* (payment for a ritual service).' I gave her the sum indicated of Rs 21 (roughly three US dollars at the time). She took the money and gave part of it back to my son, Rs 5. My 'brother' explained, 'This woman is my "sister" (she was in effect his real elder sister), and since you are my "brother", she is your "sister" too; no man can build a house unless his sister comes to perform this ritual to bring it good luck and to drive misfortune away from the family.' The woman, married into another village, had arrived the night before and had tied the thread at dawn. An unmarried 'sister' could not perform the ritual in her stead. Moreover, it was absolutely necessary to pay her for this ritual service. I was impressed by this 'sister's' forceful personality and by the respect shown her by her 'brothers', especially her real brothers. She did not have to give the money she did to my son, but in doing so, she was showing her fondness for the family of her new 'brother'.

Building the anthropologist's house

I had just taken my first steps in the Meo kinship system. To have a 'brother' is also to have a 'sister'. Furthermore, the 'brother'–'sister' relationship is unidirectional—the married sister is supposed to provide a ritual service, thus fulfilling her function as officiant, and her 'brother' is supposed to give her a ritual fee.

Moving in and people we met

Our new house was completed and we moved in. The first day, our neighbour, who had a small grocery shop, came over. He bade me welcome and added, '*Cācā* (father's younger brother), I'm going into town, can I bring you back some fruit and vegetables?' I thanked him for his offer and gave him my order. Then I asked him why he called me *cācā*. He told me simply, 'Your "brother", your *bhāī*, is my *cācā*, so you too are my *cācā*, and I am your *bhatījā* (brother's son).' That evening a small

Girls pay a visit to their 'paternal uncle', the anthropologist, to play with their 'brother'

My 'brother', Suleikha, who gave me the land for my house, and his two sons

girl asked me to look at a sore on her wrist, addressing me as *dādā* (paternal grandfather). Here again, the explanation she gave was of the same order, 'Your "brother" is my *dādā*, so you too are my *dādā*, what else can I call you?'

The next day, a young woman acquaintance from next door entered our house dressed in her best clothes and decked in her best jewellery. Her usually cheerful countenance had given way to an expression of sadness. Visibly she was expecting something from me. I asked about this. It was explained that she was going back to the village of her husband, who had come for her. As her *cācā*, I was supposed to give her my blessing and a small sum of money. My usual question received the usual reply, 'Your "brother" is

My 'brother' and assistant Abdulaziz (in the middle) with his two nephews

her paternal uncle, and so you too are her *cācā*.' This type of visit was repeated regularly, either by 'nieces', or more accurately 'brother's' daughters, by married *bhatījī*, or 'sisters', or by young married *bahin* returning to their husband's house. Each would arrive with unmarried sisters from the quarter and demonstrate her sadness with tears, thus reiterating the behaviour which marks

A 'brother's' daughter at the anthropologist's, before going back to her husband's village

the first time the young bride leaves home again after the wedding ceremony. Our kinship network was rapidly taking shape—Suleikha, who had given me the land, was a 'brother', a *bhāī*, and his children were 'brother's' sons and daughters, *bhatījā* and *bhatījī*, and his wife was 'brother's' wife, *bhābī*. As her husband was older than I, she could entertain a familiar (unveiled) relationship with me. But all the wives of younger 'brothers' and nephews would cover their face in my presence and not speak to me. These different relationships were not restricted to the close family of Abdulaziz and his brother, Suleikha; they extended to the entire village. As we gradually met more and more people, the Meo of the different quarters became kin.

In the village of Bisru there were three separate Meo patrilineages which, according to our informants, descended from the same ancestors. With a few exceptions, however, no Meo in the village could trace their genealogy back to more than two or three generations, and they were incapable of determining the exact links within and between the lineages. That did not prevent the inhabitants from knowing exactly how everyone was related. One example will show this. I had been assimilated to the Uparla lineage. One day, I was introduced to a man from the neighbouring lineage, Haweliya. My 'brother' Abdulaziz introduced him as my *potā* (to simplify: the son's son, or the 'brother's' son's son, this being either a close or a distant 'brother'), since he was also his own *potā*. Astonished, I asked him how he knew that X, who was our own age, fell into the category of grandchildren; he answered that X's father was his *bhatījā*, a brother's son. But how did he know that the latter fell into this category? He answered, 'My father called the father of X *potā*, which could not be anything but my *bhatījā*, the son of a brother; and his son, X, therefore, had to be a *potā*'. That is where his knowledge of the facts stopped. There was never any question of checking the genealogy to see if this relationship was agnatically correct. In fact, all kinship relations work this way: to establish a link with someone, all one has to do is find a third person, who can be a member of the same generation (a 'brother' or a 'sister', for instance) or of the generation above (a father or a mother). This is how we were integrated into the kinship system without it being necessary, as people themselves emphasized, for us to be inserted into a genealogy or an agnatic group.

My 'paternal uncle'

In the course of our encounters with 'relatives', we were confronted with the question of how to define the central terms, *bhāī*, 'brother' and *bahin*, 'sister'. At first, these seemed to have a well-circumscribed meaning. In the Demrot clan, for instance, from which all the lineages in Bisru descend, people had kin in both categories. Likewise, in the other clans with which marriage was proscribed, people could have consanguineous[2] 'brothers' and 'sisters'. And our informants themselves stressed that one did not marry into groups where one had 'brothers' and 'sisters'. But this claim was soon contradicted.

One day my 'brother' from Bisru introduced a woman to me as our *bahin*, our 'sister'. At first I thought she was from our village and that she had come home for a visit. But I was quickly set right. The woman came from another village and was married to my 'brother's' *cācā*, paternal uncle, and was therefore, a *cācī* (wife of the paternal uncle). But she was also my 'brother's' mother's brother's daughter, and therefore, fell into the category of 'sister', *bahin*. In effect, the children of my real or classificatory maternal uncle are my 'brothers' and my 'sisters', like my own brothers and sisters or the children of my maternal uncle and aunt, or my paternal uncle and aunt. More generally, all married women in the village were *bahin*, 'sisters', before they married and became *bhābī*, 'sisters-in-law' or *bahū*, 'daughters-in-law'. In effect, it is unusual for them to continue to be called *bahin* after they have married. It is hard to say why my 'brother' decided to singularize this woman as *bahin* rather than *cācī*: is it because she was the daughter of his first-degree maternal uncle, or did he want to attenuate the fact that a woman of his own generation had married someone from the generation above? Whatever it may be, this case showed me something important: no one saw any contradiction in the fact that *bhāī* and *bahin* designate, on the one hand, consanguines, as distinct from affines and, on the other hand, kin ties that transcend this distinction. This means that *bhāī* and *bahin* are, depending on the context, those one is forbidden to marry or those one must marry.

Calling on relatives

A visit to a 'sister'

One day we set out to call on my 'sister' (the one who officiated when the house was being built) in her husband's village. We were given a very warm welcome, fed, and shown around the village.[3] When we left, as a 'brother', I gave my 'sister' Rs 31 (it was later explained to me that this gift was for her husband too), then Rs 11 for my 'sister's' husband's sister, Rs 5 for each of her husband's parents, Rs 5 for each of my 'sister's' children who were present, and Rs 9 for the nine members of the village council. Again my 'sister' gave back Rs 5 to my son. X, my 'sister's' sister-in-law, her *nanad*, was away at the time. She was not presented to me as a sister-in-law, but as a 'sister', and it was as such that I was supposed to make her a gift. For this woman, I was a 'brother', a *bhāī*, and not a brother-in-law. I thus had 'sisters' not only among the agnates or consanguines, but also among those we usually classify as affines. What held for me did not, however, hold for my 'sisters' in Bisru: for them, X was a sister-in-law, a *nanad*. Whether the original link was composed of brother–sister or of sister–sister (and likewise, sister–brother as opposed to brother–brother) therefore, made an important difference.

This was not a ceremonial visit. But I quickly came to understand that rituals had long-lasting after-effects. As long as a 'sister' is unmarried, she receives nothing from her brother. But once she marries, the unidirectional ritual prestations begin, and continue—not only on all ceremonial occasions (rituals for the birth of the 'sister's' children, the circumcision of her sons, the marriage of her sons and daughters), but on 'secular' occasions as well, the latter being modelled on the former.

A visit to a daughter-in-law's family
A visit made in another village was just as significant. I accompanied one of my agnatic nephews, who was going to bring his young wife back from her home village. Once again I was very well received. After a fine meal, I was treated to a mocking ritual called *samdhī* pūjā. In-laws call each other *samdhī* (male) and *samdhan* (female). The word 'pūjā' means 'devotion, religious worship'. As I was the 'brother' of the young man's father, I became a *samdhī* for his in-laws. This ritual was carried out in the following manner: the young woman's mother, my *samdhan*, surprised me from behind, her face covered, rested a copper pitcher on my head and laid a blackened hand on my back, while making fun of me.[4] The scene sparked uproarious laughter all around. After which the young woman's father gave me the sum of Rs 52. Generally speaking, the *samdhī* pūjā is done on specific ritual occasions (marriage, birth, etc.). Here it was in no way obligatory, the family simply wanted to honour me,[5] since I was visiting the village for the first time and they wanted to mark our *samdhī–samdhan* relationship fittingly. Unlike the preceding visit, here I was in the position of wife-taker and I had to receive the ceremonial prestation this entailed.

Thus I began to make the acquaintance of my 'relatives' outside the village. The marriages of my 'sisters', 'brothers' and agnatic nieces and nephews linked me with Meo from other localities.

An encounter with a sālā
Far from being restricted to a limited kinship network, our integration could extend a great distance, in fact to the entire Meo community. When two Meo meet for the first time, they try to discover a kinship link before broaching any other subject. Of the many examples, I will cite one briefly, as an illustration.

Our car broke down in a small town in central Mewat. My 'brother', Abdulaziz, found a mechanic. While he worked on the car, we talked with him. He was a Meo. When he heard the name of our village, he told us that one of his sisters had married a man there who was the 'brother' of my 'brother'. When he heard the name, my informant replied, 'Why, then, you're my *sālā*' (wife's brother or 'brother's' wife's brother, for a male ego). The discussion went on. The time came to pay for the repair. The mechanic, who had married his sister in our village, for this reason refused to accept any money. He was set on his refusal. For him the economic relation came second to kinship. My informant began a new discussion and, following a different line, he discovered that the mechanic was also a *bhāī*, similar to a consanguineous 'brother'. In this case, he could receive our money pending a ceremonial occasion on which to reciprocate. The mechanic accepted, but noted that he by far preferred the first relationship.

Ceremonial relations with agnates and affines

This world of kinship into which I found myself thrust was actualized in official rites. The Meo of Bisru village belong to the Demrot patrilineal clan, and their territory backs on to that of the Chirklot clan. I became acquainted with a member of this clan and we came to entertain friendly relations. This man had just lost his father and, being the eldest son, he organized the *fatiya* festivities marking the end of the mourning period, forty days after the death. For the occasion, he had invited, as custom dictates, many of his kin who were supposed to give him a turban and a sum of money. He in turn gave them a meal. I was invited to make a gift, not as a friend of the man, but as his *bhāī*. The Demrot of Bisru and the Chirklot do not intermarry, and this man was the equivalent of a consanguineous *bhāī* of my village. I fulfilled my 'duty', and I learned that this kind of prestation implied a return gift. If I were to organize a mourning or a marriage ceremony at my house, the person to whom I had made a gift would have to reciprocate with the same sum.

A man with whom I had become acquainted while we were staying in the guest house invited me to the wedding of his two sisters with two brothers. I went to his village with one of my agnatic 'nephews'. During the ceremonies, I saw this man's two consanguineous 'brothers' give him

My 'paternal uncle's' wife setting out for a day in the fields

gifts (in principle returned by the recipient when the givers hold a ceremony). I thought that, as a friend from the outside, I should make a gesture. Seeing me reach into my pocket, my 'nephew', sitting beside me, signalled to me not to do anything. I therefore did not give. As we were leaving, our host thanked me for coming and gave me Rs 11; he did the same with my 'nephew'. On the way home, the latter explained to me that he had married one of this man's sisters; I concluded that gifts went in the same direction as the woman and could in no case go back in the other direction. The gifts that had begun at the time of the wedding must continue at subsequent meetings whether or not these are ceremonial occasions.

Other rites showed us the systematic nature of our integration into the Meo kinship. Marriage rites, especially for the village girls, are the occasion for much merrymaking. Our son liked to join in with his numerous 'brothers' and 'sisters'. After one of these weddings, he came back to the house, furious, because, he told us, several girls he did not know (they were not from the village) followed him around, pinching and teasing him. Laughing, my 'brothers' explained the situation to me. This was the joking relationship between a *jījā* (our son) and *sālī* (these girls), between the brother of a married man and his wife's younger sisters. On the occasion of ceremonies, and especially at weddings, this relationship is supposed to take a certain form, to which our son had been subjected. Usually *jījās* are well prepared and rarely let themselves be caught by their *sālīs* because, if they do, they are given a very hard time, and are supposed to endure this teasing, and not answer back even as they try to escape. This incident touched my wife and me deeply because it showed that our integration into the kinship system was not simply a manner of speaking, but that it was given concrete form in ritual action. Several times afterwards we observed similar indications.

One problem I had not thought of was raised in the course of our discussions. I was assimilated to the 'brothers' of the village, as was my son; I was integrated into a place, a lineage, with respect to which I established all my relationships. But my wife could not come from the same village because this residential unit does not intermarry. So a natal village had to be found for her, my 'brothers' joked. As the subject came up periodically, I saw that the question preoccupied them. After a few discussions, they chose a village where they regularly took wives from and with which they were on excellent terms. This satisfied them, and they subsequently acted as though my wife came from this village. The wives of my 'nephews' and those of my younger 'brothers' would come to her to complain about their husbands' behaviour, hoping she would intervene on their behalf. Alternatively, my 'sisters' kept an eye on her to see that she was looking after the house as a sister-in-law, a *bhābī*, should.

These events are only a few of the many that studded our stay in the village. Our house was assailed daily by visitors, agnatic kin or affines, and would empty out only at mealtimes. To be sure, they had been very curious about an *ingrez* (from 'English', the local term for any white foreigner) in the beginning. But we quickly realized that our house was no different from our neighbours'. There is no separation between private and public life within the Meo caste. This was in striking contrast to the Moroccan Rif: among the Iqar'iyen, only close agnates have relatively free access to a man's house; all others enter only if they have been invited by him and in his presence. Furthermore, they cannot walk about the house but sit in the reception room reserved for guests, while the women, who must not be seen by male guests, keep to another room. Among the Meo, all agnates, however remote, as well as all affines have free access to all parts of the house, and no one thinks anything about it.

THE FIELDWORK AND THE MEO KINSHIP SYSTEM

These few details of our integration into the Meo kinship network are not simply anecdotal. They testify to the constraints imposed by the various dimensions of the kinship system once one has been introduced into it. We had become quasi-Meo. This prompts several questions.

Was our integration an exception?

An example will show that this is by no means the case. One day, two Meo 'brothers' I had accompanied to Delhi introduced me to a man and told me: 'He is our *bhāī*.' We ate together in the small restaurant he owned and then went to his house, where his married sister was introduced to us as my 'sister'. As we were leaving, my two Meo 'brothers' took out the sum of Rs 11 and gave it to this 'sister'. On the way home, I asked what Meo clan this family belonged to. My informants explained to me that I was mistaken; our host was not a Meo, he was the friend of one of my companions. The two men had decided to become *bhāī* and had therefore exchanged turbans. This new relationship automatically extended to both men's 'brothers' and 'sisters'. The same gifts must be given to a non-Meo 'sister' as to one from the community. This outsider and his family were in the same situation as we were, except that we were living in the village and our kinship relations were daily, more intense, and more varied.

What was the significance of our integration into the Meo kinship network through our link with a 'brother', a *bhāī*?

In the Moroccan Rif, the spoken word played an important role; to gain access to the local culture, one had to listen to old men's stories, understand at a glance the acts and gestures of the 'men of honour'. The object of my analysis had been to decode the utterances of the elders. Contrary to my experience in the Rif, the words of my Meo informants did not need deciphering. To be more precise, that was not the crucial problem. For my main informant, calling me his *bhāī* was not a way of speaking, but a way of acting. I had to adopt the same attitudes, make gifts, receive other gifts, just as the Meo did with each other. The institution of this relationship between two people had set in motion the whole kinship network linking together the community.

I would like to make myself clear: becoming the kinsman of a Meo is not the same thing as becoming a relative in Western societies, and notably in France. In French society, there are three ways of entering the kinship network of a group or a community:

- By adoption into a family: In this case, the child loses its birth kin group and enters that of its adoptive family. Adoption implies a parent–child relationship, and therefore, a relationship between persons in two adjoining generations.
- By marriage: Anyone who marries into an extended family, in the narrow or the broad sense (the husband into the wife's family and she into his) becomes what the French call a '*bout*' or a '*pièce rapporté(e)*', literally, a patch that has been sewn on. The person is added on to, completes the relationships within this family. The relationship between families linked by marriage is not marked. It is as though marriage were a way of being 'brought in', of entering into consanguinity with the other while keeping one's own consanguines.
- By becoming a godparent: The godparent who, in the Christian tradition, holds the child (his or her godchild) over the baptismal fount creates a personalized relationship of ritual kinship with the baby (and by derivation, with its family), which is different from natural or social kinship. No one here is obliged to change his or her birth kin group or to adopt a new one.

None of these procedures for integrating someone into a kinship network adequately describes the one I encountered among the Meo. I was not adopted into a family and I did not have a Meo father or mother. Each man has his own parents, who are not those of the others. Furthermore, there is no such thing as adoption among the Meo themselves. We did not encounter a single case of someone having changed families or lineages, and someone who leaves his natal village to settle in another or even to leave the region, keeps his agnatic identity. There was no question of integrating me by marriage. The Meo community is endogamous and an outsider cannot hope to marry a Meoni (feminine of Meo), even if he becomes a kinsman. Finally, there is no procedure analogous to becoming a godfather in order to enter into a relationship with a non-Meo; I did not simply establish a relationship with a particular person, and there was nothing to distinguish the kin relationship I entered into from that linking the Meo with each other. Meo social kinship is a ritual kinship, and it is hard to separate the two. It was through a link with a 'brother', a kinsman from my generation (and not with a kinsman from the generation above, as in adoption or becoming a godparent), that I had come to be linked with a growing number of Meo. I was part of the Meo kin network and yet I had not become a Meo. To understand this apparent paradox, I shall make an analogy: we noted that the gifts given in the course of daily life are modelled on those given in ritual situations, except that they do not have all the ceremonial characteristics. There is both continuity and discontinuity between the two kinds of gifts. The same holds, in a certain fashion, for the extension of kinship to an outsider.

People had manufactured 'roots' for me, as it were; the village of Bisru, where they had built a house for my family. Each time I was called upon to act, I would imitate my 'brothers' who had taken me in, just as the Meo would model their relations with me on those they entertained with their 'brothers' in the village. But there were certain lines not to be crossed, and marriage was one of them. From this standpoint, I was an outsider, and was and always would be someone from somewhere else. My original identity was neither denied nor unknown. Integration ran up against this major fact which prevents the opening of kinship and the community to the outside world. I had in a sense been absorbed, but I remained marginal. My kinship was at once an inescapable 'reality' and an 'illusion' that had to be maintained.

What did this experience tell us from the standpoint of the Meo terminological conception of kinship?

From my privileged position, I was able to understand how the Meo put their terminology into practice. I could have been integrated into a group—as a 'brother' of the village—but it is not what happened. Each relative had to be named, and the kinship relations were constructed both within the village and outside, through the intermediacy of my *bhāī*, my 'brother', Abdulaziz. In this context, it was no accident that my integration came about in this way. Not all generations are equivalent. The 'brothers' and 'sisters' turned out to be the central generation.

Analysis of the terminology posed three problems: (a) How is one to understand that ego's generation is essential, in that the principles at work there provide the structural frame of reference for the other generations? (b) How can one account for the fact that not all terms are mutually exclusive, but that they overlap or are distinct depending on the chain of relatives? (c) And finally, should one keep the distinction between consanguinity and affinity or let it drop? And in the second case, what should it be replaced with and what importance should be assigned to the brother–sister tie and to marriage, with which it is linked? (see Chapter 2) The last question arises not only concerning the vocabulary of kinship but also concerning marriage alliance and life-cycle rites.

Conceiving the terminology without regard to genealogical relationships raises yet another question: What is the place of unilineal descent reckoning if it is not the means of determining the kin relationship? We will see that unilineal descent reckoning structures the agnatic groups by subordinating territorial organization and annexes itself to the marriage prescriptions, but that it is not the dominant point of view in the Meo kinship system (see Chapter 3).

What significance should marriage be given?

The half-serious, half-in-fun search for a place of origin for my wife showed the importance of the wife's natal village. The intermarriage unit assigned to her and in which 'her' village was located was chosen not because wives were regularly taken from there—that is a rule common to all intermarriage units—but because it was from this unit that the wives most appreciated in Bisru come. Wife-givers were distinct from wife-takers. Furthermore, asymmetrical marriage alliance proved to be a sociological reality. Generation after generation, marriages were repeated in the same directions and with the same groups.

Yet marriage with the mother's brother's daughter, the first-degree matrilateral cross-cousin, was proscribed, as was marriage with a woman from one's mother's village. In these conditions, how is one to understand the existence of enduring asymmetrical marriage when the union which epitomizes it in the literature is prohibited? To resolve this twofold difficulty, we will see first of all that the reference units of intermarriage are not the families or the people, but the more or less broad agnatic groups, extending in some cases beyond the village, and thus that the marriage alliance between groups can be translated in inter-individual terms by a formula that takes into account the above prohibitions.

But there was another problem: there are no specific terms for wife-givers and wife-takers, and the terminology is not based on the transgenerational distinction between consanguinity and affinity, which the anthropological literature deems should be congruent with the marriage alliance. Was one supposed simply to note the heterogeneity of these two dimensions, to throw into question the application of the marriage-alliance model to the Meo, or simply to acknowledge that this model could find expression other than in the distinction between consanguinity and affinity? (see Chapter 4)

How is one to understand the use of kinship, and in particular of the brother–married sister relationship, in life-cycle rites?

I have said that a 'sister' returning to her husband's house receives gifts from her 'brother', and when the 'brother' visits her in her husband's village, he once again has to make a cash gift to her as well as to her children and certain of her husband's agnates. Unlike the reciprocal gifts between 'brothers', those given a married sister are never returned. These unidirectional prestations prolong the gifts made at the life-cycle rites.

Also to be taken into account are the ritual services performed by the married sister, such as those designed to promote the prosperity of my home, for which I gave a sum (*neg*) analogous to that given a priest officiating in a temple or for a family. These services and the corresponding fees are similar to those of the marriage rites, but less developed, for, during the wedding ceremony, the married sister is the principal officiant and occupies, in relation to her brother, a position equivalent to that of a Brahmin priest, in relation to the Kshatriya warrior.

This brings us back, by another route, to the problem raised in connection with kin terms, namely the relation between marriage and the brother–sister relationship; in effect one gives the same gifts to the wife-taker as to the married sister. That being said, the gifts are usually made to the sister, or through her, and not through her husband; the ritual services are performed by the married sister, not by her husband. Is the brother–married sister relationship, therefore, a simple extension of that between brothers-in-law—which would suppose that, in marrying, the sister becomes an affine for her brothers—or is it more than an affinal relationship—which would mean that the sister becomes fully a sister through marriage? (see Chapter 5)

In sum, the Meo have unilineal descent groups and asymmetric marriage alliance, yet kinship in this community cannot be reduced to any of the theoretical models that have been constructed for either dimension, no more than it can be analysed in terms of the simple consanguinity/affinity distinction, even though it, too, is present. But does this mean a 'repressed' form of affinity, an 'incomplete' and 'unconscious' configuration of kinship with respect to the Dravidian system prevailing in south India? (Dumont 1966a: 146–7). I intend to show that the Meo kinship network forms a system. To do this, it will be necessary, first, to relativize the structural importance of unilineal descent and affinity as a manifestation of the marriage alliance and, second, to give full weight to the brother–married sister tie. This relationship will assume its full meaning when we come to the analysis of terminology and rituals, in which it will feature as the dominant structuring principle of Meo kinship.

Our integration into the Meo kin network entailed our identification with their 'caste' in their relations with other castes. We, too, became, after a fashion, Rajput. Like our 'brothers', we could not let backward castes enter our house, or fakirs, members of the caste of funeral priests; we could give food to or receive food from only those who received from or gave to the Meo. One incident is worth mentioning. One day a Brahmin from our village called and, to my great surprise, accepted a cup of tea. When he had gone, the Meo who were present told me: 'That man is no longer a real Brahmin, the proof is that he accepts food from a Meo.' The mixture of teasing and discomfort they expressed had to do with the fact that a member of the higher priestly caste did not respect the prohibition on commensality which places Brahmins above the Rajput warrior caste.

We were able to establish regular or episodic relations with certain castes on the model of the traditional intercaste relations already existing in the village. I had become a *jajmān* who employed men from the service castes (*kamin jāti*). A water-carrier from the Sakkā caste regularly brought us water, a washerman laundered our clothes, the potter provided us with earthenware, all in exchange for payment in cash, not in kind as was the custom with the Meo, because I did not own land. Relations here had economic overtones. Nevertheless, they were modelled on the principally ritual relations between a Meo *jajmān* and various service castes. A counter-example will show this clearly. It was our intention, on arriving in Bisru, to engage a cook. This turned out to be impossible. Meo do not serve other castes, and it was difficult, if not impossible, to find anyone from another caste who would be accepted as a cook. In this village, as in the others in the area, each family prepares its own daily fare; it is only on ceremonial occasions that they accept the services of the barber caste to prepare food. The idea, therefore, had to be abandoned, and the occasional help we received from a Meo could not be remunerated because cooking is a family affair among members of the same caste and cannot be paid for. Here the economic and ritual spheres were inseparable.

While the Meo considered us to be members of their kinship network and their Rājpūt caste, there was never any question of regarding us as Muslims. Yet communion through the great monotheistic religion, between 'people of the Book', as the Meo say, could have been an ideal way into the community. This raised the question of the place of Islam in this Rājpūt caste. That is a complex problem which would be difficult to deal with thoroughly here. I will merely outline the major points in Chapter 1 before proceeding to the essential part of our analysis: the Meo kinship system.

Notes

1. Rif is a mountain area in north Morocco.
2. *Cf.* p. 8, the example of the Chirklot man who invited us to a ceremony marking the end of the mourning period.
3. This village was a special case. The centre was occupied by Sikhs and the periphery by Meo. According to the inhabitants, when India became independent, the Meo of the village were afraid of being massacred by the Hindus and fled to Pakistan. The Indian government resettled Sikh refugees in their place. Later, numerous Meo emigrants came back and found their houses and lands occupied. Nevertheless, they were pleasantly surprised because the other Hindu castes in the village of whom they were the *jajmān* had saved many pieces of land, which

they returned to them. The Meo built their houses and established their quarters around those inhabited by the Sikhs. Our stay was too short for us to learn much about the relations between the two communities, but our informants stressed the absence of tension and antagonism.
4. In ordinary life, as during rituals, the *samdhan* must cover her face in the presence of her *samdhī* and make fun of him. The latter must act as though this did not concern him.
5. The mocking ritual is an obligation, and whoever undergoes this ritual in no way regards himself as having been humiliated.

The Meo: A caste and a faith

The Meo themselves say that they are at once a caste and a Muslim community. We will be asking ourselves how these two dimensions fit together within the social structure of this group, and in what sense we can speak of the Meo as a Muslim caste. Rather than begin with a series of general considerations on these two dimensions, however, we will study the way they are expressed in Meo social life and will look into the possibility of a contradiction between the system of regional castes and the brand of Islam specific to this community.

THE MEO AND MEWAT REGION

The Mewat region, where the bulk of the Meo live, occupies an area of approximately 7910 sq. km spread over three states: Rajasthan, Haryana, and Uttar Pradesh, within a triangle defined by the towns of Gurgaon (near Delhi), Alwar, and Bharatpur. In 1961, the rural population of Mewat was over 1,000,000, more than 30 per cent (350,000) of whom were Meo living in some 2200 villages.[1] The region comprises for the most part of relatively fertile plains used for growing wheat, barley, and mustard, with two harvests a year: the *sadhi* (or *rabi*) harvest in March–April, and *savani* (or *kharif*) in September–October.[2]

For the Meo, Mewat is their place of origin and reference, even if they emigrate. The region connects them with the great Hindu myths in two ways. It is close to Mathura, the birthplace of Lord Krishna, who according to legend engendered certain of the Rājpūt's ancestors. It is also identified as the location of Kurukshetra, site of the mythic battle between the Pandava and the Kaurava in the Mahabharata. The Meo are very attached to this epic, and a Meo translator has even rendered it into the local dialect. The Meo take great pride in the myths which identify them with the Mewat region and refuse to recognize the superiority of the Ashraf, who are composed of prestigious Muslim groups, 'the first two of [which], in theory of Arab origin, have honorific names: Saiyad[3] and Shaikh, while the following two have ethnic names: Pathan (that is, roughly, Afghans) and Mughul' (Dumont 1966a: 262; English trans. 1970: 207; cf. Ahmad 1973: 171–205). Finally, every emigrant Meo maintains ties with his clan and his natal village, and comes home to find a wife, in accordance with the traditional rules of the region.

The Meo as a Rājpūt Caste and as Varna Kshatriya

The Meo community claims the status of caste Rājpūts and members of the second varna (literally 'colour', but also 'category'), that of the Kshatriya or 'warriors'. Our informants proudly tell us how their ancestors refused to bow to an outside authority. They distinguished themselves as bandits, attacking caravans and plundering towns, not hesitating to set upon the city of Delhi, then capital of the Mughal empire.

But more than defining their identity, the status of Rājpūt marks their place in the regional caste system. It is not my intention to study this system here, however, but to define just how the Meo community ties in with the other castes. Following Bouglé's analytical distinction (1969), I will consider this caste system from the standpoint of three closely related aspects: status ranking, the detailed rules ensuring the separation of these statuses, and the rules of interdependence associated with the social division of labour.

Status ranking

Together with the Brahmins, 'priests', and the *baniyā*, 'merchants', the Meo belong to the three 'high castes', the *uncī jāti*. In the minds of our informants, these correspond to the first three varna, or castes, those of the twice-born: Brahmins, Kshatriya (to which the Meo belong), and Vaishya, which include the *baniyā*. The Meo recognize the Brahmin's higher rank. However, although they are meat-eaters, while the *baniyā* are vegetarians, their warrior status gives the Kshatriya second place in the hierarchy.

The 'service castes', *kamīn jāti*, are supposed to serve the *uncī jāti* and are lower. There are many of these castes, and they are ranked in hierarchical order: from the *naï*, or 'barbers' down to the untouchable *camār*, or 'leather people' and the *bhangī*, or 'sweepers'. The barber caste is treated as almost equal to the Meo's.[4] Some Meo make a distinction between the middle castes: the *kasaī* or 'butchers', the *sonar* or 'goldsmiths', the *lohar* or 'blacksmiths', the *kumhar* or 'potters', and the low castes: the *dhobī* or 'washermen', the *mirasī* or 'bards', and so forth. Among these low-status groups are the fakir, a term of Arab origin meaning literally 'pauper'. In the literature, the word generally designates a Muslim ascetic who has taken a vow of poverty. In the present case, *fakir* form a caste of funeral priests occupying a position equivalent to that of the Hindu *Mahabrahmins*.[5]

Brahmins, *baniyā*, and the backward castes are all Hindus. The other castes vary. For instance, in some villages, the barbers and the washermen are Hindus, while in others (including Bisru), they are Muslims. All *fakir*s, however, are Muslims.

Separation

Caste endogamy
Like the other castes, the Meo are an endogamous group and do not marry out of their community. The fact that they are Muslims makes no difference. Of course, there are some cases of Meo having married other Muslims, but they were obliged to leave the area. We knew of a Meo lawyer living in Alwar who had married out of his caste. He admitted that he could not come back to live in his natal village with his wife because his agnates would never tolerate such a state of affairs.

There is a myth which tells how the Mughal emperor, catching sight of a beautiful Meo girl from Bisru, carried her off and installed her in his harem. This aroused a wave of emotion among all the Meo, who found this abduction unacceptable. A man by the name of Bahar, from Kotiya village and the Chirklot clan, decided to bring back the Meo woman. He set out for Delhi. When he got there, having located the harem palace, he scaled the wall one night to reach the chamber where the Meoni was secluded. He recognized her from the particular way she slept with one hand behind her head, woke her, and took her away with him. As he had touched her, we were told, he was obliged to marry her. For ten years the emperor's forces pursued him without success. Bahar had to flee his village, but he continued to fulfil his duty brilliantly as a warrior bandit. Ultimately, he was captured, taken back to Delhi, and executed. His body was left to rot outside the town walls. A *baniya* merchant from Mewat recognized him, put him over the saddle of his donkey and took him back to his village. Bahar was buried, and the merchant was given a feast and the honorific title of *caudri*, 'leader'.

This story is rich in meaning, and some of the aspects will be analysed later. But here it should be noted that the scandal had to do not so much with the fact that a woman had been captured as that she had been abducted by a Mughal who had no right to her. That he was a ruler or a Muslim makes no difference. The rule of endogamy cannot be violated.

Castes are distinguished in two other ways: by occupation of space and by eating habits. To illustrate these points, we will take the example of Bisru village which differs little from the other localities we visited.

Occupation of village space
The village is known as *gaon* and is divided into two parts: the residential zone, also called *gaon*, and the cropping zone, called *jañgle*. The second term designates the uncultivated forest wilderness as well. The cemeteries (*kabristan*) are situated in the *jañgle*, among the uncultivated fields.[6] It is recommended not to go walking at night in the *jañgle* because one would be at risk of attack by evil spirits, or *bhūṭ*. People regarded as madmen vanish

from the village from time to time. We were told that they can be seen at night, in the distance, running to and fro in the *jañgle*, jumping and somersaulting and gesturing wildly, because they are being attacked by evil spirits.[7] On the boundary between the two zones are usually found the ponds, wells, and threshing floors.

The Meo represent nearly 40 per cent of the village population, occupy over half of the residential space, and live in three quarters. The quarters of the two untouchable castes, the *camār* and the *bhangī* lie to the east. The Brahmins and the *baniyā* each have their own quarters, west of the main street, which divides the village down the middle along a north–south axis. West of this street lie the well-circumscribed quarters of the *kumhar* (potters), the *kasaī* (butchers), the *sonar* (goldsmiths), and the *lohar* (blacksmiths), which are separated from the backward castes by a street so as to avoid any spatial contact with them. Different Muslim service castes are represented in the village by only a few families, all of whom share the same quarter and cemetery. This is the case of the *naï* (barbers), the *fakirs* (funeral priests), the *sakkā* (water-carriers), the *dhobī* (washermen), the *mirasī* (bards), and last of all, the *kazi* (Saiyad or descendants of the Prophet).

A map of the village in presented in Figure 1.1.

Diet and food contact

The Meo eat meat, traditionally mutton or lamb, and in the last few decades water buffalo. Consumption of the latter is strongly disapproved of by Hindus, and the Meo conceal its circulation so as to avoid causing conflict. This does not, however, mean that the Meo have abandoned the dietary rules of the caste system. On the contrary, they say that their warrior status allows them to be less punctilious about the food they eat. Alternatively, they are very particular about who they eat with, who they accept cooked food from and in what kind of ware.

As often in the caste system, the Meo differentiate between ordinary food and ceremonial food. The first is prepared by the women of the house, served in ordinary ware, and generally eaten by the family or by the visitor from the same caste. Ceremonial food is prepared by the barber caste, who in these circumstances serve as cooks. Whereas ordinary food is generally called *kaccā* (boiled rice, wheat or barley chapatti, i.e. flat bread cooked without animal fat), ceremonial fare must be *pakkā* (cooked or fried in butter, a purifying product from milk). On such ceremonial occasions, the Meo invite members of different castes and give them food, but only the Meo may eat in the host's house, the others must consume the food outside. Earthenware bowls replace the family's daily ware. These bowls are used only once. Afterwards, they are collected and piled outside the house to be removed by the *bhangī* caste, the only ones who can destroy (or reuse) them. It must also be said that there is

The Meo: A caste and a faith 21

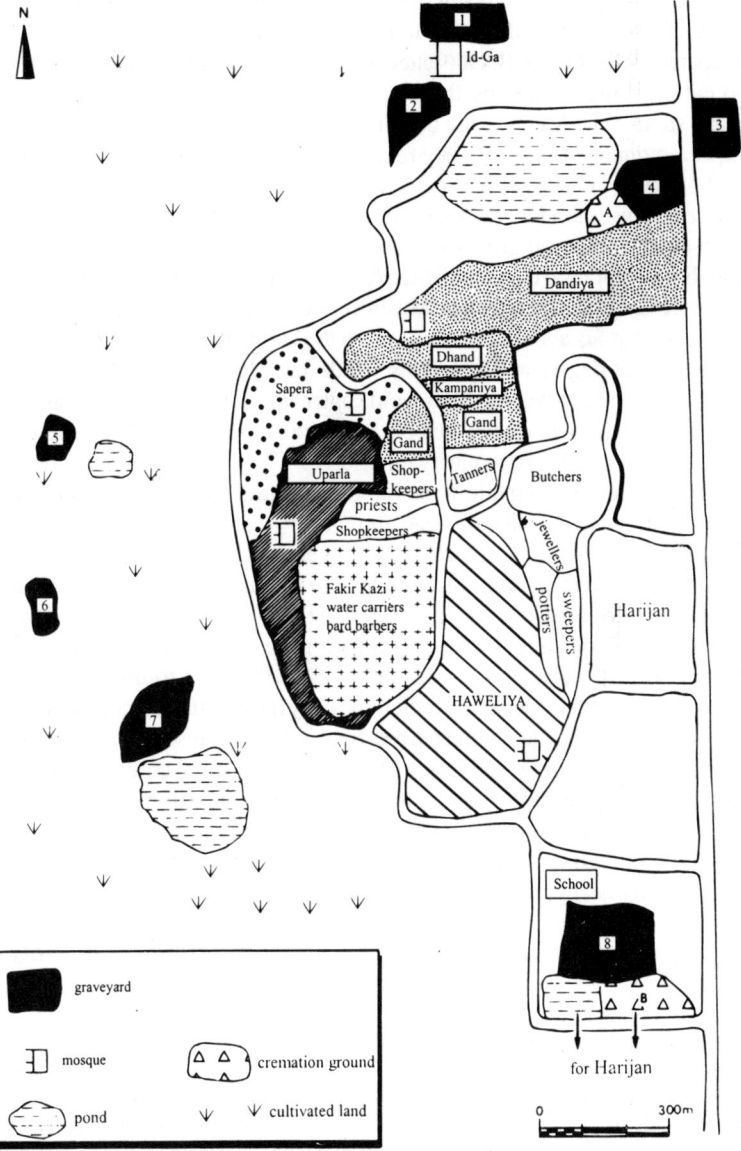

Figure 1.1: Map of Bisru village (by Sophie de Beaune)

nothing convivial about the meal taken in common. Everyone eats quickly without saying much to his neighbour and without turning towards him.[8]

In daily life, the Meo, like most other castes, accept in principle food prepared by Brahmins. But the latter, like the *baniyā*, are vegetarians and refuse to eat anything cooked by the Meo, even if they acknowledge their high-caste status. The Meo use the barbers as cooks, who prepare the *pakkā* food on ceremonial occasions.[9] They refuse to accept any food prepared by lower and backward castes. In particular, they expressly refuse to enter the fakir's house because, as a funeral priest, he is in contact with the impurity connected with death and burial grounds. Among the lower castes, only those who are Muslim accept food cooked by Meo or, in the case of the Meo, by barbers; the others refuse.[10] It seems that the Muslim castes are less punctilious about purity and less rigorous about dietary rules than the Hindu castes, but it is ultimately a question of degree and in no way affects the Meo's high status.

Like all high castes, the Meo avoid contact through food and even all direct contact with impure castes, notably with the untouchable *bhangī*, so as not to be defiled or obliged to purify themselves. These sweepers, who clean the streets and remove organic waste, in other words the leftover food thrown into the street, also deal with dead animals; they are not allowed to enter the houses of the Meo or to touch them. In certain ceremonial circumstances, the Meo ask them to feed small sticks into the fire under the pots in which the barbers are cooking food, but they must turn their back as they do this in order to avoid defiling the food with their gaze.[11] The *camār*s are a special case. A few decades ago, the group took the decision to no longer act as scavengers and they became vegetarian. They have remained cobblers (some are also tailors), but do not themselves treat hides. Because of this, their status has improved. Until recently, they were still forbidden to enter a Meo house. But following the change in dietary habits, the prohibition was lifted. This counter-example confirms the close relationship between impurity and contact. Nevertheless, while a vegetarian diet is indeed a sign of greater purity, it does not basically change the caste's status, since working with animal hides is still a source of pollution.

Dumont nicely sums up this caste segregation in terms of impurity as follows:

> The preoccupation with purity leads to getting rid of the recurrent personal impurities of organic life, to organizing contact with purificatory agents and abolishing it with external agents of impurity, whether social or other. The ban on certain contacts corresponds to the idea of untouchability, and all sorts of rules govern food and marriage. It must be pointed out that, segmented though it is, the relative degree of a group's purity is jealously protected from contacts which would diminish it. It must also be noted that each group protects itself from the one below and not at all from the one above, and that the actual separation from the one above is the result only of the exclusiveness of the superiors (1966a: 84; English trans. 1970: 59–60).

Such caste hierarchy is founded on the opposition between pure and impure, and the Meo are just as preoccupied with problems of pollution as are the other Hindu or Muslim castes, and thus with that which both separates them from and links them to the other castes, since only they have the privilege of performing certain necessary tasks for the Rājpūt Meo. Furthermore, the order which ranks the Meo just below the Brahmins calls to mind the classic image of the encompassing relationship between status and power (Dumont 1966a: 63–108; English trans. 1970: 33–91). It is this aspect I would now like to examine as it can be seen in the *jajmānī* system.

The Meo and the *jajmānī* system

This type of caste interdependence will once again be studied here from the standpoint of the Meo. The *jajmānī* system can be viewed in two ways: by focusing on the head of a house or by concentrating on the members of a caste having an eminent right on the land. In either case, each service is performed by members of specialist castes. Various authors have dealt with several aspects of this system: the village as the site of caste relations (Mayer 1960: 33–91); the differences in the nature of the service provided by a Brahmin and those provided by the service castes (Parry 1979: 84–128); and finally, the differences between the religious tasks included under the *jajmānī* system and other specifically economic tasks which form a set of employer–employee relations (Pocock 1962: 78–95). Without denying the interest of these distinctions, I feel it is more useful for my purpose to consider that the relations of caste interdependence are above all of a ritual nature and that the *jajmānī* system should be interpreted in this light, even if, from a subordinate point of view, certain relations may take an economic form.[12] It is therefore my intention to show how the *jajmānī* system is organized around the Meo as a dominant caste, the village being essentially, but not exclusively, the place where the asymmetric relations are organized into the provision of services in exchange for the provision of goods, the overall system assuming its value within the ritual setting.

Generally speaking, in villages in Mewat, the Meo have an eminent right on the land. This right is not granted from the outside by royal authority, the Meo claim it because they are Kshatriyas, members of the second varna, and because they are the founders of the villages they occupy. In Bisru, it is said that they arrived with the Brahmins, who have the same right on certain lands.[13] Each family possesses a series of plots which they hand over to their sons (daughters are excluded). Rights to a given piece of land can be ceded provided the transaction takes place between Meo or Brahmins.

In the village, any Meo with land is regarded as a *jajmān*, and has obligations to *kamin* from particular families of different service castes, including the backward castes. All these families have a right to a fixed portion of the harvest. In exchange, they must provide ritual services to their *jajmān* throughout the year, and specifically on the occasion of life-cycle rites. In addition, they receive a small ceremonial fee in kind or in cash each time they officiate for their *jajmān*.

When it comes to working in the field, especially at harvest time, the Meo may use only the members of their own family. If they must employ extra hands, they will use the services of certain *kamin* families who are bound to them by the *jajmānī* system. For these jobs, the members of the service castes receive an on-the-spot payment in kind. For example, when the wheat or barley is harvested, every evening, each agricultural worker takes one-twentieth of the sheaves he has cut, and every water-carrier takes one sheaf for the water he has brought to the workers during the day. All these remunerations are fixed by custom and can be modified only by a decision of the panchayat, the village 'council'.

The bulk of the relationship is organized by the set of ritual prestations and counter-prestations between *jajmān* and *kamin*. The use of the latter as agricultural workers is a corollary of the overall organization and not the determining factor. Not all *kamin* families necessarily work on their *jajmān*'s lands. Moreover, it is because the member of a caste provides ritual services for which he is paid that he can ask to be hired for agricultural work, and not the reverse. In other words, the economic aspect (the employer–employee relationship, the redistribution of the product of the land in the different castes) of the *jajmānī* system is modelled on the broader services–fees relationship, which is of a ritual nature, as M.L. Reiniche clearly saw in her analysis of the notion of *jajmānī*: 'every secular activity (set of actions), directed towards a material goal, is implicitly conceived on the model of a rite, carries within it the implications of a rite. That is why all technical know-how has a religious dimension, is a ritual know-how' (1977: 95).[14]

All it takes to be convinced that *jajmānī* relations are of a ritual nature are a few examples: the barbers prepare the ceremonial *pakkā* food for the Meo on the occasion of life-cycle rites, they wash those who are to be circumcised, they perform circumcisions, they wash and purify the future bride and groom, and accompany them throughout the ceremony, receiving gifts as they do. Likewise, the washermen wash not only the daily linen, but the clothes of women who are menstruating and those of the members of the family of the deceased for the duration of the mourning period.

The fakirs wash the bodies of the dead, help bury them, and tend their grave for forty days, washing it down regularly with water and lighting a candle to ward off evil spirits. They occupy the position of funeral priest, custodian of the burial ground, and of the dead.[15] The importance of the backward castes with respect to impurity is well enough known not to be reviewed here.

The technical skills of certain artisan castes, which they alone possess, are also considered to be of a ritual nature: for instance, the potter supplies his *jajmān* with everyday ware as requested, but also, during certain life-cycle rites, notably marriage, when the Meo house has been purified, with new pots because the old ones can no longer be used.[16] The analogy of the potter's work with the ritual work of the wedding is recognized as a source of prosperity for the newly-weds (Biardeau 1971–72: 33–5).[17] The goldsmith makes bangles, necklaces, etc., upon request, and must be remunerated. His professional activity is, to be sure, a matter of caste, but at first sight is not properly speaking of a ritual nature. However, the Meo use the jewellery chiefly as part of the dowry, which the bride must wear when she leaves home for her future husband's house, adorned as a proper *kanyādān*, 'gift of the maiden', the sacred gift par excellence, similar to the gifts that can be given a Brahmin (see details, Chapter 5).

As a rule, in this system the Brahmin officiates as a priest, *purohit*, for his *jajmān*; his ritual service is different from those provided by the *kamin*, for it flows downwards. It so happens, however, that the Meo, who are Muslims, do not use the services of the local Brahmins in their rites. To be sure, in the past, some served as astrologers, but it is not certain that they took a direct part in the rituals, as they do for Hindus. This failure to call upon the Brahmins slightly alters the *jajmānī* system in which the Meo are involved, but it does not change it in any fundamental way.

Things are not all that simple, however, for this warrior caste uses the services of Brahmins called Jagga as genealogists. The Jagga live outside the village in a region bordering on Mewat district. Regularly, every year or two, they call on their *jajmān* in order to collect recent genealogical data (essentially deaths, births, marriages, but also certain important facts of family history to be recorded for memory). These they consign in big books that no one can read, people say, except these wise men, the Jagga. In exchange for their services, they receive remuneration in cash and kind.

What is genealogy for the Meo and why do they have Brahmin genealogists? The Meo are divided into a number of patrilineal clans, some of which are connected with territories. They think the Brahmins know the deities who engendered the five great Rājpūt groups (*vamsh*), how the founding ancestors of the different clans descend from them, and how, at various times and in various places, the intervening ancestors established the sub-clans, lineages, and villages, and the lines.[18]

Determining relationships with the ancestors, the deity, and the status of Rājpūt is therefore the work of these Brahmin knowledge-specialists. Genealogical ties are not a secular affair as they are for us; their consignment by Jagga Brahmins in exchange for gifts and fees is analogous to the work done by the other caste specialists in the *jajmānī* system. Therefore, every birth, every marriage, every death in the family of a Meo, *jajmān* is not only marked by specific ceremonies in which a group of specialists provide their services, but also transcribed by the wise men, thus attesting that an unbroken chain links the dead and the living, the gods of Hindu mythology and present-day humans. The knowledge attributed to the Brahmin genealogists envisages kinship in its two basic dimensions: the passage of time through the succession of the generations and the movement through space of various founding ancestors from different localities. It inscribes the Meo in their high-caste status. In short, theirs is a global knowledge, for it embraces a total vision of the world, human and divine, and so distinguishes itself from the partial knowledge of other ritual specialists.[19] In this sense, it is useful to situate the Mirasī, the bards, by contrast. The Mirasī are regarded as low caste; at life-cycle rites in particular, they sing the praises of the families whose *kamin* they are. The songs are about the words and feats and acts of someone, living or dead, but they rarely go back more than three generations and retain only a few striking deeds on which they embroider. Here we have an example of partial knowledge connected with a low caste, analogous to that of the ritual specialists of the other service castes, but different from the all-encompassing knowledge of the Brahmins.

The Meo are thus linked to the knowledge specialists par excellence, the Brahmins, as well as to the specialists of a ritual know-how in the persons of the members of the service castes. They stand at the centre of a web of asymmetric relationships, some with a higher caste, others with lower castes, implying a prestation in the form of service provided by the different specialists and counter-prestation in the form of retribution or a ritual fee. In this ternary pattern, the asymmetric relationship between the Brahmin and the *jajmān* provides the model for the other relationships of this type (Reiniche 1977: 71–107).

According to Nesfield (cited by Dumont 1966: 129 n. 42b), the term *jajmān* comes from *yajamāna*, which designates 'the person' who employs the genealogist (*bhāṭ*), identified with the sacrificing priest. With this etymology we must associate the etymology which makes the *yajamāna*, a 'sacrifier', the person who offers a sacrifice, usually a Kshatriya, but who calls upon an officiant for the actual sacrifice, a Brahmin, who receives for his ritual service a fee called *dakṣiṇa* (Malamoud 1976: 155–204). The asymmetrical relationships we have identified in the *jajmānī* system thus send us back to the articulation between the opposition pure–impure and the sacrificial-type relationship deployed in the rites.

This explains the Meo's insistence on their status as both Kshatriya (which is connected with the varna and the sacrificial system) and Rājpūt (which gives them their place in the caste system and supposes the articulation between the opposition pure–impure and the *jajmānī* system).

Although we will not carry this analysis of the *jajmānī* system any further, it is already becoming clear that the Meo as members of the Rājpūt caste are perfectly integrated into the system of relations between the regional castes, of which they are one of the essential cogs. Given these conditions, how is it that they are Muslims?

THE MEO AND ISLAM

A number of hypotheses are propounded by Aggarwal concerning the dates of the Meo's conversion. Some advance the eleventh century CE, others the thirteenth or even the seventeenth century, at the time of the Mughals, as the result of the action of Emperor Aurangzeb (1971: 37–8). Neither do we know whether the Meo were a single caste before their conversion nor whether they belonged to different Hindu groups and were brought together and welded into a single caste by their adoption of Islam at different periods (ibid.: 39–40). The hypotheses of another author, Hashim Amir-Ali, are just as conjectural and do not bring any decisive elements to bear on the Meo's history (1970: 18–31). All we know for certain is that the Meo are converted Hindus and that they put forward this quality to distinguish themselves from the Mughals, the Pathans, and other Muslim groups which arrived from outside India.

The features which, until 1920–30, differentiated the Muslim Meo from the Hindu Rājpūts were the following: prayer at the mosque, even if it was irregular; use of Muslim names, which seems recently to have become generalized; burial of the dead according to the Islamic rites in cemeteries (*kabristan*) located in the agricultural zone; circumcision of boys. But alongside these characteristics, a whole series of features indicate that the Meo have remained deeply attached to their Hindu origins: active participation in all the Hindu festivals and ceremonies; an asymmetric marriage system related by its main aspects to that of their Hindu neighbours and which proscribes marriage with the patrilateral parallel cousin; life-cycle rites whose sequences unfold much like those of the Hindu rites; the institution known as *got*, or patrilineal clans, into which the Meo are divided and whose founding ancestors are said to have descended from mythological heroes or Hindu

Id-Ga, mosque reserved for Muslim festivals

goddesses and gods like Sita or Krishna; lastly, the worship of wells, *kuan pūjā*, with which is associated a Hindu god, Bherū, child of the god Shiva and his wife, the goddess Parvati.

This mixture of sporadic Islamic practice and solidly established Hindu traditions has given the Meo the reputation of being a superficially Islamicized community, of having but a veneer of Islam. Some Hindus, members of a religious reform movement, tried to reconvert the Meo to Hinduism during the troubled period of independence, but they had little success.[20] Others, Muslims, on the contrary urged the Meo to become better followers and members of the community of the faithful, the *Umma*. Because the latter movement had a greater and more enduring impact than the reverse efforts of the Hindu reformists, we will dwell for a moment on its action and the reactions it aroused among the Meo.

The objectives of the 'Tablighi jama'at'

The 'Community for the Propagation [of the faith]' was a movement established in the 1920s by Maulvi Mulana Ilyas and continued by his son, Mulana Yusuf.[21] But it did not achieve any real influence among the Meo until after 1947.[22] Its primary objective was to persuade the Meo to become better Muslims. It asked the Meo:
- to pray (*namaj*) five times a day
- to fast (*roza*) during the month of Ramadan
- no longer to take part in the Hindu festivals
- not to sing at festivals
- to abandon all rites of a Hindu character
- to abandon the clan system based on the originally Brahmin *got* in which the Meo saw themselves as descendants of mythological heroes and Hindu gods
- no longer to forbid marrying within the clan, but on the contrary to marry between patrilateral parallel cousins, a frequent practice among Muslims.

The means used

H. Amir-Ali describes the movement's action, and our informants confirmed his description. Several movement members, Meo but Muslims of other origins as well, would visit a village. They would bring their own food and set up camp in the mosque. Then they would go from door to door, encouraging the Meo to come and pray at the mosque. There they would lecture them and preach the good word. After a few days, they would leave the village, asking to be accompanied by one or several men who would continue the visits with them in other villages so as to learn, in the space of one or several weeks, the basic rules of Islam. Sometimes certain of these Meo would be sent to Delhi, to the Nizamuddin *dargah* (mausoleum)[23] where the headquarters of the movement is housed. There they would receive religious training in the hope that, when they came back, they would lead other Meo in the village to become better Muslims and to join the movement.

The results

The movement's action bore its fruits: Koran study, the five daily prayers, the Ramadan fast all interested more and more people, as we ourselves witnessed. But there are still many whose religious practice remains irregular. Both categories of believers can coexist, however, in the same family without giving rise to conflicts of a religious nature.

The construction of new mosques seems to be gaining ground. In the village of Bisru there are no less than four, three of which are recent. But there is something worth pointing out here. Each mosque is located in the quarter of a specific Meo lineage, which paid for its construction and with which it is connected. It is of course open to all Muslims, from the village or elsewhere, but it is used by practically no one but the members of the lineage which owns it, a phenomenon similar but not identical to the Hindu lineage temple, which defines the identity of those who worship there.

At the instigation of the Tablighi movement, many Meo stopped taking part in such Hindu festivals as Dassera and Holi. We observed at the time of Holi that Bisru's Meo went about their business as though nothing was happening. Whereas the Hindu quarters were animated late into the night, the Meo quarters were by contrast strangely quiet. On this level, the Meo demonstrate a clear will to set themselves apart from Hindus.

But in other areas, for everything touching directly on the social structure, the Meo have refused, sometimes subtly, sometimes violently, to submit to the injunctions of the Tablighi jama'at movement and have stuck to their traditions.

Kuan pūjā, 'worship of the well', was practised on different occasions (birth, circumcision, marriage) by the Meo women, the Meoni. They would go in procession to the lineage or village well to worship the god Bherū, represented by a stone monument erected next to the well.[24] The Tablighi jama'at asked the Meo to cease this heretical practice and to remove the monument. The members of the movement who visited the village sometime later saw to their satisfaction that the monument had indeed disappeared. In reality, however, the Meo had not removed it but had buried it next to the well. They could thus continue their cult without offending their visitors from the Islamist movement.

There was a more violent reaction to the attempt to make them abandon their marriage prohibitions and their organization into *got*. As we will see, the Meo do not marry in their villages, nor in their clan, nor with parallel or patrilateral cross-cousins, nor even with the first-degree matrilateral cross-cousin. The

Tablighi jama'at tried to persuade them that these prohibitions had nothing to do with Islam and urged them to practise marriage between parallel cousins. Certain informants told us that the visitors from the Tablighi movement were nearly driven out of some villages by the Meo, who forbade them to bring up the subject. People also say that certain movement members in one village managed to persuade two brothers to exchange their children in marriage. The marriage lasted only a few days because the couple and their families were totally isolated and shunned by the village; no Meo would talk to them or even have contact with them any more. In the village of Bisru, the Meo staunchly refused to abandon their marriage prohibitions and, in our records of the matrimonial unions over several generations, we do not have a single example of marriage with the parallel cousin, an alliance which contravenes traditional rules.

The Meo refused just as staunchly to abandon the *got*. The Tablighi jama'at tried in vain to explain that one cannot adore at the same time the God of Islam and the Hindu gods, be monotheistic and polytheistic. When asked about this, the Meo are very clear: how can one deny the obvious, namely that their ancestors are descended from these gods or from the heroes of mythology? These existed, just as humans, the trees, the forest, the animals, etc., exist. For the members of the movement, the relationship with the universal God of Islam and that with the Hindu gods are of the same order: both involve an act of faith, but the first is true, the other false, and analogous to that of the time of ignorance, *Jahiliya*. The Meo do not see things this way. Even though the gods inhabit a celestial world and are more powerful than humans, they are not basically different from the rest of the universe. This means that the relationship between humans and the gods is not simply a matter of belief, as the great monotheistic religions claim. The notion of belief is a complex concept, to be sure, but, as Pouillon has emphasized, it is the great universal religions that make a fundamental distinction between 'the kingdom of God and this world', between a supernatural world to which we subscribe by an act of faith, and which is beyond all law, and the natural world where the human condition is determined by divine law (1979: 43–51, esp. pp. 48ff).

Islam and Meo social morphology

But the issue is more complex yet. In Christianity or Islam, an act of faith is primarily a relationship between an individual and God, or, to borrow a formula from Dumont, an individual-in-relation-with-God (1983: 40). The social order of the world is diminished in value or becomes the means of applying divine law. According to the Tablighi jama'at movement, the act of faith and social practice should be harmoniously and perfectly coordinated. For the Meo, the act of faith does not jeopardize existing social traditions but is added to them and must, through certain of its manifestations, become a local fact. They do not deny belief in God, but they do not make him the centre of everything, thereby throwing into question the rest of life in society. In this context, and essentially, Islam is merely one dimension of local social and religious life.

A series of examples will make this easier to understand. Like all Muslims, the Meo practise circumcision. However, this practice is not designated by the Arabic term *khitam*, nor by an equivalent term in Urdu or Hindi, but by the term *musulmani*.[25] This choice signifies that a Meo becomes a Muslim not only at birth, but by this important ritual act. And it is significant that the different rites involved engage the different service castes and are modelled on the wedding rites. The father's married sister comes to officiate, just as she does for the marriage of her brother's children, and the boy's maternal uncle must bring the *bhāṭ*, the ceremonial gifts. Furthermore, the children to be circumcised undergo ritual baths and are prepared like bridegrooms. Before the circumcision proper, they receive, like the bridegroom upon leaving to fetch his wife, the gifts from the village women. Circumcision and marriage are not simply equated though; for the Meo, the circumcision cannot be performed unless all the kinship relations and all the caste relations are activated within the ritual framework.

Tomb of a saint (pir)

The festival of Muharram, celebrated only by the Meo and the other Muslim castes of the area, has meaning only within the local context. Aggarwal provides a long description similar to the one given to us, with the exception of a few details which sometimes have their importance. Muharram is the first month of the Muslim calendar. The festival evokes the battle of Karbala in which Hassan and Hussein, the two sons of Ali, the Prophet's son-in-law, died. For Shi'ites, it is a sort of commemorative festival during which they flagellate and mortify themselves in a forceful reminder of the schism that has separated Sunnis and Shi'ites for centuries.

The Meo, who are Sunnis, celebrate this festival in their own particular way.[26] Aggarwal quotes the critical opinion of one non-Meo Muslim from Mewat, talking about the Meo practice: 'These Meo claim to be Sunni Muslims.

They should not celebrate Muharram. Actually, they do not mourn at all. To them this is another festival and an excuse to cook rice pudding. These Meo are animals' (1971: 161).[27]

The festival, held in only certain villages, lasts several days and is the occasion of a huge celebration. The main roles are taken by certain young Meo boys who play Hussein's soldiers, called *paink*. Frequently, families who have lost several children wish their remaining sons or those yet to be born to play *paink* at Muharram. These characters wear special costumes, go barefoot and sleep on the ground throughout the festival. For a period of several days, these 'soldiers' go from village to village dancing and collecting money from different families.[28] The main ceremony takes place on the ninth day. We will describe the festival in Bisru.

The Meo build a several-metre-high bamboo structure and cover it with coloured paper. At the top they make a small dome. This cenotaph-like edifice is called a *tajiā*; it rests on a platform mounted on long horizontal poles which enable the *paink*s to carry the whole construction around on their shoulders. Some Meo say it represents Hussein's mausoleum, others add that it also stands for mankind in general, with a head (the dome) and a body, the feet being the poles. Construction takes place in front of the Dhaja lineage house, which stands in one of the village's three Meo quarters: Bicharla, 'the central one'. The other two quarters and lineages are: Uparla, 'the upper one', and Nicharla, 'the lower one'. The procession follows the *tajiā* carried by the *paink*s. It begins at the centre and follows a clockwise circular route, passing in front of the houses of the upper lineage and then that of the lower lineage. Then it makes a wider circle through the other quarters of the village and comes to a halt near a pond outside the residential zone. The *tajiā* is carried into the water and sunk. This marks the end of the ceremony and the festival.

I do not intend to go into detail, but I will point out some features of interest to the matter at hand. Nothing in these ceremonies connects the Meo with the Sunni Muslims, for whom this is not a festival, or with the Shi'ites, for whom the ceremonies are associated with a sort of violent expiation. The primary meaning for the Meo must be sought in the local setting. During this festival of mourning, the *paink*s, who represent the soldiers of Hassan and Hussein killed at Karbala, are supposed, on the contrary, to gain a new lease of life. In addition, the procession ensures the prosperity of the village. To this effect, the circular procession ties in the three lineages of the village (first the centre, which is opposed to the two ends, then the upper, and finally the lower), then the pond where everything is purified and dissolved. The final moment displays a striking analogy with the end of certain Hindu festivals, quite common in India, when a procession accompanying the idol of a god immerses it in a body of water. This is not meant to say that Muharram is a Hindu festival, but simply to show that the Hindu festival provides the model for translating the Muslim festival into local ritual terms.

I have said that the Muslim fakirs form a caste of funeral priests, and we have seen how they ritually remove the impurity connected with the dead and hold them at a distance from the living.

One last fact is worth pointing out. The village of Bisru is home to families of *kazi* (or Saiyad), descendants of the Prophet. They are educated men and their function is to teach Muslim law. Generally speaking, they constitute the most prestigious group in Islamic society. The Meo, however, do not recognize their superiority. On the contrary, they regard the *kazi* as a service caste. In effect, they live in the same quarter as these castes and share the same cemetery.[29] Once again we see how an Islamic feature imported into a Meo setting becomes an attribute of the local system and not something which transforms it.

In such conditions, one understands why the Meo refuse to reconvert to Hinduism as well as to abandon certain Hindu traditions, as the Tablighi jama'at would like them to. It is as though Islam were meaningful for the Meo only because it is for the most part localized. Inasmuch as it is a local phenomenon, nothing can call it into question. But this does not mean that the two dimensions of Islam and caste coexist on the same level: the Meo are not Muslims and Rājpūts; they are Muslim Rājpūts, which is an altogether different matter. They are Rājpūts like all the other groups having the same name and status in the region, but they stand apart from them by their original manner of articulating their membership in the caste system and their adoption of the Muslim faith. That being said, the problem cannot be reduced to opposition between Rājpūts in terms of their internal characteristics (Muslims on the one hand, Hindus on the other). The essential feature is the system of relations between the castes within which the 'position' of Rājpūt is located and becomes meaningful.[30]

What does this mean if not that the Meo brand of Islam is meaningful because it is part and parcel of the local social structure, of the local ritual system, and not simply because it ties this caste to the rest of the Muslim community.

Notes

1. Population density in 1961 was nearly 150 inhabitants/km^2 with a sex ratio of 884 women to 1000 men (Aggarwal 1971: 18–31).
2. For details, see Aggarwal 1971: 80–91.
3. The Saiyads are recognized as the descendants of the Prophet.
4. In the south, the barbers who serve as funeral priests have low status (Dumont 1966a: 71; English trans. 1970: 57–8), while in this part of the north, they rank almost with the high castes. In Kangra, Himachal Pradesh, barbers have an elevated status, occupying the position of priest (*purohit*) and *kamin*; they even have the right to wear the sacred thread, like the members of the first three varnas, even though they are Śudra (Parry 1979: 72–4).

5. The *Mahabrahmin*, or Great Brahmin, a sort of priest who presides over funeral rites, is 'in fact an untouchable of a particular kind, inspiring such an aversion that care is taken not to have the slightest relation with him beyond the circumstance in which he is indispensable as representative of the deceased' (Dumont 1966a: 71; English trans. 1970: 58).
6. The tombs of certain holy men (*pir*) are often placed in the agricultural zone, but sometimes also in the residential zone.
7. The best refuge from evil spirits, *bhūṭ*, is the cemetery. This probably has to do with the fact that the *bhūṭ* are, for Muslims and Hindus alike, people who have died a violent death without having completed their destiny and who wander the earth without a grave or who are unable to stay in their tomb. From this standpoint, *bhūṭ* are incompatible with cemeteries. Yet it is said that they try to assault the dead before they have had time to make their journey to heaven. There is a contrast here between the cemetery and the cremation ground which is haunted by ghosts, *bhūṭ*.
8. When we described a meal taken together in Morocco to the Meo, they expressed astonishment that Muslims could behave in such a manner and share the same dish.
9. The Meo claim they eat *pakkā* food prepared by *kasaī* (butchers) or *kazi* (Saiyad). But we did not have the occasion to witness this type of contact.
10. The well built by a Meo group is used by them and by the service castes, with the exception of the backward castes. The latter are supposed to have their own well. The *hukka* (water-pipe) can be smoked in common provided the end of the pipe does not touch the mouth, the hand being used as a 'mouthpiece'. It is shared with the members of one's own caste. The young men prepare it; the old men, sitting on the charpoy (rope bed) or squatting on the ground by order of age, pass it around in this order. The Meo accept that Brahmins, *baniyā*, and barbers smoke this pipe with them, but we have only observed the presence of barbers. Brahmins refuse to smoke with other castes. Among the service castes, things are more complex; one accepts to share the pipe only with those considered to be of equivalent status.
11. Obviously in these circumstances, the food is cooked outside the house.
12. On this theme we will continue the perspective developed by Dumont (1966a: 128–42; English trans. 1970: 92–108) and Reiniche (1977: 71–107).
13. In other parts, if the village has Jats or Thakurs, who are of equivalent status to the Meo, eminent right on the land is attributed to all these groups. The Meo say that the land belongs to them because they registered it in their name with the land office. There are even records of land sales between Meo. Some having grown rich outside the community have thus purchased land which they claim to be able to use in a non-traditional manner. Since 1947, Punjabi refugees have been resettled in Mewat and have bought land which they own in full as private property.
14. As for the meaning to attribute to the ritual act, let me quote this author again: 'Every activity is suited to the goal aimed at .... No act is innocent, because every act exercises violence and is in itself dangerous and a source of impurity. In other words, if the rite is by definition effective (positive), it is so to the extent that it is capable of cancelling out its dangerous, negative consequences'

(Reiniche 1977: 94). Impurity danger cannot be eliminated by the actor himself, the sacrifier in the texts; this must be done by ritual specialists, who have a different status.

15. The fakirs remove all of the deceased's belongings, and notably the charpay, the four-legged bed which was used to carry the deceased to his grave. They rid the deceased's family of the impurities connected with his death. The Meo refuse to enter the house of a fakir, to share food with him or to sit on the same charpoy, the bed which is also used to seat guests. For the first year following the death, the fakir attached to the family acts as a go-between in the family's relations with the deceased. Every Thursday, the family makes *khir* (rice pudding) and gives some to the fakir who, by eating this food, also feeds the deceased, appeases him, and keeps him from coming back to haunt the living. The *khir* can then be consumed by the deceased's family, and it is good to give some to the agnates as well. This period of mourning is a time for accompanying the deceased on his journey to heaven and for warding off the danger that the deceased might be tempted to return to his house. The fakir is a funeral priest, a sort of intermediary agent who makes it possible to maintain a distance between the living and the dead.

Two observations are in order. First, we have here a process like that of the offerings made to the gods through the agency of the Brahmins, the leftovers from which are regarded as consecrated food (*prasad*) and can be widely distributed. But whereas the offerings are made to the gods, therefore to pure beings, here we are dealing with the dead, who, in this in-between period, can be dangerous. And only a man from an impure caste, but nevertheless a priest, can keep the danger at bay and make the 'offering' consumable. In reality, it is probably less a question, in this case, of purity or impurity than of the idea of ceremoniously sharing a meal with the dead through the agency of the fakir. Second, in the village of Bisru, there are abandoned houses occupied by *bhūṭ*, evil spirits. From this standpoint, all funeral rituals, and especially the actions of fakirs, have one objective, which is to prevent the deceased from turning into a *bhuṭ*.

16. On this occasion, a procession of women arrives with gifts in kind. The pot maker has already prepared his pots, which always come in pairs; the analogy with marriage is obvious to the Meo. Formerly, the mother of the groom or the bride was supposed to consecrate the potter's wheel by drawing around the outer edge, with her right hand, swastikas representing the god Ganesh, who smoothes away all difficulties connected with any new undertaking. Nowadays it is the potter himself who makes these designs, after which the women present him with the gifts they have brought, called *neg*, and carry away the new pots.

17. M. Biardeau offers a very perceptive analysis of relations between Brahmins and potters, notably concerning the cult of Aiyyanar, and shows the meaning of the reference to the potter and his workshop in the episode of the *Mahabharata* which relates the marriage of Draupadi to the five Pandava brothers. It is useful to quote this author's conclusions at length because they seem to me to apply perfectly to the Meo case: 'The potter is not only the man who fashions the clay into the requisite shape. He is also the man who, by firing the clay, turns the earth from black to red, an operation which, Hindus say, consists in combining earth with fire. The red of the fired earth comes from the fire liberated by the

potter from the wood where it was in a latent state. It matters little that, in practice, the pottery is usually fired in the open air, where the clay is also shaped, with or without a wheel. ... The potter who changes the earth from black to red is one of those stereotypes that classical mythology could not help but use, especially since the pot itself frequently symbolizes, in rites as well as in myths, the human womb. That is effectively what is going on in the story we are examining here: the place where the union is to be decided of the Pandava—who symbolize the reign of *dharma*—with Kṛṣṇā Draupadi, the black princess who smells of earth, is also the place which will seal the alliance between the same Pandavas and Dhṛṣṭadyumna-Agni, Draupadi's brother; this alliance is a promise of prosperity for Draupadi herself, that is to say for the kingdom and its inhabitants.'

18. For details, see this vol., Ch. 3, 'Kinship and territory'.
19. I am indebted for this whole section to a suggestion made by M.L. Reiniche, to whom I also owe the analysis of specialization as a form of ritual knowledge which acquires its meaning in asymmetric relationships.
20. Aggarwal tells how the members of the religious reform movement, Arya Samaj, urged the Meo from the Alwar region to reconvert by going through *suddhi*, 'purification'. Fearing for their lives, the Meo accepted to return to Hinduism; but, as one of Aggarwal's informants said, it was a bad experience because, 'they had destroyed our faith' (1971: 40–50).
21. Kepel (1987: 179–90) indicates that this movement did not limit its action to the Meo; it exerted its influence on other Muslims as well, even beyond India's borders. In his book, Kepel studies the introduction of the Tablighi jama'at among Muslims in France.
22. For an analysis of the movement's impact, see particularly Amir-Ali's book (1970: esp. 34–45). Aggarwal also devotes a few pages of his ethnographic study to the same subject (1971: 226–7).
23. This mausoleum is the burial place of a Muslim saint and mystic, founder of a religious brotherhood.
24. A number of songs tell the following legend: a woman reproached her husband because he had forbidden her to go to the well to make *kuan pūjā*, since the village was surrounded by Mughals; she told him that her own father would not have hesitated to go with her to ensure her safety, for nothing, not even war, should keep such a ritual from being performed. The husband yielded and escorted his wife to the well with his men. The Mughals killed them all. No condemnation of the woman for her obstinacy is pronounced in these songs. They simply tell the story as though it were obvious.
25. Aggarwal (1971: 175–6) records analogous phenomena for the region he has studied.
26. They are not the only Sunni group which celebrates this festival. Nor is it a matter of celebrating a victory over the Shi'ites. In the Muslim villages of central Nepal, this ceremony is performed in a similar manner (see Gaborieau 1977: 121).
27. For Nepal, Gaborieau mentions that, despite the action of the reform movements, the Muslim curates continue to celebrate this festival in its traditional form, even though they say: 'We shouldn't; next year we will stop' (1977: 182–3).
28. According to Aggarwal (1971: 162), the money collected is used for religious

projects or to repair the big village drum. He does not say what these projects are, and our informants were vague about the matter. One of them mentioned an incident he had witnessed. At the end of each day, the *paink*s were supposed to return to their village. But when the seventh day came, they did not return for the ceremony which was supposed to take place in their village. When they returned on the eighth day and were dancing, a young Meo fell into a trance and was possessed by Hassan. He criticized the *paink*s for their behaviour. Then he fell to the ground and was still. To bring him out of his trance, an earthenware pot containing slowly burning cow-dung was set beside him.

29. And when one asks why these descendants of the Prophet are inferior to the Meo, certain informants answer that the former are outsiders while the latter are from the area. But in a report written by a Meo and destined for external use, we saw that the *kazi* were classified as a very high-status group. This is not accepted in the village, however, and, whatever certain Meo may think or say, the *kazi* continue to be regarded as a caste, live in the service-caste quarter and are, therefore, assimilated to these low-status groups, to *kamin*, with whom they share the same cemetery.

30. In saying this, we are doing no more than recalling what Dumont already wrote in 1953: 'Ultimately, in the caste-based society, there are no natural truths, there are only positional truths, there are no essences, there are only relationships. "Caste" means "structure". Hence the so-often recognized impossibility of making universal judgments in India: here there is no law, no principle, no truth, as long as one considers the particular as existing' (1953: re-edited in 1964a, ed. 1975: 105).

Meo kinship vocabulary

In the last few decades, a number of analyses of Hindi kinship vocabularies have been produced, but, for the most part, Dumont's and Vatuk's interpretations still dominate this literature. It is, therefore, useful to provide a brief look at these two types of analyses and point out the questions they raise, so as to clarify our own approach.[1]

In an early article on the subject, Dumont showed the special nature of the north Indian Hindi kinship vocabulary when he contrasted it with the Dravidian and the French systems (Dumont 1972). The kin terms in these systems are organized around a simple opposition: complementarity between consanguinity and affinity in the Dravidian system; distinction within filiation between the direct line and the collateral line in the French system. The basic opposition is a transgenerational one, or to be more specific, it classifies kin homologously in the three central generations (parents' generation, ego's generation, children's generation).

In the north Indian Hindi vocabulary, on the contrary, ego occupies a central position within this generation, and it is the double sibling relationship between 'brother' and 'sister' which provides the structural principle determining the configuration of a whole series of other kinship relations. According to Dumont, this vocabulary can be analysed using the 'descriptive' method: beginning with the first-order relationships (the double sibling relationship), the second- or third-order relationships are constructed by 'augmentation and combination' (basic rule + affinity, or basic rule + filiation), which yields the other distinctions in the same generation and those in the other generations.[2] Filiation and affinity are only means, we shall call them 'relays', permitting extension, not of the terms, but of the distinctions within the double sibling relationship. One can see the difference between this type and a Dravidian classificatory logic or a French-type descriptive logic (which bases its central portion on a simple, distinctive, transgenerational logic).

Dumont remarks: '[Hindi] terminology cannot be reduced to a simple system of oppositions ... it is in a way only partially systematic' (1962: 25). Its complexity stems from the fact that the sibling relationship, though dominant, must, in order to construct the other relations, combine with filiation and affinity without these having a structural role.[3]

Of course, it is difficult to analyse the Hindi vocabulary as one would the Dravidian or the French, but why presuppose that only a simple, distinctive opposition permits the construction of a system? If the double sibling relationship predominates, while the other types are subordinate and, more specifically, shaped by the dominant principle while being different from it, do we not in this case have a situation in which a hierarchical opposition, defined by Dumont in other contexts, can apply? Yet this solution has not been retained, and we will need to return to it.

But the essential problem in Ðumont's initial analysis of the Hindi kinship vocabulary resides in the very way he characterizes the double sibling relationship. For him, the term *bhāī*, 'brother' (which is, together with *bahin*, 'sister', the central term for this generation) designates those who share at least one common ascendant with ego. As a consanguineous kin term: 'The sibling link *refers to a double relationship of filiation with a common ancestor*' (1962: 28; italics in the text). This definition, which is in accordance with one common use of the term 'sibling', thus implies reference to filiation. One wonders exactly how a dominant principle can construct distinctions internal to filiation when it depends on this for its definition. If we are to avoid this contradiction, we need either to recognize that consanguinity must here be given a different definition from our own or even from that used in south India (Proposition 1) or say that the so-called sibling links are not consanguineous links—but in this case how should we characterize them (Proposition 2)? We will consider these two propositions in turn and will see that they are not exclusive.

Proposition 1 If we want to preserve the dominance of the double sibling relationship as the basic principle and define it as a relationship of consanguinity, we must consider that my 'brothers' and my 'sisters' are primary or first, real consanguines and that relatives in the ascending and descending generations are only secondary or derived consanguines. In other words, before we have parents or other kin, we have 'brothers' or 'sisters', and it is through them that we will define the other relationships of filiation. The order of consanguinity between the two components is different from that with which we are familiar in the French or Dravidian systems.[4]

Nevertheless, we gain nothing from defining the sibling link in this way if we do not distinguish it from the affinal relationship. To speak of a consanguineous sibling is to speak of a relative whom or the children of whom ego cannot marry; therefore, the terms for 'brother' or 'sister' must be different from those designating relatives by marriage, or affines. But does this not bring us back by another route to the consanguinity/affinity opposition which Dumont did not consider to be relevant in the Hindi vocabulary? Vatuk has found this type of opposition among the Gaur Brahmin in Meerut. Here, she tells us, the sibling terms are different from those for brothers- and sisters-in-law: a male speaker has a consanguineous *bhāī* who is distinguished from his *sālā*, his wife's brother or his brother's wife's brother, and from his *jījā*, his sister's husband; a female speaker has a *bahin*, sister, who is distinguished from her *nanad*, her husband's sister or her sister's husband's sister, and from her *bhābī*, her brother's wife (1969: 105–6).

Beginning with this central opposition between consanguines and types of affines, Vatuk constructs different chains of relatives in ego's generation (1969: 107), finding corresponding links in the other generations. The question is what ego calls the affines of affines (in either direction). There are two scenarios, depending on whether the first affinal link is composed of same-sex or of opposite-sex siblings. In the first case, the affines of ego's affines are ego's consanguines (which makes it possible to say that the affines of two same-sex siblings are consanguines to each other). In the second case, the affines of affines are still affines (in other words, gender difference within affinity preserves and extends affinity). The interest of these chains of relatives is that they show how the consanguine/affine opposition is confirmed and extended in the chains of relatives and how the difference within affinal kin between brother–brother or sister–sister on the one hand and brother–sister on the other permits construction of the series of relationships.

Vatuk's analysis makes an important contribution to the understanding of the Hindi vocabularies. But she raises more problems than she actually solves. I will not dwell here on the difficulties of making the chains based on the consanguine/affine opposition in ego's generation correspond with those in the other generations which lack terms for affines. We will come back later to what is, at first sight, the absolute character of this opposition in the generation of ego. This seems to be contradicted by different indications. First, a female speaker has no term for her brother's wife's brother (her brother's *sālā*) and vice versa, a male speaker has no name for his sister's husband's sister (his sister's *nanad*) (ibid.: 106–7). In other words, when the initial link is composed of brother–sister, one has a hard time finding affines among the in-laws (Figure 2.1).

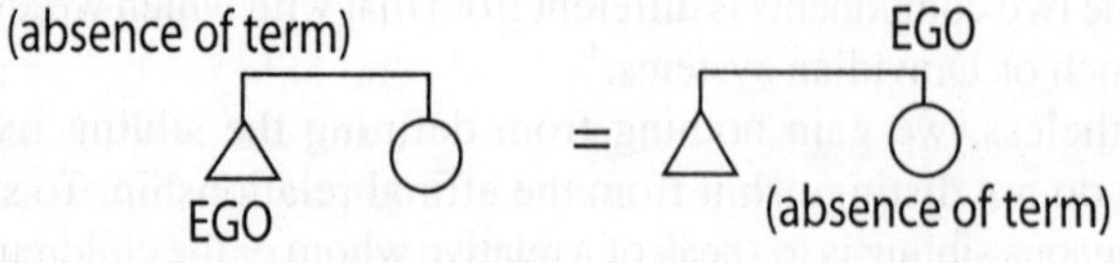

(absence of term)   EGO

△──○   =   △──○

EGO   (absence of term)

Figure 2.1: Chain of brother–sister relations in Meerut (S. Vatuk)

Vatuk treats this lack of terms at the two ends of the chain (or between BWB[5] for a female speaker and ZHZ for a male speaker) as an anomaly in the system. Upon closer inspection, one notices that it is when one starts with a brother–sister relationship that there is difficulty in naming the affinal link, whereas the brother–brother or the sister-sister relationship establishes the consanguine/affine link without any ambiguity at all. This indicates that, when it comes to affinity, there is a difference between the brother–sister link and the same-sex sibling link which needs to be accounted for. For the Meo, unlike the Gaur Brahmins, there is no hesitation: a male speaker calls not only his sister, but his sister's husband's sister, *bahin;* and vice versa, a female speaker calls not only her brother, but her brother's wife's brother, *bhāī*. One can show that, even for the Gaur Brahmins, everything in the environment indicates that the absence of the terms is of the nature of an unspoken presence and that here, too, these kin are *bhāī* and *bahin*. In short, certain chains of relatives—starting with same-sex siblings—distinguish between consanguines and affines (*bhāī* and *sālā*, *bahin* and *nanad*), while others, starting with the brother–sister relationship, are not based on this opposition. But how are we to qualify this second type of chain then and, more generally, how are we to understand that the central terms, *bhāī* and *bahin*, on the one hand, apply to consanguines to the exclusion of affines and, on the other hand, are used without distinction for consanguines and affines?

Another difficulty brings us back to the same problem. When Vatuk opposes one category of kin like *bhāī* to another like *sālā*, she is working from the idea that, at least in this chain, there is no possible overlap. But, as Dumont has pointed out, everything depends on the context:

> In Hindi, *bhāī* is susceptible of extremely wide use, and at the other end it designates a male consanguineous relative of Ego's own generation, to the exclusion of others like *sālā*, wife's brother. At this level, *sālā* is opposed to *bhāī*. On the next level, all male relatives of one's own generation fuse as *bhāī* in opposition to those of other generations, including non-kinship usages. This combination bothered me at first, in the study of kinship nomenclature, because it is different from the neat (South-Indian) 'distinctive opposition' which alone I was prepared to admit as a 'structural' feature and able to treat as such. Actually, it is what I now call a 'hierarchical opposition' similar to (but not identical with) the Adam/Eve or man/woman opposition (1971b: 69, n.33).

We will return to the hierarchical opposition that Dumont intuitively saw in this terminology, but which, in my opinion, he failed to define adequately. As far as our subject goes, we note that *bhāī* and *bahin* apply to ego's own generation overall in opposition to the other generations, whereas within this generation, the same terms are used for consanguines as opposed to affines, *sālā* and *nanad*. In a sense, every *sālā* is a *bhāī*, but the reverse is not true: not every *bhāī* is a *sālā*. Here, as for the chains of relatives, the same problem arises: how do we define the term *bhāī* when, at the global level of the generation, it does not distinguish between consanguineous and affinal kin?[6] This leads to a concrete statement of our second proposition.

Proposition 2 To interpret the complexity of this data, we can either (a) distinguish between a primary meaning of the terms *bhāī* (and *bahin*), designating consanguineous siblings, and secondary, derived meanings for relatives by marriage, or (b) call into question, for these terms, the absolute distinction between consanguinity and affinity.

The first term of alternative (a) tempted proponents of componential analysis, for whom the nuclear family and genealogical ties are central.[7] It is our intent to show that the second term of alternative (b) is what we need if we want to understand the Hindi vocabularies. As there is no concept to express it, we have found it useful to construct one for the purposes of our analysis. By convention, we will use the notion of *metasiblings*, notably for *bhāī* and *bahin*, when, for ego's own generation, these terms do not distinguish between consanguineous and affinal kin; and the notion *metasiblingship* when, on a more abstract level, we want to speak of a level of value which transcends the distinction between consanguinity and affinity. Alternatively, we will keep the notions of consanguineous siblings (in the sense defined in Proposition 1) and of affines when distinctions of this order are necessary.

If our proposition makes any sense, we will be able to identify two levels: a global one, which recognizes only metasibling *bhāī* and *bahin*, and a more restricted one, which includes marriage ties in which the same principle of metasiblingship is applied when one starts with a brother–sister relationship; whereas the consanguine/affine opposition is meaningful only if one starts with the brother–brother or sister–sister relationship. It is in this context that we will speak of 'hierarchical opposition',[8] using Dumont's term but with a slightly different meaning from the one he outlined above.

I am now ready to set out my plan for analysing the Hindi kinship vocabulary used by the Meo. I will attempt to delineate a system whose consistency is not of the classificatory type but is, at first sight, more akin to a descriptive logic, since we start with a series of what are immediate or first-order relationships in ego's own generation in order to obtain, by a process of 'augmentation and combination', the second- or third-order relationships.

I have chosen to use the notion of a *basic cell* around which the terminology is organized rather than that of first-order relationships starting with ego, to indicate that the whole set of these terms constitutes a structure built on a hierarchical opposition between metasiblingship and the consanguine/affine distinction located in the generation of ego. Second-order relationships are not constituted by extension of the terms of this basic cell or by rules of equation (as componential analysis would suppose), but rather by the translation of the structural properties of this basic cell by one or several intermediaries (the added links of marriage or filiation, ascent, or descent), which serve simply as bridges and, therefore, occupy a subordinate place in the system. The basic cell must consequently be considered as the key to the terminology. We will, therefore, try to characterize it in terms of its internal properties, those of ego's generation, and by the external application of these properties to other generations.

MEO KIN TERMS

The generation of the grandparents and those above (or G-2, G-3, etc.)

(1) *dādā*: FF; FFB; FMB; FZHF; MZHF (this term is also used for kin of *dādā* preceded or not by the prefix *per-*)
(1bis) *dādī* = wife of *dādā*, sister of *dādā*
(2) *nānā* = MF; MFB; MMB; MBWF; FBWF (As for *dādā*, this term is also used for a kinsman of *nānā*, preceded or not by the prefix *per-*)
(2bis) *nanī* = wife of *nānā*; sister of *nānā*

Parents' generation (G-1)

(3) *bāp* = F
(4) *maī* = M
(5) *tāū* = FeB; all S of *dādā* or *dādī* older than F
(5bis) *tāī* = W of *tāū*
(6) *cācā* = FyB; same application as for *tāū*
(6bis) *cācī* = W of *cācā*
(7) *phūphī* = FZ; MZHZ; more generally any D of *dādā-dādī*
(7bis) *phūphā*: H of *phūphī*; HB of *phūphī*
(8) *māmā* = MB; MBWB; FBWB; more generally any S of *nānā-nanī*
(8bis) *māmī* = W of *māmā*; WZ of *māmā*
(9) *mausī* = MZ; FBWZ; ZHM (m.s.)
(9bis) *mausā* = H of *mausī*; HB of *mausī*
(10) *sasur* = WF; BWF; HF; ZHF (f.s.)
(10bis) *sās* = W of *sasur*

Figure 2.2 shows the kinship terms for the parents' generation. Figures 2.3 and 2.4 present the affinity and kinship terms for the ego's generation (male and female respectively).

Ego's generation (G0)

(11) *bhāī* = own B; various first-, second-, third- degree cross- and parallel-cousins; any S of the generation of own F and M; WZHB; BWZHB; ZHBWB; BWB (f.s.); HBWB (f.s.); BWZH (f.s.) (for broader uses, refer to Analysis of Ego's generation)
(12) *bahin* = own sister; the different parallel- and cross-cousins; any D of generation of own F and M; WZHZ; BWZHZ; ZHBWZ; ZHZ (m.s.); ZHZHZ (m.s.); HBWZ (f.s.); ZHBW (f.s.) (for broader uses, refer to Analysis of Ego's generation)
(12bis) *behnoï* = H of *bahin*; HB of *bahin*; a *behnoï* of a *behnoï* is a *behnoï* (reference term used by m.s.)
(13) *jījā* = women use this term instead of *behnoï* for H of *bahin* and HB

44 Kinship and Rituals among the Meo of Northern India

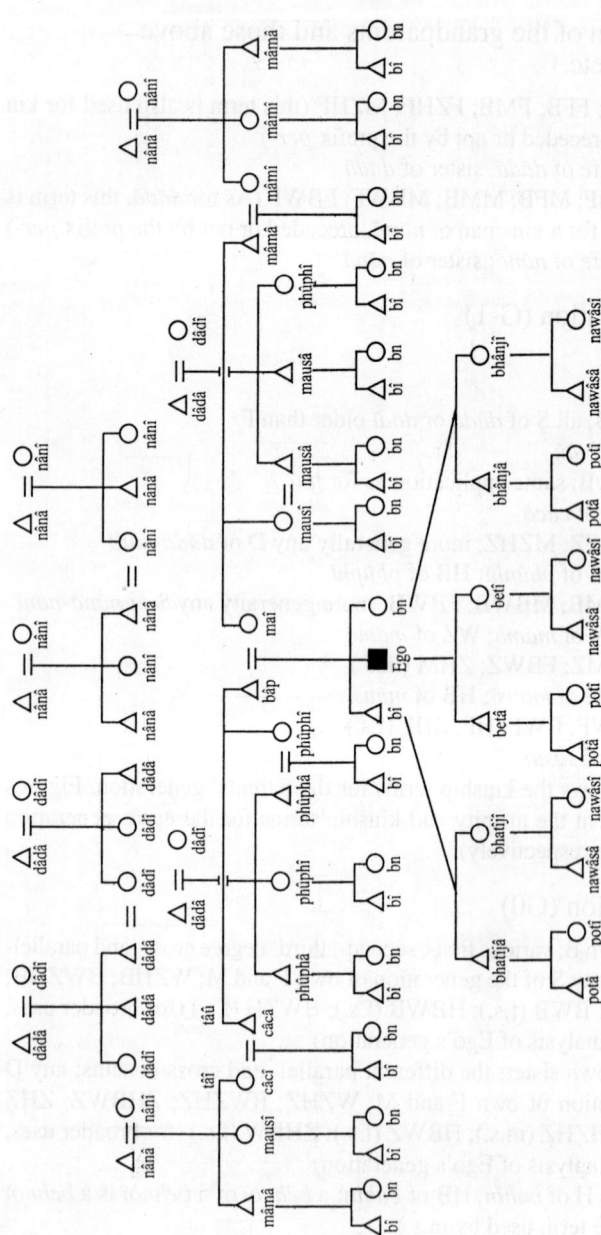

Figure 2.2: Kinship terms for parents' generation

bi = bhāī
bn = bahin

The children of bhāī are bhatijā/jī and those of bahin are bhānjā/jī

Meo kinship vocabulary   45

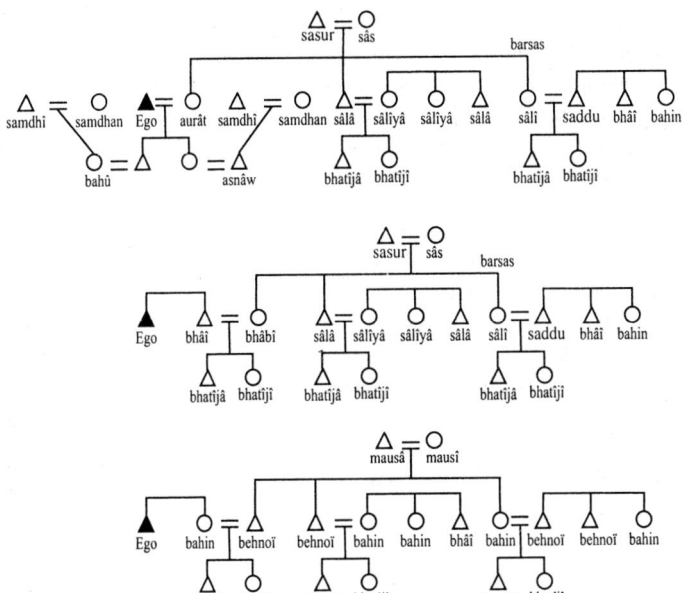

Figure 2.3: *Affinity and kinship terms by marriage for ego's (male) generation*

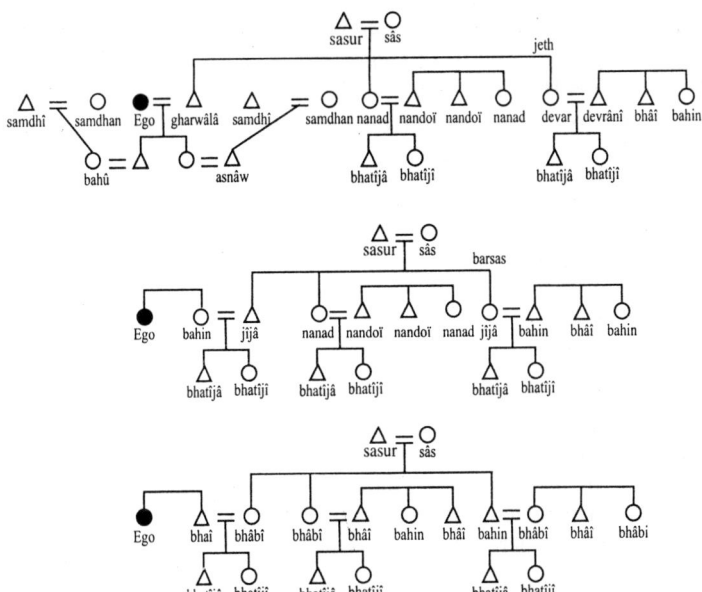

Figure 2.4: *Affinity and kinship terms by marriage for ego's (female) generation*

of *bahin*. (This term does not have the same extension as *behnoï*; one cannot say that the *jījā* of my *jījā* is my *jījā*. While *behnoï* carries connotations of respect, *jījā* has overtones of teasing.)

(14) *bhābī* = eBW; BWZ (f.s.); BWBW (f.s.); BWBWZ.
(15) *sālā* = WB; BWB (m.s.) (as in the case of *behnoï*, the *sālā* of my *sālā* is my *sālā*).
(15bis) *sālīyā* = W of *sālā*.
(16) *sālī* = WyZ; BWyZ (m.s.).
(17) *barsas* = WeZ; BWeZ (m.s.).
(18) *samdhī* = SWF; DHF.
(18bis) *samdhan* = SWM; DHM.
(19) *aurat* = W.
(20) *gharwālā* = H (literally, 'master of the house').
(21) *saddu* = WZH.
(22) *jeth/jethānī* = HeB/HeBW.
(23) *devar/devrānī* = HyB/HyBW.
(24) *nanad* = HZ; HZHZ (as for *sālā* and *behnoï*; the *nanad* of my *nanad* is my *nanad*).
(24bis) *nandoï*-H of *nanad*; HB of *nanad*.

Children's generation (G+1)

(25) *beṭā/beṭī* = S/D (another term: *ladkā/ladkī*).
(26) *bhatījā/bhatījī* = S/D of *bhāī*, *sālā*, *saddu*, *devar* and *jeth*.
(27) *bhānjā/bhānjī* = S/D of *bahin*, *nanad*.
(28) *asnāw* = H of *beṭī*, *bhatījī*, *bhānjī*, *potī* and *nawāsī*.
(29) *bahū* = W of *beṭā*, *bhatījā*, *bhānjā*, *potā* and *nawāsā*.

Grandchildren's generation (G+2)

(30) *potā/potī* = S/D of S, *bhatījā*, *bhānjā*.
(31) *nawāsā/nawāsī* = S/D of D, *bhatījī*, *bhānjī*.

ANALYSIS OF EGO'S GENERATION

It is useful to recall that, for the Meo, determination of kinship and use of the corresponding terms is not an abstract or formal matter (see Introduction, this vol.). The following analysis, therefore, attempts essentially to restore the meaning of the distinctions they themselves make.

Let me briefly review certain general features of the Meo kinship vocabulary, pointing out wherever necessary how it differs from the other Hindi vocabularies:

• All terms are used for kin in specific generations (with the exception of *bhāī* and *bahin*).

- Distinctions made in one generation do not automatically transfer to the next, as in the Dravidian vocabularies: thus a man's children and those of his brothers-in-law do not make distinctions among themselves as their respective parents did; they are all each others' *bhāī* and *bahin*. This Hawaiian feature already explains why a classificatory logic is impossible, for the distinctions within the different generations are not equivalent.
- Certain terms are used for the husband–wife couple or for the brother–sister pair. In this case, the root of each of these terms is followed by a different ending to indicate gender, as, for example, *cācā-cācī* for FyB and FyBW, *māmā-māmī* for MB and MBW, or *bhatījā-bhatījī* for S-D of *bhāī* and so on. Other terms—all in ego's generation—apply to only one gender: these are *barsas* and *sālī*, WeZ and WyZ; *saddu,* their husband; and finally *jījā*, which in the Meo terminology, is always used with *bahin* by a female speaker only, the two terms being radically different, whereas a male speaker uses *behnoï* with *bahin*, which are the same term with different endings.
- In ego's generation, only two terms, *bhāī* and *bahin* (plus a third, *bhābī*, which poses a special problem to which we will return later) are used by both men and women. All the rest are used exclusively by one or the other. But the specification *bhāī* and *bahin* is clearly inadequate. The two terms, as we have noted, have extensions which vary with the context.[9]

We will first study the different uses of *bhāī* and *bahin* according to these contexts. Then we will look in detail, from the standpoint of a specific ego, at the chains of relatives in G0 in which these two terms appear. For the construction of the basic cell, we will take into account only two links, ego plus a person to whom ego is related by marriage. It is our hypothesis that additional links (the third in particular) in ego's generation do not add any new properties to the basic cell, but can be constructed from it using simple rules of composition. The same procedure will be followed for ascending and descending generations.

On the most general level of kinship, *bhāī* and *bahin* are used with all members of the Meo caste, without distinction of generation or age but keeping the gender distinction. This comes down to designating all kin, without specifying genealogical or marital ties: people never say that all Meo come from a single ancestor. In this context, *bhāī* and *bahin* designate the members of an endogamous group, of a group within which one must obligatorily marry, but they do not allow one to distinguish between a Meo whom one can marry and another whom one cannot. French has the term *parents*, which in English translates as 'relatives', to designate all those with whom one is linked in one way or another, without specifying whether it is by blood or by marriage. *Bhāī* and *bahin* are thus 'relatives' in this broad sense, divided into male and female. This level will be understandable only when we have examined the relationship between the generations.

On the global level of ego's own generation, *bhāī* and *bahin* refer to all members of this generation, as opposed to members of the other generations, and do not distinguish between those one can marry and those one cannot. Here, too, the two terms are not consanguineous kin terms which could be opposed to affinal kin terms. In this context I will use the term 'metasiblings' for the *bhāī* and *bahin* of this generation, adding that here we are differentiating this level from the general level.

At a more restricted level, the use and the meaning of the two terms differ with the speaker's gender. To understand this variation, we will start with the relationship marriage creates between two brothers-in-law or two sisters-in-law (Figure 2.5a,b).

When male Ego 1 marries, his wife's brother, who is Ego's *bhāī* at the global level of G0, becomes his *sālā* at this more restricted level. The situation is the same for male Ego 2, brother of Ego 1: his brother's wife's brother is his *sālā*. Between the two same-sex siblings, Ego 1 and Ego 2, the relationship remains that of *bhāī*. But in this context, *bhāī* is distinguished from *sālā*, and we can thus oppose same-sex siblings and affines. But when we go on to female Ego 3, the brother's wife's brother is *bhāī*. Her brother's marriage does not fundamentally alter the situation for this woman, since, at this level, she finds herself with two *bhāī*s and not consanguines and affines.

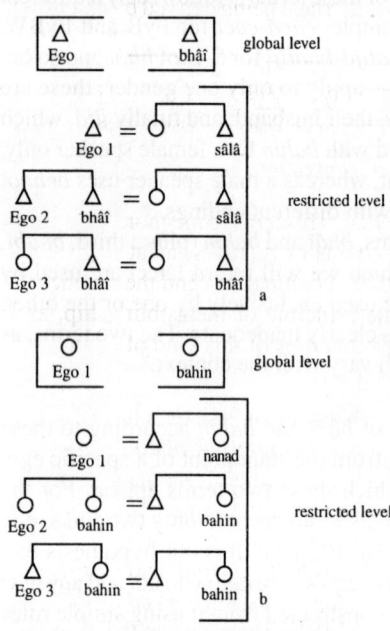

Figure 2.5: Relationship marriage creates between two brothers-in-law/sisters-in-law

The same reasoning can be followed starting with the link between two sisters-in-law: female Egos 1 and 2 remain *bahin* to each other, whereas the husband's sister or the sister's husband's sister becomes a *nanad*, and for male Ego 3, the sister's husband's sister remains a *bahin*, like his real sister.

There are two kinds of chains of relatives to examine: one opposing same-sex siblings to affines, the other made up of two brother–sister pair linked by a marriage and expressing a relation of metasiblingship similar but not identical to that on the level above. I will indicate the properties of these two kinds of chain before going on to situate the basic cell of ego's generation.

Chains of opposite-sex metasiblings

The principle of metasiblingship
In the case of two brother–sister pairs linked by a marriage, a man calls his sister and his sister's husband's sister *bahin*. Conversely, a woman calls her real brother and her brother's wife's brother *bhāī* (Figure 2.6). There is nothing to support the assertion, as componential analysis would have it, that the first meaning of *bhāī* and *bahin* are consanguineous brother and sister with the second meaning used for a relative by marriage being derived by extension

Figure 2.6: Chains of two brother–sister pairs linked by a marriage

in accordance with the rules of equivalence.[10] It seems to me more satisfying to acknowledge that, in both of these chains of relatives, as at the overall level of ego's generation, the terms *bhāī* and *bahin* transcend the distinction between consanguines and affines. The principle of metasiblingship, as I have defined it, is associated with four properties of this kind of chain.

Spouse's status
In both of these chains, the terms designating a man's sister's husband and a woman's brother's wife are respectively *behnoï* and *bhābī*. *Behnoï* is considered to be a contraction of *bahin-noï*; it is, therefore, made from the same root as *bahin*, but with a different ending; the same goes for *bhābī* with respect to *bhāī*. We will see later that the meaning of these two terms is more complex. Used for couples, the terms *bahin-behnoï* and *bhāī-bhābī* resemble other terms used in the other generations, such as *cācā–cācī* for FyB and FyBW, or *māmā-māmī* for MB and MBW. This indicates that marriage is not marked by special terms and that it is hard to describe *behnoï* and *bhābī* as affinal kin as distinct from consanguines. As they are closely associated with *bahin* and *bhāī*, I will say, and this is the first property of these chains, that they are metasiblings by marriage. L. Dumont, who underscored analogous phenomena in Gorakhpur, speaks of 'neutralization of the marriage relationship' (Dumont 1962: 22). This seems excessive, precisely because it results in privileging consanguinity. The first property of these chains can be stated as follows: *marriage is important not because it points to an affinal relationship, but because, by linking two brother–sister pairs, it expresses an aspect of metasiblingship*.

Equivalence of spouse and spouse's same-sex sibling
The brother of the *behnoï* is a *behnoï* and the sister of the *bhābī* is a *bhābī*. In the metasiblingship chain, the brothers or the sisters of the alternate link to

50 Kinship and Rituals among the Meo of Northern India

that of ego (ego's spouse's same-sex sibling) are assimilated to the same term. Therefore, the only relevant distinction and hence the relationship in these chains is that of brother–sister.

The brother–sister pair or the husband–wife couple

Articulation of the two links reveals equivalent pairs and couples. In effect, a man calls *bahin/behnoï* both the couple Z/ZH and the pair ZHZ/ZH. A woman calls *bhāī/bhābī* the couple B/BW as well as the pair BWB/BW. In other words, when a male speaker refers to *bahin–behnoï*, he can be talking about a couple as well as a pair. The same is true for a female speaker with *bhāī–bhābī*. This property of the metasiblingship chain will take on its full meaning and scope when we study the compositions of the vocabulary.

Reciprocity of viewpoints in the chains

The last property shows perfect reciprocity between a female and a male speaker placed at the far ends of the chains and who are *bhāī* and *bahin* to each other. The brother–sister and the sister–brother vectors are equivalent and articulate with each other. As a result, the two shorter chains actually form one long chain (Figure 2.7).

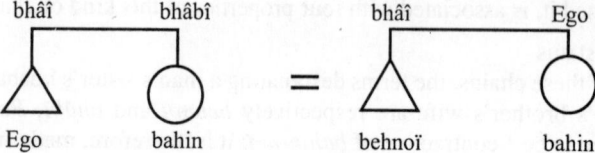

Figure 2.7: Chain of metasibling reciprocal terms

Briefly, this chain of opposite-sex metasiblings, consisting of two brother–sister pairs linked by a marriage, expresses, at the level of interpersonal relationships, the principal features of the global level of ego's generation, non-distinction between consanguines and affines, although with certain specifications proper to the generation: identification between the husband–wife couple and the brother–sister pair of the link alternate to ego's. In this context, marriage is central, not as a manifestation of affinity, but as that which welds the brother–sister pairs into an unbreakable chain of metasiblingship.

Chains of same-sex siblings

When the initial link is composed of brother–brother or sister–sister, the structuring principle and the properties associated with it are entirely different (Figure 2.8).

The principle of the consanguine/affine opposition
First of all, here *bhāī* and *bahin* designate exclusively ego's consanguines by opposition to the terms *sālā* and *nanad*. In this context, the first two terms apply to consanguineous siblings and the last two to affines. Once again we

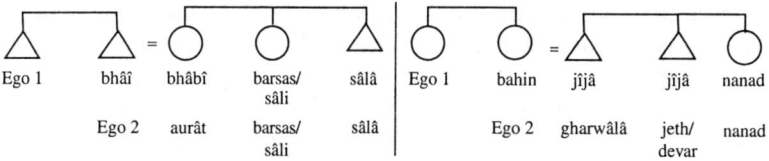

Figure 2.8: Chain of same-sex siblings/affines

have a distinctive opposition which is absolute in other vocabularies, whereas it is relative for the Meo and encompassed in metasiblingship, in the sense that the *sālā* and *nanad* are also respectively *bhāī* and *bahin* at the level above, while the converse is not true.

Spouse's status

The terms for ego's same-sex sibling's spouse are *jījā* and *bhābī*. Let us look at the second term first. The term *bhābī* is used by both a female speaker in the opposite-sex metasibling chain and by a male speaker in the chain opposing siblings and affines. This variation on the meaning of the term appeared in the contradictory statements of our informants, some claiming and others denying that *bhāī* and *bhābī* were a single term. What are we to deduce except that *bhābī* has two different meanings depending on the context? We can now compare and differentiate the terms *bhāī* and *bahin*, on the one hand, and *bhābī*, on the other. Whereas, depending on the context, *bhāī* and *bahin* designate metasiblings or consanguines, *bhābī* applies, in a similar but not identical way, to metasiblings by marriage and to affines. That being said, *bhāī* and *bahin* are present on both levels of ego's generation, whereas *bhābī* is used only at the restricted level of the chains of relatives.

The term *jījā*, used only by women (while *behnoï* is used only by men), is different from *bahin* and applies therefore to affines. Thus the *behnoï*/*jījā* distinction applies to the distinction between metasiblings by marriage and affines. But this proposition needs to be refined. It is only among the Meo that this distinction is so clear-cut. In the Meerut region, studied by Vatuk, whose terminology is very close to that under consideration here, both genders use *behnoï* and *jījā* interchangeably in the two kinds of chain. Furthermore, even among the Meo, *behnoï* and *jījā* are used as equivalents in certain composed chains to characterize affines (see Figure 2.12). As for *bhābī*, but with a slight difference, *behnoï* can be regarded as both a term for metasiblings by marriage and a term for affinal kin. In short, these two terms, like *bhāī* and *bahin*, have different meanings depending on the chains of relatives in which they appear.

Non-equivalence of spouse and spouse's same-sex sibling

While in opposite-sex metasibling chains, the brother of the *behnoï* is a *behnoï*, and the sister of the *bhābī* is a *bhābī*, in the chains opposing siblings to affines, some special features appear (see Figure 2.8). Sisters of the *bhābī* are designated by other terms and a distinction is also made between elder, *barsas*, and younger, *sālī*; this is true for male Ego 1 as well as for his brother, Ego 2. The elder/younger opposition between persons of the same sex thus appears in relation to affines but not to consanguines. In an analogous manner, but only for female Ego 1, her husband's brothers are divided into elder, *jeth*, and younger, *devar*, whereas for her sister, Ego 2, sister's husband and sister's husband's brother are both *jījā*.[11] The relative age distinction can, therefore, not be generalized, and the specific difference from the viewpoint of two sisters has no equivalent in the case of brothers. To account for these facts, we need to bring in factors not contained in the terminology: special attitudes and common residence. A man will have a joking relationship with both his *sālī* and his *barsas*, but will show more respect for the latter and be more familiar with the former. The two women for whom he is a *jījā* can tease or mock him in the same way. A woman (Ego 1) who comes to live with her husband's family, will cover her face in the presence of her *jeth*, her husband's elder brother, and will avoid speaking to him, whereas she will be close to and familiar with her *devar*, her husband's younger brother, whom she will treat like a little husband or a son. This woman's sister (Ego 2) will not have this kind of problem and will fuse the two men into one category. That being said, we must not lose sight of the fact that the elder/younger opposition within affinal kindred concerns same-sex parallel-cousins or siblings and is not significant for opposite-sex cross-cousins or siblings: *sālā* or *nanad* are never differentiated into elder and younger. As we will see later, these terms are extended beyond the second link, while the terms for same-sex siblings, accompanied by the elder/younger distinction, are localized in this second link and are in a sense residual from the terminological standpoint.

The brother–sister pair and the husband–wife couple
In contrast to the opposite-sex metasibling chain, the same-sex sibling chain differentiates for the alternate link between the husband–wife couple and the brother–sister pair. So a male speaker distinguishes the couple *bhāī–bhābī* from the pair *bhābī–sālā*, and a female speaker distinguishes the couple *bahin–jījā* from the pair *jījā–nanad*.

Reciprocity of viewpoints in the chains
In the above chains, reciprocal terms and relationships have different forms depending on whether the alternate link is made up of same-sex or opposite-sex siblings (Figure 2.9).

In the first case, a man's *barsas* or *sālī* will call him *jījā*, and his *bhābī* will call him *jeth* or *devar*. These are all terms of affinity. We remain within the consanguineous siblings/affines opposition when both chains are composed of same-sex siblings.

In the second case, the man whom a male speaker calls *sālā* regards him as a *behnoï*, and the woman whom a female speaker calls *nanad* regards her

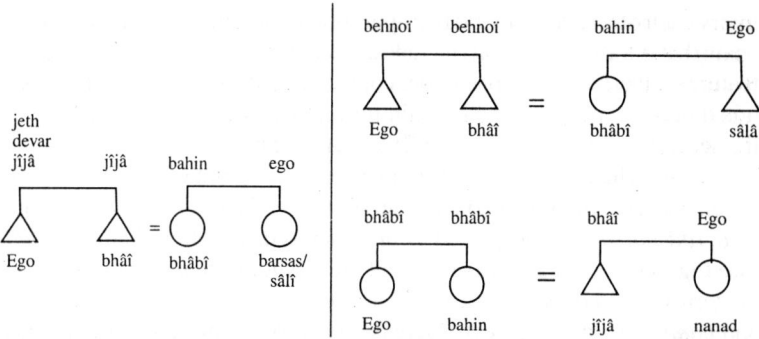

Figure 2.9: Reciprocal terms in the siblings/affines chain

as a *bhābī*. Thus, in one direction we go from a sibling (first link) to an affine (second link), while in the opposite direction, we stay within the metasiblingship chain. There is, therefore, a certain articulation of the two types of chain owing to the presence of a brother–sister pair in the first link. The *behnoï/sālā* opposition is merely a partial form of the opposition between the two chains of relatives. When we come to the analysis of marriage rituals, we will see the importance of this last proposition.

In short, the chains built from a brother–brother or a sister–sister pair have the following properties: consanguineous siblings are opposed to affines, a sibling's spouse is an affinal kin and the husband–wife couples are distinguished from the brother–sister pairs. The elder/younger opposition appears only through the intermediary of certain affinal relations. Finally, residence, as a factor external to the terminology, intervenes only to mark a woman's position with respect to the men of her husband's village.

Hierarchical opposition of the basic cell

We are now ready to construct the basic cell.

At a higher level (what we have called the global level of ego's generation), two terms marking gender difference, *bhāī* and *bahin*, trace the outline of this generation and express the metasiblingship which transcends the distinction between consanguineous and affinal kin.

At a lower level (called the restricted level of ego's generation), two chains of interpersonal relationships established by a given ego oppose each other: one, made up of two brother–sister pairs linked by a marriage, reproduces for ego the non-distinction between consanguineous/affinal kin found on the higher level, that is metasiblingship; and the other, formed by an initial link between same-sex siblings and a second between affines, introduces a distinction between *bhāī* and *bahin* regarded as consanguineous siblings (that is who cannot marry each other), and other terms appropriate for affinal kin. It is in this last chain that the affinal relations include a whole series of secondary or residual features (elder/younger opposition, considerations of residence). It must be noted that the metasiblingship chain forms an unbreakable whole, whereas the second chain is made up of differentiated links.

In these chains, we always begin with the viewpoint of a particular male or female ego. All those whom a male speaker calls by affinal kin terms like *sālā, sālī-barsas*, are designated by his sister as metasiblings *bhāī* and *bhābī* (see Figures 2.3 and 2.4). Likewise, all those whom a female calls by affinal kin terms: *jījā, jeth-devar* and *nanad*, are designated by her brother as *behnoï* and *bahin* (see same figures). There is, therefore, a fundamental difference, depending on whether the starting point is a brother–sister pair or a same-sex sibling pair, brother–brother or sister–sister. *While two brothers or two sisters are alike and can generally be substituted one for the other, a brother and a sister do not make the same kinds of distinction.*

What is primordial is not only the way ego designates different categories of kin, but also the context in which the terms are used and for what kind of relationship. In short, it is the whole set of brother–sister or sister–brother and brother–brother or sister–sister links which are decisive in constructing the basic cell.

If we take *bhāī* and *bahin*, we see that these are pivotal terms because they alone designate both metasiblings and consanguineous siblings as distinct from affinal kin. All other terms (with the exception of *bhābī*, which is a special case) are used only in a specific context and have one unequivocal meaning. The polysemy of *bhāī* and *bahin* does not result from the fact that they have a primary meaning and a secondary derivative meaning, but is instead explained by the fact that they are used at both the global and the restricted levels.

The brother–sister or the same-sex sibling links are essential, to be sure, but we must add marriage if we want to move from the higher level to the one below. Marriage is, therefore, not a secondary feature and cannot be analysed unequivocally as being interchangeable with the term affinity. There are two ways of conceptualizing marriage: either as an expression of metasiblingship, in chains beginning with a brother–sister link, or as an expression of affinity, in same–sex sibling chains. It is in this context that one understands the difference of perspective between an ego in relation to his *behnoï* and conversely between the latter and his *sālā*. In the first case, ego gets to his *behnoï* through a brother–sister link, while in the second, the reverse of the first, ego gets to his *sālā* either through his wife or through a brother–brother link; the two are equivalent owing to the fact that two brothers in the chain have the same point of view.[12]

The different properties of the hierarchical opposition in the basic cell can be summarized in the diagram shown in Figure 2.10.

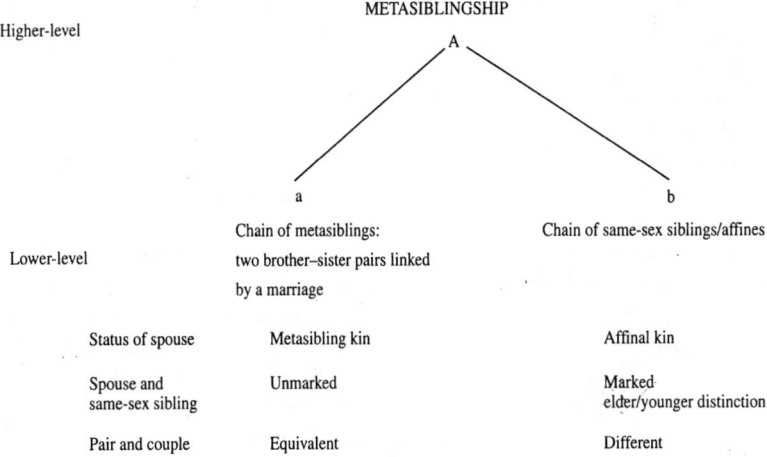

Figure 2.10: Properties of hierarchical opposition in the basic cell

To further develop the structure of the basic cell, we need to define the whole and the parts, and to specify their relationship. The higher-level metasiblingship of ego's generation constitutes a partial whole A encompassed within the greater whole of the Meo kinship system. The term 'whole' refers to boundaries, in this case those of the generation of ego, which is distinct from the other generations which form the set not-A. Within the partial whole A, we distinguish two kinds of lower-level chains as follows: a designating the opposite-sex metasiblingship chain, and b the chain opposing consanguines and affines. There are four kinds of relationship which must be distinguished in the analysis: A and not-A, A and a, A and b, and finally a and b. I intend to show that the structure of these relationships reflects hierarchical opposition and not the distinctive opposition recognized in the segmentary model or in taxonomical classification.

In all these forms of opposition, we recognize at least two levels, a higher and a lower, plus the four kinds of relationship. For the moment we will set aside the relation between the whole A and the set of not-A, for it is a difficult problem.[13] Where things become clearer is in the internal relationship between the whole and its parts. In the segmentary distinctive opposition, the lower-level components are units of the same nature which are equivalent even though they have different names. In this way, we can say that tribe A is divided into tribal factions or sections a1, a2, and so on. Each named unit is defined in relation and by opposition to the other units of the same level. None has a privileged relationship with the whole A from which it stems. The relation between the whole A and its parts a1 and a2 is usually explained by the process of fission and fusion. To use a less empirical language, we will say that the structural relativity of the groups in the segmentary models implies, as Dumont saw, the principle of distinctive opposition.[14] The same sort of reasoning applies to the taxonomy, which recognizes the level of a whole (for instance the species of rose A) and its parts (subspecies a', a", etc.). These, as subclasses of a higher level, are equivalent to each other, the differentiated gap between the subclasses again referring to the distinctive opposition. None of the parts considered has a special status with respect to the other parts (Figure 2.11).

The particularity of hierarchical opposition is that it cannot be understood as a simple process of dividing the whole or as a relationship encompassing units of the same nature in a greater whole. The whole A has a special, privileged relationship with a, which is different from its relationship with b. Thus the relationship between a and b cannot be one of equivalent subclasses within a class. The components are not units of the same kind, and the asymmetry we are obliged to acknowledge, the pre-eminence of component a over component b, comes from the difference in their relationship with the whole A.

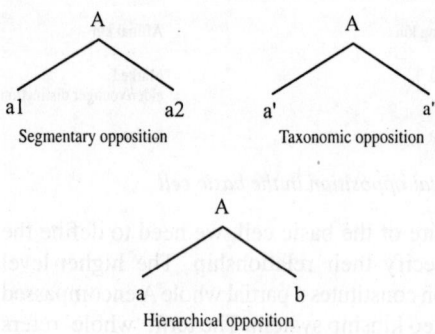

Figure 2.11: Different sets of opposition

This first difference between distinctive opposition and hierarchical opposition must be further developed, and only the analysis of our example with respect to those provided by Dumont will enable us to do this.

Component a does indeed have this privileged relationship with the higher-level whole A in the sense that it can be characterized by metasiblingship. Whereas element b is differentiated by the distinction it introduces between consanguines and affines. It is not-A while still being a part of A. It is in this sense that, between A and b, we will speak, following Dumont, of a relationship of encompassment of the opposite. But that is not sufficient. When we go from the higher to the lower level, we are obliged to recognize some differences: ego's differentiated viewpoint according to gender is not relevant for the whole A, but it becomes relevant for the two chains of relatives a and b; the marriage perspective is not recognized in A, but becomes important in the two chains; and gender difference is not recognized on the higher level, but is crucial on the lower. A defines a whole characterized by 'undifferentiated' metasiblingship of reference, whereas a inserts this metasiblingship into the chain of relatives of two brother–sister pairs linked by a marriage. One can, therefore, not simply speak of identity between A and a because to do so would cancel the difference of level. In chain a, metasiblingship is specified by the brother–sister relationship and by marriage. In the b chains, the brother–brother or sister–sister relationships and marriage are indeed present, but they are based on the opposition between consanguines and affines.

In short, on the one hand, metasiblingship defines the contours of a partial encompassing a whole and, on the other hand, it is the structuring principle which subordinates consanguinity and affinity.

If I now allow myself to speak of metasiblingship as a value, it is not because it is explicitly named as such, as a substance whose effects on the relationship one might subsequently study, but rather because it is the reference inscribed in a structure that it specifies as a hierarchical opposition.[15]

In this context, the components or the poles of the hierarchical opposition are not simply kin terms; they are sets of relationships. That is why I felt it necessary to extend the hierarchical relationship Dumont (1971b: 69, n.33)[16] proposed between *bhāī* and *sālā* to the entire set of relatives in ego's generation, and to clarify the significance I give to this opposition. In the formula *bhāī/sālā*, the encompassing viewpoint is provided by *bhāī* and the encompassed by *sālā*, which enables us to say that every *sālā* is a *bhāī*, but not every *bhāī* is a *sālā*; it is therefore from the broader category of *bhāī* that we take its opposite category, *sālā*. This view is nevertheless incomplete. In the *bhāī/sālā* opposition, we can distinguish only the encompassing level of *bhāī* and the encompassed level in which *bhāī* is distinguished from *sālā*, in other words a consanguine opposed to an affine. We now find ourselves faced with a difficulty. The *bhāī* of the encompassed level is the same term as that of the encompassing level, but its principal characteristic is different: it partakes of consanguinity whereas the higher-level *bhāī* transcends the distinction between consanguines and affines. The meaning is therefore not the same at the two levels. There is no way out of this difficulty unless we see the hierarchical opposition as being, not between the kin terms, but between the principles which underpin the kinds of relationships, the relation between the terms being only one aspect of the structure. In our basic cell, the term *sālā* concerns only a male speaker and through the intermediary of an initial link comprises same-sex siblings. In relation and in opposition to a consanguineous *bhāī*, he is differentiated not only on the global level, where *bhāī* (and *bahin*) is exclusive of all other terms, but also on the lower level of opposite-sex metasiblings.

This is not to say that the opposition between the terms is inadequate, but rather that it is insufficient to qualify our hierarchical opposition. It is merely a partial expression of the more fundamental opposition between types of relationships. In other words, *it is not the logic of the kin terms, but that of the chains of relatives which is essential in this type of vocabulary.*

The other kin terms and relations of this vocabulary can now be set in place. The descriptive method we will use proceeds by 'augmentation and combination', beginning with the internal structure of the basic cell and going on from there to construct the other kin terms. I will show that the operant distinctions depend on those identified within the basic cell. The analysis will begin with the marriage relay and go on from there to construct the chain of relatives for ego's generation. This will show, if not new properties of the chains, at least the characteristics that have until now not been specified or apparent. Then we will study the filiation relay for the distinctions in the adjacent generations, which translate and amplify the distinctive properties at work in the generation of Ego.

There are two kinds of composition rules: relay + basic cell and basic cell + relay:

• The first kind applies to the whole chain of relatives in ego's generation and to the ascending generations, ego taking into consideration the viewpoints of own spouse, father or/and mother: *ego will take into account the marriage or filiation link with an Ego 1 and, depending on the construction of Ego 1's basic cell, ego will define own relationships with the members of this cell while respecting the structural properties of Ego 1's basic cell.*

• The second kind applies to the descending generations: *ego takes into account its own distinctions in the basic cell in order to compose the terms for the descending generations.*

These two rules of composition echo each other so as to construct reciprocal terms and relationships: between relatives in ego's generation, between parents' and children's generations, and between grandparents' and grandchildren's generations. For the construction of the basic cell, the composition of the peripheral terms will take into consideration the way the Meo themselves proceed.

When the analysis is finished, we will take an overall look at the relationship between the basic cell and the peripheral terms so as to define the hierarchical opposition on the global level of Meo kinship terminology.

Constructing the end links in Ego's generation

To construct the relationship between ego and a third link, we will use the following method: marriage of ego + the different chains of the spouse's basic cell. We will consider these compositions one by one, beginning with the different chains of relatives.

Compositions starting with chains of opposite-sex metasiblings

For clarity of exposition, we will call the principal referent EGO, the spouse Ego 1, the same-sex sibling Ego 2, and the opposite-sex sibling Ego 3 (Figure 2.12).

The relationships between the viewpoints of EGO and Ego 1 are as follows: the *bhāī* of my wife is my *sālā*, and the *bhābī* of my wife (wife of first *bhāī*

Meo kinship vocabulary 59

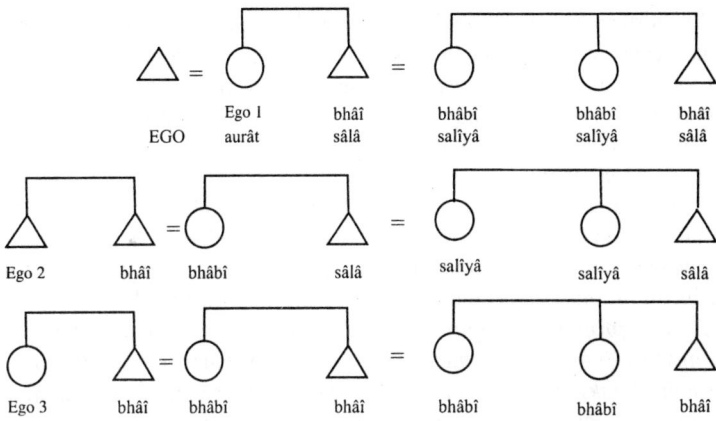

Figure 2.12: Sister–brother vector

or sister of second *bhāī*) is my *sālīyā*. To *bhāī–bhābī*, applied to a pair or a couple in the chain of Ego 1's metasiblings, correspond the affinal kin terms *sālā–sālīyā*, used for a pair and a couple by EGO and by his brother Ego 2. Alternatively, Ego 3, the sister of EGO, will set herself apart from her brothers and will, as it were, adopt the perspective of Ego 1, her brother's wife, and like her, use the metasibling chain.

Equivalent distinctions appear in the other metasibling vector (Figure 2.13). The *bahin* of my husband is my *nanad*, and the *behnoï* of my husband (husband of the first *bahin* or brother of the second *bahin*) is my *nandoï*. To the equivalence between pair and couple for *bahin–behnoï*, corresponds the equivalence between *nanad* and *nandoï* in the third link for EGO and his sister. Ego 3, the brother of Ego 2, distinguishes only metasiblings, *bahin–behnoï*, as does Ego 1.

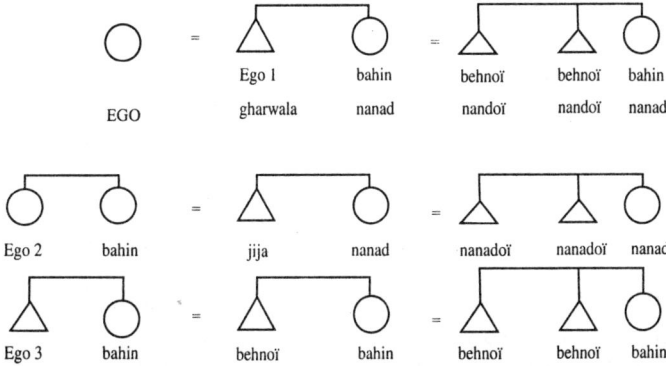

Figure 2.13: Brother–sister vector

In short, in compositions beginning with EGO and adding the chains of spouse's opposite-sex metasiblings, the equivalence of the brother–sister pair and the husband–wife couple in the second link of this spouse's chain is extended by an analogous equivalence to the third link in relation to EGO, but this time within the affinal system: *bhāī–bhābī* become *sālā–sālīyā*, and *bahin–behnoï* become *nanad–nandoï*.

It is as though, in a chain of brothers–sisters linked by marriage, the affinal relationships introduced by EGO were modelled on metasiblingship and were, therefore, modulated by it. This does not apply to all affinal relationships, only to those mediated by a brother–sister link.

By this property of equivalence between pair and couple (whether it belongs to the opposite–sex metasibling chain or that in which affinity appears in the third link) the viewpoints of EGO and his spouse are coordinated: they are united because they use the same structural properties in viewing this kind of chain, while differing in the terms they use.

In this construction, EGO uses the same terms as his same-sex consanguineous sibling (Ego 2); but the viewpoint of his spouse (Ego 1) and the opposite-sex consanguineous sibling (Ego 3) are identical and different from EGO's. That being said, there is more involved than the perspective of a specific EGO. In the two chains obtained by composition, the brother–sister pair, EGO–Ego 3, and the husband–wife couple, EGO–Ego 1, are alike in their treatment of the pairs and couples (metasiblings or affines) of this additional chain. In other words, in these chains, the pair and the couple EGO regards as equivalent will adopt, in the other direction, similar coordinated perspectives (Figure 2.14). It is not only in the way they are viewed in a chain, but also in the way they view a chain that a pair and a couple are equivalent. This important property of the basic cell assumes its full extension in these composed chains.

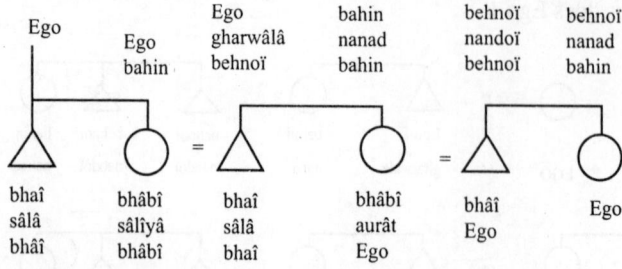

Figure 2.14: Global configuration of brother–sister chains

Compositions starting with same-sex sibling chains

It is in these chains that we find, sometimes in an accentuated form, residual features of the vocabulary. In these constructions, Ego 1 (Figures 2.15 and

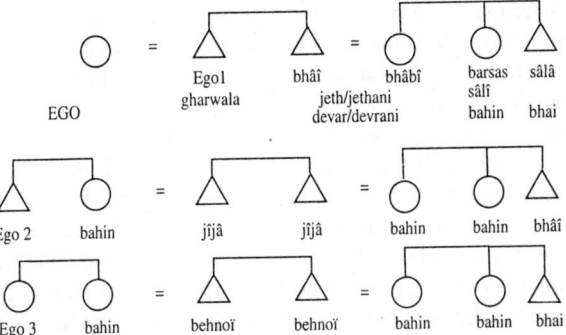

Figure 2.15: Brother–brother chain

2.16), spouse of EGO, distinguishes between siblings and affines. EGO adopts the opposite order: siblings of Ego 1 are affines to EGO, and affines of Ego 1 are siblings to EGO (marriage with these is prohibited). Ego 2 and Ego 3, EGO's brother and sister, will have the same perspectives as EGO. The rule of thumb in these chains has been given by Vatuk: *affines of two brothers or two sisters are siblings to each other.* We will look at this rule in more detail before going on to the ambiguous cases of *saddu* and *jethānī–devrānī* and their consequences.

In the basic cell, the viewpoints of two same-sex siblings with respect to their affines in the second link are similar (except for the special case of a woman who distinguishes *jeth* and *devar*, while her sister assimilates them to *jījā*). For instance, Ego 1 (m.s.) has *barsas*, *sālī*, and *sālā* both on his wife's side and on his brother's wife's side. These different *barsas–sālī* and *sālā* are therefore logically *bahin* and *bhāī* to each other. In this context, the last two terms should not be seen as indications of metasiblingship, but as true

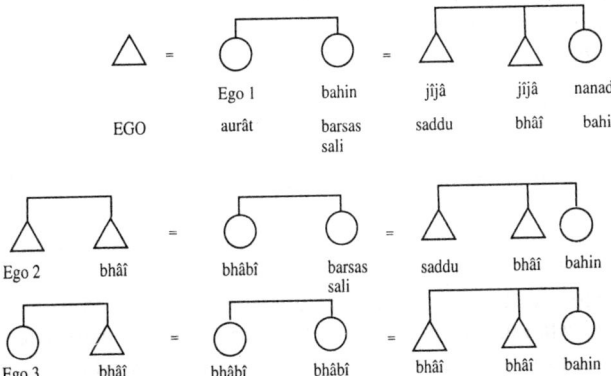

Figure 2.16: Sister–sister chain

consanguineal terms since they are opposed to terms of affinity.[17] It is as though we had here two brothers who had married two sisters (a form of marriage practised by the Meo), and it is no accident that the *bhāī* and *bahin* of the first and third links do not marry each other.

What is decisive is the viewpoint of the initial link of same-sex siblings in the basic cell, and not that of the persons joined to this link by the relay so as to form a composed chain. The change in the gender of EGO in the first link does not fundamentally alter the viewpoint of the third link: EGO, Ego 2, and Ego 3 have the same kind of *bhāī* and *bahin* in the first and third links. Here Ego 3 does not identify with Ego 1, the spouse of her direct opposite-sex sibling EGO, as she would be in an opposite-sex metasibling chain.

This confirms that only the presence of two brother–sister pairs linked by a marriage expresses metasiblingship. All that is needed is that a pair of same-sex siblings (brother–brother or sister–sister) be introduced into a chain, once again to obtain the opposition consanguines/affines.[18]

Let us now examine the ambiguous cases of *saddu* and *jethānī–devrānī*. Unlike the term for spouse, *saddu* is a reciprocal term. Two men married to two sisters call each other *saddu*. One might deduce from this that *saddu* is an affinal kin term, but this would be to overlook the fact that the brothers and sisters of *saddu* are *bhāī* and *bahin*, kin whom it is forbidden to marry. The Meo are aware of the ambiguity of the term *saddu* and say that he is like a 'consanguineous' *bhāī*. But *saddu* cannot be made the equivalent of *bhāī*: first of all, the term appears in only one specific chain and it can be taken as a term of affinity or of consanguinity, depending on whether the man is considered with respect to his wife or with respect to his siblings, without the term ever transcending this opposition, as is the case with *bhāī* in the chain of metasiblings.

Unlike the couple *sālī* (or *barsas*)–*saddu*, that comprised by *jeth* and his wife *jethānī*, or by *devar* and his wife *devrānī*, use a single term built on the same root plus a different ending. Between two women married to two brothers, the relationship can be nothing but *jethānī–devrānī*. Here, too, the ambiguity of these terms stems from the fact that the consanguineous brothers and sisters of *jethānī* or *devrānī* are *bhāī* and *bahin* to EGO.

The terms *jeth–jethānī*, *devar–devrānī*, *sālī* (or *barsas*)–*saddu* apply to 'localized' or individualizing' relationships in the second or third link; they have no extension, unlike *sālā* and *nanad*, which appear in the second as well as in the third link and therefore, have a more 'collectivizing' character.

In other words, these affinal kin terms are differentiated from each other according to whether they apply to a brother–sister relationship or to a same-sex sibling relationship. In one case, they are shaped in their extension by metasiblingship, while, in the other, they remain localized and so relate to the dominant principle without being modulated by it. We can now identify an important feature of hierarchical opposition, namely that the encompassed component b (Figure 2.10) has two aspects: one which is modulated by the dominant principle (cf. *sālā* and *nanad*), and the other, which remains residual, not having any structural relationship with the rest of the terminology (see the other affinal kin terms).[19]

An important corollary of the basic cell structure appears when one compares the perspectives of two spouses (EGO and Ego 1) in the different types of chain. In the chain opposing consanguineous siblings to affines, the two spouses make a distinction between the husband–wife couple and the brother–sister pair: on the one hand, *bhāī–bhābī* and *bhābī–sālā* go with *jeth–jethānī* (or *devar–devrānī*) and *jeth* (or *devar*)–*bhāī* (Figure 2.15); and on the other hand, *bahin–jījā* and *jījā–nanad* go with *sālī* (or *barsas*)–*saddu* and *saddu–bahin* (Figure 2.16). But this correspondence is clearly far from complete. Ego 1 (m.s.) has brothers, *bhāī*, which his wife EGO differentiates into elder brother (*jeth*) and younger brother (*devar*); or again, Ego 1 distinguishes between the elder and the younger sisters of his wife or his brother's wife; but his wife EGO assimilates them to the category *bahin*. Ego 1 (f.s.) calls her sister's husband and her sister's husband's brother by the affinal term *jījā*, while her husband EGO differentiates them into *saddu*—an ambiguous term—and consanguineous *bhāī*. In other words, where one of the spouses opposes elder to younger, the other does not make this distinction; where one uses the same term for same-sex affines, the other plays on the ambiguity between consanguine and affine. In short, *a couple does not identify in the distinctions it makes within the chain of siblings/affines*.

All these irregularities and differences of perspective disappear *in the opposite-sex metasibling chains: the two spouses make similar distinctions and use the same structural properties when establishing an equivalence between a brother–sister pair and a husband–wife couple, but using different terms*: *bhāī–bhābī* and *bahin–behnoï* go respectively with *sālā–sālīyā* and *nanad–nandoï*.

The distinctions between the different chains of the basic cell continue in the compositions made for additional links. Marriage as a relay amplifies and clarifies the structural difference between the two kinds of chain and articulates them according to the distinctions effected by the two spouses.

In concluding this analysis of ego's generation, it is important to retain the following facts. If *bhāī* and *bahin* are at the same time terms of metasiblingship and of consanguinity, and *bhābī* and *behnoï* are metasiblings by marriage or affines, it is precisely because they appear in different chains of relatives. These different chains also enable us to differentiate affinal kin terms. Only *sālā* and *nanad* do not contain any possibility of ambiguity and, through the brother–sister relationship, can be extended infinitely (at least in theory). On the contrary, the other terms—*sālī* or *barsas*—which go with *saddu, jeth–jethānī*, and *devar–devrānī*, individualize more and play on a certain ambiguity between consanguinity and affinity. Therefore, what is primary in this vocabulary is not so much the perspective of the terms as the chains of relatives in which they feature. The terms can vary in meaning without affecting what seems essential to us: namely the hierarchical opposition between metasiblingship on the one hand, and the relative distinction between consanguineous siblings/affines on the other.

CONSTRUCTING THE GENERATION ABOVE (G −1)

In this generation, the couples are not usually differentiated by special terms but are called by a single term which has a different ending for masculine and feminine. This treatment of marriage makes it impossible to distinguish between consanguines and affines of EGO in this generation. EGO's father and mother are the only couple which takes different terms. Through them, EGO will define own relationship with all relatives in this generation using the following composition: filiation + basic cell. To do this, EGO will observe how the two parents go about designating their metasiblings, their siblings, and their affines, and will construct his own relationships accordingly (Figure 2.17).

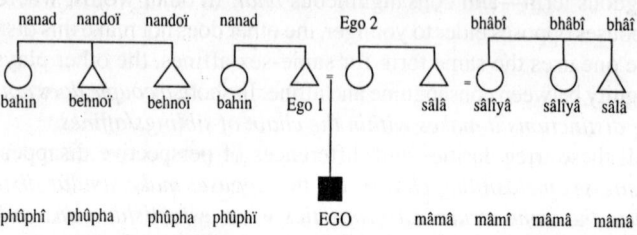

Figure 2.17: *Metasiblings chain of relations and generation −1*

Hence the following rule: My father's *bahin* (and therefore my mother's *nanad*), is my *phūphī*. And my father's *behnoï* (therefore my mother's *nandoï*) is my *phūpha*. In a symmetrical fashion, my mother's *bhāī* (and therefore my father's *sālā*) is my *māmā*, and my mother's *bhābī* (therefore my father's *sālīyā*) is my *māmī*. *Phūphī–phūpha* form a husband–wife couple and a brother–sister pair in the second link on my father's side, as do *bahin–behnoï* and *nanad–nandoï* in G0. Likewise, *māmā–māmī* constitute a husband–wife couple and a brother–sister pair on my mother's side, exactly like *bhāī–bhābī* and *sālā–sālīyā* in G0.[20]

Figure 2.18 shows the particularities of the chains constructed from same-sex siblings. Just as father and mother do not have the same vision of their chains, so EGO cannot adopt both perspectives because it would lead to two different naming systems. A choice must be made. Wherever the two

Meo kinship vocabulary   65

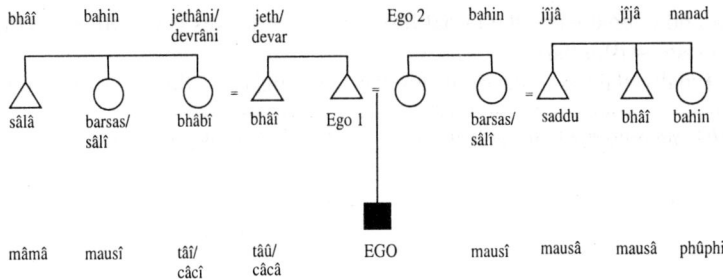

Figure 2.18: Same-sex chain of siblings and generation −1

perspectives diverge, EGO will adopt own mother's rather than father's point of view. Indeed, while EGO's father calls all his brothers and their wives *bhāī* and *bhābī*, EGO's children distinguish between father's elder and younger brothers, together with their respective wives, following the distinctions made by their own mother: *jeth–jethānī* becomes *tāū–tāī* and *devar–devrānī* becomes *cācā–cācī*. EGO, like own mother, assimilates to a single category, *mausī*, the persons the father differentiates into *barsas* and *sālī*, brother's wife's elder and younger sisters. Lastly, wherever the father makes a distinction between *saddu* and brother of *saddu*, whom he calls *bhāī*, while the mother sees only *jījā*, the couple's child follows the mother, designating both categories of kin by the term *mausā*.

In connection with the dominance of the mother's perspective, we note that the two kinds of father's *bhāī*, his real brother and his wife's sister's husband's brother, are distinguished by EGO: the first is a *tāū* or a *cācā* and the second is a *mausā*. Thus, wherever a man does not make a distinction between his *bhāī*, his child will, by introducing a differentiation between *bhāī* who are father's agnates and other *bhāī*. It is interesting to note that it is through a woman, the mother, that the agnatic feature is underscored and not directly in the father–son link.

Alternatively, at the end of the second link composed of an opposite-sex relative, the unity of parents' perspective is restored with the rule for the preceding diagram: my mother's *bhāī* (therefore my father's *sālā*) is my *māmā*, just as my father's *bahin* (and therefore my mother's *nanad*) is my *phūphī*.

A child does not distinguish, therefore, between father's and mother's perspective when the chain of relatives in the first ascending generation is made up of brother–sister pairs linked by marriage. Alternatively, being obliged to choose between the two viewpoints when the chain of relatives is made up of same-sex siblings, the child chooses the mother's.

EGO uses the other properties of the parents' basic cell: equivalence of brother–sister pair and husband–wife couple when the chain of relatives is made up of two brother–sister pairs linked by a marriage, and difference between pair and couple when the initial link between relatives is a brother–brother or a sister–sister pair.

Finally, the first ascending generation retains the following distinctions:

Chain of opposite-sex metasiblings	Chain of same-sex siblings/affines
Pair = couple	Pair ≠ couple
(Viewpoints of father and mother interchangeable)	(Viewpoints of father and mother divergent with mother predominating)

CONSTRUCTING THE GENERATION BELOW (G+1)

In the case of the first ascending generation, there is no translation of the global level of ego's generation with a distinction equivalent to that between *bhāī* and *bahin*. Alternatively, the first descending generation globally retains this distinction alone. Apart from the terms reserved for Ego's own sons and daughters, *beṭā–beṭī* (or *ladkā–laḍkī*), corresponding to the terms designating ego's father and mother, there are only two other sets of terms: *bhatījā–bhatījī*, for the sons and daughters of a *bhāī*, and *bhānjā–bhānjī*, for the sons and daughters of a *bahin*.

To know which terms to use, we must go back to the chain of relatives in the basic cell. The composition follows the rule: basic cell + filiation. As for the first ascending generation, we again obtain two scenarios: one with opposite-sex metasiblings and the other with same-sex siblings.

Chains of relatives starting with two brother–sister pairs linked by a marriage

We will distinguish between the perspectives of an Ego E, own father m and own mother f. The short vertical line (Figure 2.19) designates children of *bhāī* (*bhatījā–bhatījī*) and the long vertical line, children of *bahin* (*bhānjā–bhānjī*). Under each of these individuals of G+1, the m or the f indicates which relatives of the two genders call them *bhatījā–bhatījī* or *bhānjā–bhānjī*.

In these chains, the pattern of correspondences is perfect. The top of the figure sums up the main features of the metasiblingship chain and its applications to the first ascending generation. On the right side, a male Ego m has *bahin–behnoï*, who are *nanad–nandoï* for his wife f and *phūphī–phūphā* for his child E; on the left side, a female Ego f has *bhāī–bhābī*, who are *sālā–sālīyā* for her husband m and *māmā–māmī* for her child E. Egos m and f call *bhatījā–bhatījī* those who call them *phūphā–phūphī*, and the same egos call *bhānjā–bhānjī* those who call them *māmā–māmī*.

Furthermore, couple m and f adopt an identical perspective to qualify persons in the first descending generation: the unity of the husband–wife couple is thus constituted through two brother–sister pairs linked by a marriage.

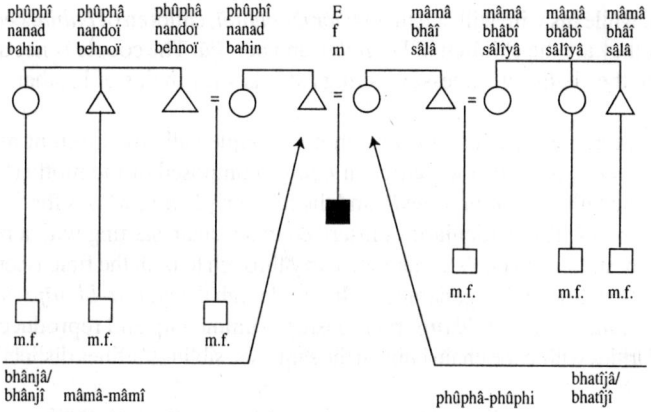

Figure 2.19: Metasiblings chain of relations and generation + 1

We have also seen that E regards them as forming a united couple by making their viewpoints interchangeable when E names own ascendants. The couple thus finds its unity not only in the composition filiation + metasibling chains but also in the opposite direction, in the chains metasiblings + filiation.

There is one question which enables us to verify what has just been said: why are the children of a man's *sālā* his *bhatījā–bhatījī*? The answer can be: m follows his wife, for whom they are children of *bhāī*, or m follows his sister, for whom they are also children of *bhāī*, or finally, for ego, the *sālā* is also a *bhāī* at a higher level and therefore, his children are children of *bhāī*. One does not have to choose among the three solutions because they go together in this diagram of the dominant principle, in which the brother–sister pair and the husband–wife couple are identified with each other and translate, on the subordinate level, the metasiblingship of the encompassing level. A perfectly equivalent example can be given for the relationship between a female ego and the children of her *nanad*, her *bhānjā–bhānjī*. These examples thus allow us to verify the special relationship between the encompassing principle of the basic cell and its translation in the chain of opposite-sex metasiblings.

Chains of relatives starting with pairs of same-sex siblings, brother–brother or sister–sister

In this scenario, the irregularities established for ego's generation and for the first ascending generation (see in Figure 2.20 the summary of the viewpoints of m and f for persons of their generation and the viewpoint of E for parents' generation), namely that spouses' perspectives do not always coincide, are once more confirmed here. The members of the husband–wife couple, m and f, are distinct from each other in the following cases: a man calls children of *bhāī*, children of the *sālī–saddu* couple, and children of *saddu*'s brother *bhatījā–*

bhatījī, while his wife will call them *bhānjā–bhānjī*, children of *bahin*, because for her they are the children of her *bahin* and her *jījā*. The couple is not united through the chains of same-sex siblings as it is with chains of brother–sister pairs.

Furthermore, persons in G+1, whom a couple calls by different names, will call *mausā–mausī* the particular couple composed of the mother's *jījā*, who is the father's *saddu* or *bhāī*, and the mother's *bahin*, who is the father's *barsas* or *sālī*. The particularities inscribed in the chain starting with a pair of same-sex siblings in ego's generation carry through to both the first ascending and the first descending generations. It is as though the *mausā–bhatījā–bhatījī* and the *mausī–bhānjā–bhānjī* relationships summed up and reproduced the irregularities within the chain built on the same-sex siblings/affines distinction.[21]

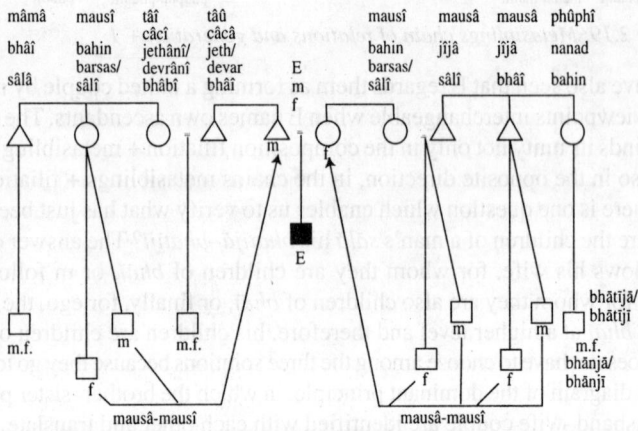

Figure 2.20: *Same-sex chain of relations and generation + 1*

A woman follows her husband for his brother's children and calls them by the same names as he. Once again, we find here the residential influence mentioned above, since a woman comes to live with her husband's family and adopts his perspective on his descendants and his uterine consanguines.

Lastly, for children of a woman's *bhāī*, who are children of a *sālī* for her husband, and for children of a man's *bahin*, who are children of a *nanad*, for his wife, the couple m and f shares an identical viewpoint, and we come back to the preceding pattern, with a brother–sister pair through which a couple is constituted as a unit.

The properties of this basic cell are, therefore, determining for the construction of the terms and the relationships in the generations adjacent to ego's in two ways: (a) in the choice of distinctions—the lower level of hierarchical opposition (the different chains of relatives) is selected for the parents' generation, while the higher level of metasiblingship with *bhāī* and *bahin* operates for the children's generation; and (b) in the method of composition—filiation + basic cell for the parents' generation, basic cell + filiation for the children's—both generations correspond perfectly, whether in the properties of the opposite-sex sibling chains or those of the chains which distinguish same-sex siblings from affines (as shown in Figures 2.19 and 2.20).

CONSTRUCTING G–2 AND G+2

To construct the distinctions in the two most remote generations, filiation (for G–1 or G+1) must be added into the equation: basic cell + filiation, to arrive at the far generations of grandparents and grandchildren.

The following distinctions operate (see Figures 2.21 and 2.22):

• The parents of ego's father are *dādā–dādī* to ego, while the parents of ego's mother are *nānā–nanī*. Correspondingly, the children of a son are *potā–potī* to ego and those of a daughter are *nawāsā–nawāsī*.

• For ego, the parents of own father's *bhāī* (ego's *tāū–cācā* or *mausā*) and *bahin* (ego's *phūphī*) are *dādā* and *dādī* to ego; own mother's parents as well as those of all her *bahin* (ego's *mausī*) and of her *bhāī* (ego's *māmā*) are *nānā* and *nanī*. There are no exceptions. The particularities of the first ascending generation (particularly with *tāū–cācā* and *mausā*) are cancelled.

• Correspondingly, for ego, all children of a *bhāī* of a direct descendant are *potā–potī*, and all children of a *bahin* of a direct descendant are *nawāsā–nawāsī*. No exceptions appear here either (Figures 2.21 and 2.22).

Thus to name own grandparents or grandchildren, the speaker goes through a man or a woman and their respective *bhāī* and *bahin*. To be sure, one uses

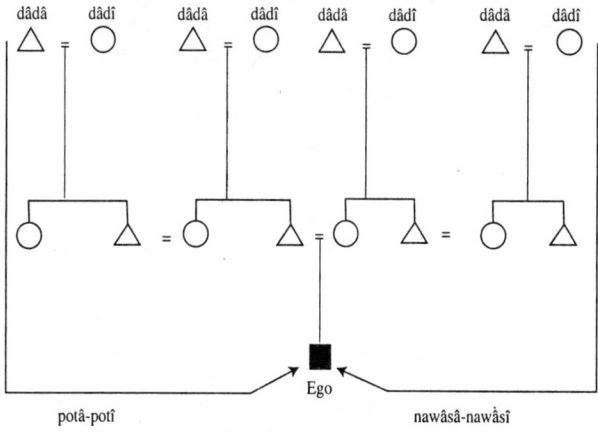

Figure 2.21: Brother-sister and generation – 2, + 2

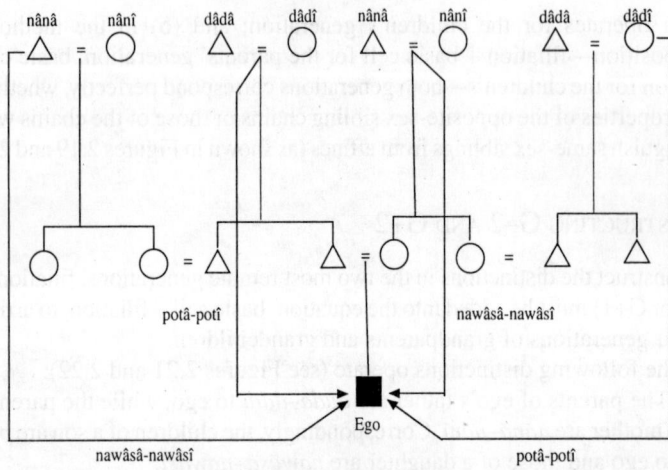

Figure 2.22: Same sex siblings and generations –2+2

the chains of relatives, but the distinctions retained are subject to the dominance of *bhāī* and *bahin*.

In this context, it becomes apparent that the suggestion of a distinction between a direct line and a collateral line, with special terms used between parents and their children, disappears in generations G–2 and G+2.

Finally, the distinction made within these two remote generations are the following: all brothers and sisters of a *dādā* or a *dādī* and their respective spouses are also *dādā* and *dādī* and, in a perfectly equivalent manner, all brothers and sisters of a *nānā* and of a *nanī*, and their respective spouses, are also *nānā* and *nanī*. The equivalence between brother–sister pair and husband–wife couple is perfect. The distinctions within same-sex sibling chains no longer operate. In a corresponding fashion, the grandchildren's generation recognizes only one brother–sister pair not distinguished by different terms as it is in the children's generation. This, I repeat, fits with the identical viewpoint adopted by siblings to define their relationships with the ascending generations.

Whereas the distinctions made in G–1 and G+1 retain the particularities associated with same-sex sibling chains, in G–2 and G+2, the encompassing level with the major *bhāī/bahin* distinction and the subordinate level of the opposite-sex metasibling chain become exclusive.

Hierarchical opposition in the global terminology

We can now come back to the more general use of *bhāī* and *bahin*, as simply distinguishing male and female relatives without considerations of generational difference. Here again, as we have said, the difference between consanguineous and affinal kin is no longer relevant.[22] It is possible to identify, for the kin terminology as a whole, a hierarchical opposition between a higher level (1) at which *bhāī* and *bahin* define all Meo, divided into male and female relatives with no distinction between consanguines and affines, and a lower level (2) at which metasiblingship in ego's generation reproduces, as it were, the encompassing level, while the distinctions in the other generations requiring the relay of filiation constitute the encompassed viewpoint (Figure 2.23).

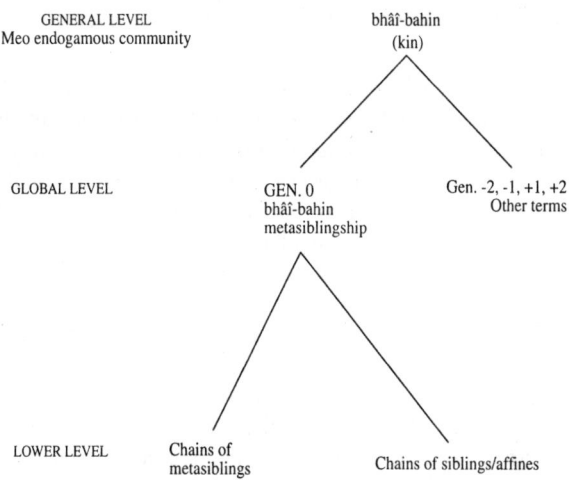

Figure 2.23: Different uses of bhâî *and* bahin

The most fine-grained and elaborate distinctions appear in ego's generation; the further one moves from this centre, the more subordinate features blur until they finally disappear. The two generations immediately adjacent to ego's decompose the higher level of metasiblingship into *bhāī* and *bahin*, and the lower level of the different chains of relatives, and establish correspondences between them. In the most remote generations, the only distinctions which appear are opposite-sex metasiblings on the one hand and the *bhāī/bahin* distinction through its expression as male and female relatives, that is, as marking absolute gender difference, on the other hand. Thus, whether we move from the centre of the terminology towards the periphery or from the periphery towards the centre, metasiblingship prevails, whether in the form of *bhāī* and *bahin* or in that of chains of two brother–sister pairs linked by a marriage; the complementary opposition between same-sex siblings and affinal kin is relegated to an encompassed position. In this context, filiation, while present and indispensable for constructing the distinctions in the ascending and descending generations, remains subordinate with respect to the basic cell structure.

In the logic of the Meo vocabulary, what appear at first sight to be residual elements turn out to have their place in the encompassed aspect of the terminology. For example, the elder/younger opposition, the emphasis on an agnatic feature (in the difference between *tāū–cācā* and *mausā*), and the expression of a perspective external to the terminology—residence—have a purely local value and appear for the most part only in the same-sex sibling chains, and more specifically, in the second link when it is composed of a brother–brother or a sister–sister pair. Furthermore, the hint of a distinction between a direct and a collateral line remains limited and is not given global expression.

A distinction must be made between certain affinal kin terms which remain localized and others which are extended: *sālā* and *nanad*, for instance, do not have the same standing as such terms as *barsas/sālī*, *jījā*, *jeth/devar* or *saddu*. And this is not only because the latter are more individualized and the former more collective. The terms *sālā* and *nanad* are used beyond the second link in accordance with the rule that pair and couple in the metasibling chain are identical, whereas the other terms have no extension.

We thus arrive at a basic rule of the Meo vocabulary: each time a brother–sister pair plus a marriage appears in a chain, the rest of the chain unfolds in accordance with the rule: pair equals couple. Consequently, a couple is united by retaining the same kinds of distinctions in these chains and in the descending generations. Continuing the unity of the parental couple, their children will regard the father's and the mother's perspectives as equivalent.

The theoretical approach adopted here differs from that of componential analysis. It is not my intention to reject the idea that terms undergo extension—for this is an observable fact—but to challenge the generalized use of this action. Furthermore, it is difficult to accept the two postulates associated with the notion of extension, namely, on the one hand, that of the *nuclear family as constituting the quasi-universal and primordial unit of reference* in which the primary meaning of certain terms is expressed and, on the other hand, that of *genealogical ties*, in other words, consanguinity, as practically the only paths by which the different rules of equivalence establish extension.[23] These universalistic claims which privilege blood ties, that is ultimately biology, seem to me unacceptable because they leave only a residual place for local categories (in the rules of equivalence) and abusively extend the categories produced by starting from a Western viewpoint. This perspective, which privileges blood ties, family, and consanguinity in the reckoning of kinship,[24] cannot constitute the universal frame of reference to which all societies must be referred. It is not a matter of simply turning this approach around and succumbing to cultural relativism by claiming that only local categories are relevant for understanding each vocabulary. Comparison must take into account both similarities and differences if it is to arrive at more general propositions about kinship vocabularies.

Thus we cannot say that the facts privileged by componential analysis do not exist; however, they do not take up as much room as they do in our Western kinship system. Family, consanguinity, the extension of certain terms well known in our culture are, of course, also realities which enter into the Meo vocabulary, but they do not prevail as they do in our system; they remain subordinate and under the sway of the structural properties of the basic cell. As I have pointed out, the unity of the family is conferred by the chain of metasiblingship, and not the other way round. Likewise, consanguinity is itself a function of the chain of relatives, since it appears only in the chain of same-sex siblings. Lastly, the extension of the terms is only one aspect of the composition of the peripheral terms through the agency of the structural properties of the basic cell.

But this comparison cannot be achieved solely by looking at the place occupied by one aspect of kinship or another in the different vocabularies. It will be necessary to put into perspective the different systems of relations that characterize them. To situate this type of problem properly, let us come back to Dumont's comparison between the Dravidian classificatory system and the French descriptive system (1962: 32–6).

The first is based on the opposition between consanguinity and affinity, both having equal status, while the second devalues affinity, retaining only consanguinity and more specifically filiation (with distinction between direct and collateral lines). Dumont underscores the paradox of the latter vocabulary, which seeks to express the viewpoint of substance—filiation—in terms of relationships.[25] The Meo vocabulary advances neither distinctive opposition nor substance as the dominant principle, but rather hierarchical opposition. It does not privilege either complementarity between consanguinity and affinity or consanguinity in the shape of filiation, but instead metasiblingship, which subordinates the binary distinction between consanguines and affines, and goes on to relativize filiation (which is here nothing more than a relay).

In conclusion, let us come back to the dominant relationship in this vocabulary, that of two brother–sister pairs linked by a marriage. If in this case I speak of metasiblingship, it is because I want to indicate a certain similarity with our own idea of siblingship; but among the Meo, marriage is the centrepiece. In this chain, marriage is not seen as a mark of affinity, as it is in same-sex sibling chains, but as that which transforms the brother–sister relationship by joining with it: the two pairs of brothers and sisters are then no longer simple consanguines, but form, with this spouse who connects them, the central kinship relation, which is expressed at the global level by the exclusive use of the two terms *bhai* and *bahin*. In this chain, neither the brother–sister relationship nor marriage as such is the primary component, for this would be tantamount to consanguinity or affinity as elsewhere. Instead, the primary component is the set of the two brother–sister pairs plus marriage.

Here a comparison with south India is in order. In his analysis of the Dravidian vocabulary, Dumont underscores the importance of marriage, which can be expressed as the relationship between two brothers-in-law (or two sisters-in-law), the sister (or the brother) of one serving as a link. In the Meo formula I propose, the relationship between brothers-in-law (or sisters-in-law) exists, but one needs to add the sisters (or brothers) on each side.

The two formulas presented in Figure 2.24 clearly show, as Dumont stressed (1961, 1964b, 1966b), how central marriage is to an understanding of kinship in India. But it would be erroneous to reduce marriage to affinity and to consider that the form taken by the latter in north India is incomplete. The brother–sister relationship must be included in the comparison. In the south, this relationship is not marked, and it is the opposition between consanguinity and affinity which predominates. Among the Meo, the brother–sister relationship becomes crucial, but this means that marriage takes on a different meaning and the pre-eminent opposition of the south becomes subordinate.

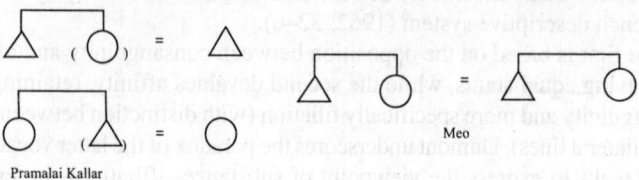

Figure 2.24: Brother-in-law and brothers–sisters
Note: *Pramalai Kallar is a subcaste in south India.*

We will have to get used to recognizing this asymmetry between the opposite-sex metasibling chain and the same-sex siblings/affines chain in the rest of the kinship system and to studying its contours in the chapters which follow. It is in the marriage alliance and in the life-cycle rituals that it will assume its full importance, and it is in these contexts that we will see how the opposite-sex metasibling chain constitutes the essential operator for articulating both the caste system and the Meo kinship.

NOTES

1. The reader unfamiliar with the study of kinship terminology, particularly that of India, may wish to skip to our analysis of the Meo vocabulary and return later to this introduction, the purpose of which is to situate our analytic method with respect to those already in use (Dumont 1962, 1975b; Vatuk 1969).
2. Returning to a distinction made by Morgan, Dumont establishes 'a contrast

between systems which distribute into classes indicated by simple words the totality of the world of kinship, and which one can continue to call "classificatory" in this sense, and systems which proceed by "description", that is to say which define a number of immediate relationships starting with the subject and proceed from these relationships by "augmentation and combination" to designate, as needed, more complex relationships, or if one wishes, more distant kin ..., while, we should note, never exhausting or even considering the world of kinship' (1962: 6–7).
3. When Dumont compares the French, Dravidian, and Hindi systems, he writes: 'It is as though the three elementary relationships between kin—filiation, siblingship and (marriage or rather) affinity—served respectively as the organizing principle for the three systems' (1962: 33). In laying the stress on siblingship, the north Indian system 'leaves room for filiation, like the European system, without giving it a properly structural role, and it does the same for affinity with respect to the Dravidian system. ... The north Indian system looks rather like a compromise between two logics, and it has the complications of a compromise: accepting as its structuring principle neither affinity nor filiation, it calls on the third principle, which is ill-suited to simplicity' (ibid.).
4. I am indebted to Charles Malamoud for this idea (personal communication).
5. B stands for brother, Z for sister, W for wife, H for husband, F for father, M for mother, D for daughter, S for son, y for younger, e for elder, m.s. for male speaker, f.s. for female speaker.
6. Generally when we have two kinship categories, we observe that they are called either by a single term or by two different terms. Here, however, the two possibilities are associated: the two categories of kin can be called by a single term in one context and by two different terms in another. In this instance, things are more complicated. This is not a situation where we have a term A for the global context and two terms B and C for the internal viewpoint. The same term A is used in both contexts: in one, it denotes the two categories of kin and, in the other, it applies to one relative to the exclusion of the other, who is designated by the term B.
7. For the theories proposed by componential analysis, see Lounsbury 1964a: 381–6; on the applications of these to Indian kinship vocabulary, see Carter 1974 and Scheffler 1980.
8. Later we will see in what sense I use the notion of hierarchical opposition for this vocabulary. As a first approximation, though, I will say here that we are concerned with a relationship of encompassment (and not simply of inclusion) between a whole and elements of this whole of which one appears to be its opposite. This supposes we distinguish two levels: (a) the global level of the whole which we must characterize and (b) a lower level, where the distinction is between one of the elements which reproduces, prolongs as it were, the whole, and another which is its opposite. Furthermore, the relationship between the two levels of hierarchical opposition is located in the realm of values (cf. Dumont 1966a).
9. Given the variation in their uses, Fruzetti and Östor thought these terms designated any relative—and therefore, none. A bit like the 'floating signifier', these terms eventually become 'empirical' as well as 'ideological', 'hierarchical', and 'descriptive' without our ever knowing what status to give them (cf. Fruzetti

and Östor 1984: 44). In fact, once again, because we have in mind an unequivocal definition of the terms, we tend to consider variation in different contexts as a sort of aberration, or rather as a lack of consistency. However, in my opinion, what is aberrant here is not this variation, but, on the contrary, the process which consists in not regarding it as relevant.

10. Scheffler and Carter similarly justify the distinction between the primary meaning of *bhāī* and its equivalent in Marathi applied to the brother, and the derived meaning. For Carter: 'In its primary sense *bhāī* denotes one's full or true brother, one's *saka bhau*. Other denotations of *bhau* are marked by adjectives which indicate the manner in which the kin types are connected to Ego' (1974: 36). Scheffler extends this idea to the whole terminology, underscoring what he feels to be fundamental for characterizing the terms: 'the focal or structurally primary denotations of the terms (those specified in Hindi as the *sage*, "true referents" ...)' (1980: 136). In other words, the use of the adjectives 'true' or 'own' are taken into account rather than the sense of the term itself, and the analysis of the terminology ultimately comes to focus no longer on the terms, but on the adjectives, prefixes, or suffixes that go with them. We see just what degree of aberration already denounced by Hocart (1952: 175) can be attained by the will to impose the ethnocentric view of the extension of kin terms on societies which make other distinctions. Inversely to these two authors, I shall say that the use of the adjectives 'true' or 'own' added to *bhāī* clearly indicates that this term does not have the restricted meaning of brother but carries a broader connotation.

11. This difference between the two sisters is linked to that between *bhābī* and *sālī*. A man will call *bhābī* the woman who refers to him as *jeth* or *devar*, and will call *sālī*, the woman who calls him *jījā*.

12. This analysis of the Meo basic cell seems to me to apply to the kinship vocabulary of the Meerut community (Vatuk 1969), even if there are notable differences at first sight.

In Meerut (Parry reports analogous findings in Kangra; 1979: 297–313), a male speaker has no name for his ZHZ, Vatuk tells us, and reciprocally, a female speaker has no name for her BWB; whereas among the Meo, these are respectively *bahin* and *bhāī*. Yet it appears that these persons are also *bahin* and *bhāī* to each other in the Meerut community. In effect, a male speaker calls his ZHZH by the same name as his ZH. Furthermore, this couple's children are *bhānjā* and *bhānjī*, like the children of the couple formed by his sister and her husband; lastly, ego's child will call *bua* (like his FZ) the woman whom the father refuses to name. The same reasoning can be followed for the relationship between a female speaker and her BWB. It is, therefore, not so much the absence of the term as the fact that it is not pronounced, the taboo on naming these categories, which characterizes the Meerut case. Vatuk is well aware of the problem and justifies this so-called absence of reference terms, not on the terminological level, but on the level of attitudes. The very fact of seeking such justifications shows that the failure to pronounce these terms cannot be placed on the same footing as the terminological reference for these relationships, which are in every way analogous to those of the Meo. Of course, we need to ask ourselves why, in Meerut (and in Kangra), there are these taboos which the Meo do not have, but this question goes beyond the scope of terminology proper. In other words, the first difference arising from the comparison is not really a difference if we keep within the framework of the vocabulary *stricto sensu*.

The second difference, which arises at the level of the basic cell, is more complex. Whereas, among the Meo, the term *behnoï* is used by a male speaker and *jījā*, by a female speaker, in Meerut (as in Kangra), the terms are used without distinction by both genders. Thus a male speaker can call his ZH by a term identical with *bahin*, or by an altogether different term. In other words, he has the choice between what I call a metasibling by marriage and an affine. However, once again, things are not that simple. We need to recall what I said concerning *bhābī*, namely that, depending on the chain in which she features, she can be assimilated to a metasibling by marriage or to an affine. It seems that for *behnoï* and *jījā* the case is similar. Finally, the determining factor seems to be the viewpoint of the chains, and not simply that of the terms: for in Meerut, as among the Meo, we have identification between couple and pair (whether these are *bahin–behnoï* or *bahin–jījā*) when the chain of relatives starts with a brother–sister relationship (obviously provided the analysis of the preceding point is accepted).

13. The set not-A can be of the same nature as the whole A when tribe B is distinguished from tribe A in a segmentary setting, but it can be of a different nature, as for example, the Muslim community in Morocco (headed by a sultan), which includes tribal units, while being different from them (see Jamous 1981). In one case, we stay within a relationship of equality between like wholes and, in the other, we are obliged to put into perspective the difference between a partial whole and a more global whole. I have shown that this difference takes the shape of a hierarchy. But until we have studied the relationship between ego's generation and the others, it is hard to say how the relationship between the partial whole A and the set of not-A can be defined. The only thing we can say formally, and therefore provisionally, is that the viewpoint of A supposes an outside which is not included, and this holds for hierarchical opposition as well as for distinctive opposition.

14. Dumont, writing about the analysis of the Nuer, underscores: 'Actually, careful reading shows that Evans-Pritchard has really discovered on his own account the structural principle of the "destinctive opposition"—which is conceptual—even if he expresses it for the most part in the language of oppositions of fact, of conflict' (1966a: 62; English trans. 1970: 41).

15. Some may wonder about the desirability of introducing hierarchical opposition into a world of categories when it usually applies to a set of ideas and values associated with social practices. To this, I reply that the notion of hierarchical opposition was introduced by Dumont to show the inadequacy of distinctive opposition for characterizing the category system. It should be formulated in conceptual terms if it is to have any sense at all. Furthermore, the Meo kinship vocabulary is not simply a formal system, it defines the framework of social relations, and I will show how this hierarchical opposition also manifests itself in ritual action. I do not intend to oppose a formal model which the terminological analysis enables us to characterize to a social practice put in play by rituals. In

both these dimensions of social life, we will need to recognize the same kinds of relationships and values, without seeking to establish any relation of cause and effect.
16. See also the introduction to this chapter, p. 41 where the same reference is quoted.
17. We have seen that a man's *sālā* is his sister's metasibling *bhāī*, while here a man's *sālā* is his wife's consanguineous *bhāī*. The first case is equivalent to opposing the two kinds of chain, while the second refers us back to the chain distinguishing siblings and affines.
18. This context enables us to understand the apparent anomaly of the *behnoï*. He appears in both an opposite-sex metasibling chain (Fig. 2.13) and in a chain opposing siblings to affines (Fig. 2.15). It is important to note here that, like *bhābī*, this is not in itself a metasibling term. Depending on the chain, it takes on different colourings, being closer to *jījā* when consanguines are opposed to affines, and more distant when in an opposite-sex metasibling chain.
19. Can we not say the same thing in the relationship of encompassment between status and power in the caste system? Power has no meaning unless it is modulated by status, while maintaining a subordinate position. But, on the other hand, it is not entirely absorbed by status and remains, as a manifestation of might, a residual empirical fact (*cf.* Dumont 1966a: 101–8).
20. Once again I must point out a difference between the Meo community and the Meerut group: in effect, among the latter, the FZ is called *bua* and the FZH, *phūphā*, whereas, among the Meo the couple is named *phūphī–phūphā*. But that does not stop *bua–phūphā* from applying to a husband–wife couple as well as to a brother–sister pair. The essential property of the metasiblingship chain is preserved even if we now have two terms and no longer one, as the Meo do (Vatuk 1969: 98).
21. It is important to know that *mausā* is my father's consanguine but my mother's affine, and that *mausī* is my mother's consanguine and my father's affine.
22. In a way, the limits of the terminology are expressed by the two most remote generations. The only distinctions retained by the opposite-sex metasibling chains in the grandparents' and the grandchildren's generations are those between children of a daughter and of her *bahin*, and children of a son and of his *bhāī*.
23. All that is needed to be convinced of this is to look at Lounsbury's conclusions on the Crow and the Omaha systems, in which he comes out in favour of an '"extensionist" theory of kinship systems', adding: 'Secondly, it can be noted that this view is, in certain of its aspects, at once Murdockian and Malinowskian: Murdockian in its accord with the assumption of the importance and near universality of the nuclear family as a social institution, and Malinowskian in its deriving the relations of kinship from the primary relations within the nuclear family. (The real "father" is F, the "real" mother is M. These are the basic meanings, others are extensions. Real "uncles" and "aunts" are (unmerged) siblings of parents, etc.)

Thirdly, in this view, kinship reckoning is based squarely on genealogical reckoning. Extensions are not seen as blanket labelings of "social groups" characterized by lineage, locality, age grade, etc., but rather as resulting from a series of derivations, reckoning genealogically from one individual to another in accordance with the principles that are normal for any given system' (Lounsbury 1964a: 381). See also a similar statement on the following page: 'I incline strongly to the assumption that the primary function of kinship terminologies is to delineate the relation of ego to the members of his personal bilateral kindred in such a way as to express some socially and legally important aspects of each of these relationships. From the kindred, these terms can be extended and re-extended till they reach the sky' (ibid.: 382). For one use of this method and its presuppositions, see Carter (1974) and Scheffler (1980). Unlike his emulators, Lounsbury (1964b: 1073–92) has considered that a different way of approaching kinship, starting with a global definition of the terms and not with their more restricted sense, could be used.

24. As D. Schneider showed in his *American Kinship* (1968).
25. If affinity is residual in this instance, all that is left is consanguinity and, more particularly, filiation; in other words a substance, as Dumont stresses in two passages (1962: 35–6), into which a distinction is introduced between direct and collateral liens. Schneider's (1968) work substantiates Dumont's proposition here. Showing the central importance of the family (which we can express in the language of terminology by the direct line) in American kinship, Schneider insists that this kinship unit is defined internally by 'an enduring diffuse solidarity' (1968: 49–54). This notion conveys the substantivist conception of kinship, which is valid not only for the American case, but for the French case as well. One only has to hear how a French family calls its daughters-in-law and sons-in-law 'pièces rapportés' (literally, patches sewn on to the original garment), which indicates a devaluation of affinity and a regard for consanguinity alone.

Kinship and territory

THE THIRTEEN *PAL* AND THE FIFTY-TWO *GOT*

The Meo say they originally came from the Mewat region, even if some no longer live there. This region calls itself the land of the thirteen *pal* (territorial units)—in reality twelve *pal* plus one *pallakra*, or 'little' *pal*—and the fifty-two *got* (agnatic kin units). To help understand the meaning of this formula often repeated by the Meo and by those writing about them, we need to define *got* and *pal*.

The *got*, which we will call 'patrilineal clan', is a more or less vast exogamous group whose members claim to share a common origin and ancestor. Very few know the name of this ancestor, however, and no one is capable of tracing their genealogical ties with the other members of their clan. But all affirm that the Jagga Brahmins have recorded the agnatic relations among the families, the clan lineages.

A Meo never loses his agnatic identity, his affiliation to a *got*, even if he moves to another location in the Mewat region or leaves the area altogether. Agnatic identity is thus independent from territorial identity. We know of no case of a Meo having abandoned his original clan and being adopted by another.

Within the territorial space, the *got* are divided into two kinds of units: *got-palya* and *got-nepalya*. The first are clans connected with a territory known as a *pal*, which bears their name and where the bulk of their members live. The second do not have a territory of their own, at least not in principle. They are simply *got*, and live in villages dispersed around the territories of the *got-palya*.

It would be a mistake, however, to believe that the Mewat region is the sum of the different *pal* territories. It is, as I have said, the land of the thirteen *pal* and the fifty-two *got*, but the conjunction 'and' does not express addition since the units are not of the same kind. Most Meo know the names of the *pal*, but no one can recite all the *got*. Furthermore, it is impossible to find out whether the thirteen *got* associated with one *pal* (of the same name) should be added to the fifty-two others to give a total of sixty-five *got* or whether the fifty-two *got* are a totality, of which thirteen are *got-palya*. Depending on the informant, we have obtained one version or the other, but most Meo admit they have no idea. The sociologists who have studied the Meo are far from agreeing on the answer. Aggarwal lists sixty-seven *got* plus thirteen more about which he has doubts. Sharma gives a list of thirty-nine *got* and thirteen *pal* for a total of fifty-two (Aggarwal 1971: 241–5; Sharma 1982: 97). Our findings do not allow us to decide between the two types of proposition. In reality, the authors are confusing two factors: empirical reality and ideology. The only way of ascertaining the exact number of *got* would be to make a survey of the entire Mewat district. Even then it is very unlikely that that would affect the way the Meo see their region. When they say thirteen *pal* and fifty-two *got*, they are giving a certain idea of their identity. When they speak of these two kinds of units, the Meo are indicating that their territory is not a sum of territories but rather a relationship between a territorial fact with which the number thirteen is associated and a fact of agnatic kinship associated with the figure fifty-two.

THE *PAL* CREATION MYTH

Legend locates the division of the Mewat region into the thirteen *got-pal* in the era of the Mughal Emperor Akbar (therefore, somewhere between 1556 and 1605). It tells that the different Meo clans were fighting among themselves over occupation of the lands. Then they realized that their fratricidal quarrels made them vulnerable to outside enemies, and a meeting was arranged in which the clan representatives discussed what steps to take. After much deliberation, it was decided that the Mewat region should be divided among twelve clans. Each received a territory in proportion to the size of its population. At that point, the representative of the Pahat clan arrived. He was indignant that the council had been held without him. He nevertheless obtained a thirteenth territory but decided that it would not be a *pal* but a *pallakra* ('little' *pal*).[1]

Table 3.1: Allocation of villages to clans

Clans	Number of villages	Clans	Number of villages
1. Demrot	357	8. Singhal	210
2. Chirklot	386	9. Punglot	84
3. Dehngal	360	10. Derwal	84
4. Pahat	360	11. Balot	12
5. Landawat	355	12. Ratawat	12
6. Dulot	352	13. Kelasa	12
7. Naï	210		

This territorial division entailed an allocation of villages which tradition has maintained (Table 3.1).[2] According to this legend, the Meo divided the territories among the thirteen clans by common agreement. No outside authority was involved in the process,[3] and it is said that the division was made so as to put a stop to the feuding and to be better able to fight the Mughals or the neighbouring Rājpūt states. At the level of the Mewat as a whole, as well as that of its territorial subdivisions, the Meo mark their political autonomy. We will return later to this particular aspect of the situation.

Even now the Meo give the same number of villages for each *pal*, continuing the tradition. After having studied the question, the Meo geographer, Abdulaziz, arrives at different figures. For instance, he indicates that Demrot is composed of 160 villages, Landawat of 93 and Dulot 101. The author retains only those villages dominated by Meo from the *got-palya* under consideration, whereas the legend includes in the *pal* villages dominated by Meo from other clans as well—whether *got-palya* or *got-nepalya*—or by other castes of similar status (such as Jat or Thakur) integrated into the Mewat region. The legendary figures and those from the empirical study can therefore not be compared. A sketch of the Mewat country based on the empirical study is presented in Figure 3.1.

For the geographical distribution, we have two maps, one established by Aggarwal and the other by Abdulaziz. To the best of my knowledge, Aggarwal's corresponds to the legend but not to empirical reality. For instance, on this map the Demrot territory is all of a piece, located not far from Alwar, near the site of Lachmangarh. However, I was able to verify that there is a second Demrot territory in the vicinity of Firozpur Jhirka, and a third near the Chirklot territory. Moreover, it is in this last section that we carried out our fieldwork. The Demrot in this section say they came from the region near Lachmangarh. The map made by the Meo geographer, who has travelled widely in the Mewat region, thus fits the present-day situation better. One apparently paradoxical feature appears here: some territories are linked to *got-nepalya*, such as Gorwal, Balyan, Badgujar, Besar, and Blawat. The author relied on the claims of the members of these *got*. Thus the Gorwal territory around the little town of Nagina seems to have been a recent creation (traditionally, most of the villages of this *got* were attached to Derwal *pal*). But the fact that the members of Gorwal or other *got* claim to have a territory does not mean they therefore form a new *pal*. According to the legend relating the creation of the *pal*, the clans existed before the territory was divided, and it was the council of the representatives of these clans which established the divisions of the Mewat region for all time.

Can it be said for certain that the territorial organization was modified at a recent period when *got-nepalya* began to demand a territory? If this were true, if there were indeed certain correspondences between myth and history, between representations of the territory and empirical findings, we would need to identify the conditions which led to the modern alterations. However, we are not in possession of historical documents which would enable us to verify this hypothesis. Furthermore, as I said, the *got-nepalya* which say they own a territory do not claim to form a new *pal*. There is thus a gap between the territorial units of reference and the empirically constituted ones. Finally,

Kinship and territory 83

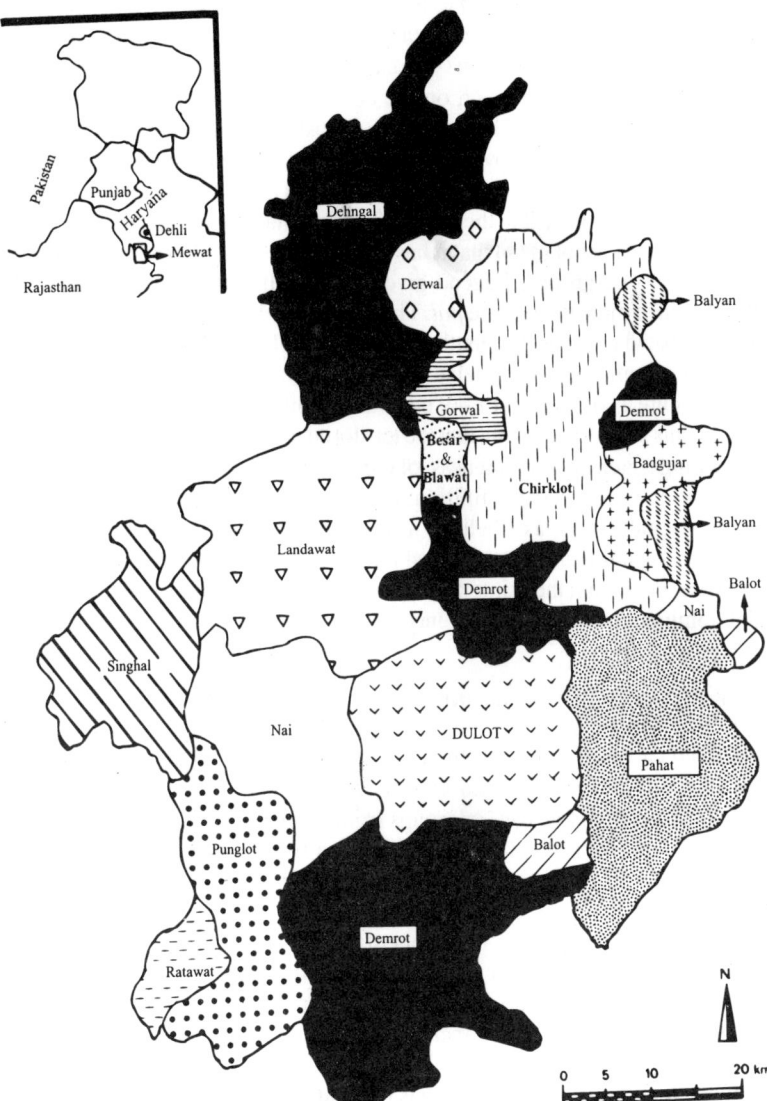

Figure 3.1: Sketch map of Mewat region, empirical division (by Sophie de Beaune)

there is a myth which tells how Balot was obliged to give up its territory without this meaning that they ceased to be a *pal*. There is, therefore, a discrepancy between the territorial division established by the myth and the facts on the ground. What is the explanation? One can say that the representations are merely a sort of misapprehension, or, on the contrary, that the observable facts are secondary to the rule. But I believe that to choose one term of the alternative over the other would be to impoverish the social facts. We must hold on to both the mythic statement and the empirical possibility of creating new territorial units.

Now let us turn back to the legend. The fact that Pahat was called *pallakra*, or little *pal*, does not mean that it has fewer villages or a lower status than the other territorial groups. Legend gives it 360 villages, whereas others, like Balot, with a mere twelve, are *pal*. The reason for this term must, therefore, be sought elsewhere. The thirteenth, which is the 'plus one', is not simply added on to the regular series of twelve. It is as though the myth indicated a refusal to constitute a complete series of equivalent units.[4] The ideological statement would thus seem to be saying that the territorial units form a sort of composition indicating a lack of completeness, of closure. It opens up further possibilities, whereas an unequivocal definition would be closed. In these conditions and if this hypothesis is, as I believe it to be, correct, there is no contradiction between the myth and the empirical facts. The number of territorial units can increase, but within the framework of the ideological statement which remains the dominant principle of reference.

THE *PAL* AS TERRITORIAL UNITS

Each *pal* carries the name of the *got* to which it was assigned. Not all of the members of this *got-palya* necessarily live in the territory with which their clan is associated; lineages, or groups from other Meo *got* (*palya* or *nepalya*), or Hindus of like status (Jat or Thakur) also live there. To take an example: Chirklot *pal* has agnatic groups from Chirklot *got*, lineages from Demrot *got-palya* and various *got-nepalya* lineages (like Sukeriya *got*) as well as primarily Thakur villages. Members of the *got-palya* take a certain pride in being associated with their territory but this does not afford them a special status. *Got-palya* are in no way superior to clans without a territory. From this standpoint, their situation is analogous to that of the Nuer studied by Evans-Pritchard.[5]

The founding ancestor of a *pal* is reputed to have founded the first village from which all the rest sprang. This place of origin is usually an abandoned mountain site, and very few people know its name or even its exact location.[6] The important thing to remember is that there was an original village and that the rest of the localities of the *got* were founded afterwards, by migration. The

Kinship and territory 85

relationship of the other *got* living in the *pal* is fixed in the form of an ancient political alliance.

The *pal* forms a political unit which confronts other units of the same kind. At its head is a *caudri*, a term usually translated as 'headman' (we will look at his role later on). Until recently, all members of a *pal*, whatever their clan, were supposed to stand together against those of other units of the same kind in the event of violent conflict. The fact that the Demrot, for example, live in the Chirklot territory does not change their agnatic identity, but it does determine their political alliances. In the event of a clash between Demrot and Chirklot *pal*, they are bound to help the latter, even if they must fight their own agnates. According to certain informants, it is accepted that they remain neutral, but never will it be accepted that they side with Demrot *pal*. We will return to this point.

THE *THAMBA*: SUBCLAN AND TERRITORIAL DIVISION

The *got* is subdivided differently depending on whether it is *palya* or *nepalya*. Here I will present the first type of subdivision.

The *pal* is divided into a certain number of territorial sections each containing several villages connected with a segment of the *got*, a subclan. The term *thamba* designates both the territorial group and the kin group. According to the Meo, each *thamba* is composed of either eleven or twenty-one villages. But empirical reality does not always concur with these claims. These figures, like the ceremonial fees of eleven or twenty-one rupees, are indications of an open and living relationship.

Territorial division of the *pal*

The segmentation of the clan territory is not presented unequivocally. I will give two examples: the *thamba* of Chirklot *pal* and certain *thamba* of Demrot *pal*.

Chirklot *pal* is divided into seven *thamba*. The largest is Kotiya, founded by Bahar, the Meo hero who fought the Mughals (Kotiya comes from Kot, this *thamba*'s village of origin). His two brothers, Pipla and Palam, founded two other *thamba* which carry their names. In this case it is the names of the founders of these subclans that have been retained and not that of the village of origin (except for Kotiya). The members of these *thamba* are called Pipla *pote* and Palam *pote*, *pote* being the kin term for the son's son. The four other *thamba* of this *pal* stem from Bahar's different sons and carry their names in the same way.

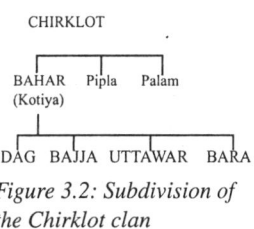

Figure 3.2: Subdivision of the Chirklot clan

There is a mythico-historical story about Bahar, regarded in this context as the original ancestor of all Chirklot. Beginning with this man, the foundation of the different *thamba* are traced through two generations. This is probably a reconstruction for the purpose of connecting all of the subclans with the mythic hero Bahar, an important figure not only in the history of this clan but in that of the Meo people as a whole.

There is nothing analogous for the Demrot clan. As I said in Chapter 1, the informants from Bisseriya did not know how many *thamba* there were in their Demrot clan. Here once again are the facts provided by the informants. Four or five *thamba* lived in the original region of Lachmangarh, near the village of Alwar. One day a Demrot man left his agnates and went to live in the vicinity of Firozpur Jhirka and founded a *thamba* close to the village of Ghata. One of his descendants left in turn and went to live in the region of Punhana; he established the village of Pausar and Aliya *thamba*. It was from this last subclan that the founding ancestor of Bisseriya *thamba* came. These last two Demrot *thamba* border on the Chirklot territory. Thus the Demrot clan is split into three separate, non-contiguous zones. Unlike Chirklot, the foundation of the different subclans is not presented genealogically, and the names of the different ancestors who gave rise to these *thamba* have not been retained. They are usually designated by the name of the first village established in the area: Bisseriya (from Bisru), Ghatiya (from Ghata), and so on, except for Aliya (hard to explain) which does not take its name from Pausar, the village of origin, but from one of the later villages.

In these two examples, apart from the exception of Bahar, the founding ancestors of the different levels of kin group are, to use a felicitous expression, 'faceless dead', coined by Malamoud (1982a: 441–53). They have no mausoleums, no altars, and are worshipped by no one. All the Meo feel the need to know is that each territory and each territorial section is linked with a clan and a subclan. The genealogical details matter little.[7]

The different subclans are presented as having come from each other, but this does not produce any kind of asymmetry or difference of rank or status. There is no such thing as an elder *thamba* regarded as superior to a younger *thamba*. Kotiya, founded by Bahar, is no different from the other *thamba* established by his brothers or his sons. The fact that the ancestor who started the *thamba* of Aliya and Bisseriya came from Ghatiya *thamba* has no consequences for relations among these three subclans. Seniority or the succession of generations has no effect on relations between the sections of territorial units. All *thamba* are equal, whatever the mythico-historical order of their creation.

Every *thamba*'s founding ancestor is reputed to have come from somewhere else.[8] Working back up the chain in this way, one eventually comes to the clan's place of origin, which is an abandoned site and beyond that, one hears of the various Rājpūt groups whose ancestors were engendered by the Hindu gods. The chain of ancestors appears as an articulation of space and time, making it possible to link clan subdivisions to sections of a territory and to indicate their relationship with the gods, and not as a form of genealogy associated with the worship of an ancestor.

Internal make-up of the *thamba*

Informants present the constitution of this kind of unit as follows. For each *thamba* the subclan's common ancestor founded a village of origin in which his descendants established several lineages. Subsequently, members of these groups left their agnatic group and created new villages nearby, which were joined by those founded by lineages from other *got* (*palya* or *nepalya*). Thus the *thamba* is made up of an original village generally located at the centre and surrounded by satellite villages located around the periphery. The original location of the *thamba* is not an abandoned site which merely serves as a reference; it is an inhabited place, and the head of the territorial sections, also called *caudri*, always comes from there.

The *thamba* as a territorial section is a political unit, a smaller version of the *pal*. It includes lineages and even villages which are not from the same *got-palya*. As a subclan, it is made up of the descendants of the unit's founding ancestors in the agnatic line and therefore, includes groups or individuals no longer living in the territory where their subclan is dominant. In order to clarify this dual aspect of the *thamba*, I will present the example of Bisseriya, where our study was carried out.

Bisseriya *thamba* takes in the original village of Bisru—where the founding ancestor of the clan settled when he left Pausar—and the satellite villages of Rahira, Naharpur, Nagla, Khachatan, Barka, Dallapas, Khayka, Fardari, Mubarikpur, which radiate out from Bisru (Table 3.3).

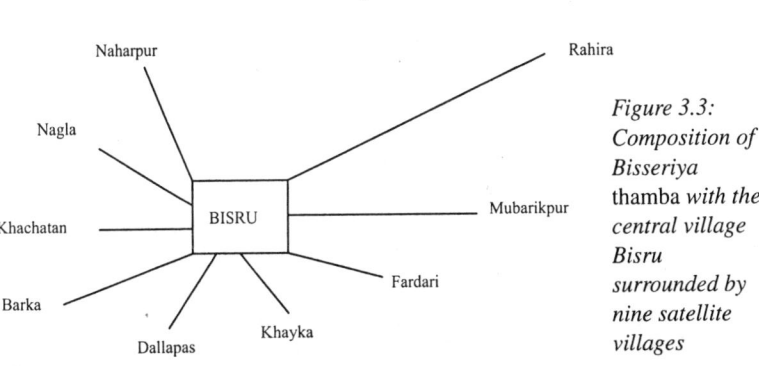

Figure 3.3: Composition of Bisseriya thamba with the central village Bisru surrounded by nine satellite villages

The information we have on the village of Dallapas is contradictory. Some regard it as part of Bisseriya; others, while acknowledging the close relationship between this village and Bisru, link it with Badgujar *got*. This is how the story goes.

In revenge for the murder of their *caudri*, Ahmed from Bisseriya *thamba*,[9] the people of Bisru attacked the village of Singhar, inhabited and dominated by lineages from Badgujar *got* whom they held responsible for this death. Thirty-two people from this *got* were killed. The heads of the dead were brought back to Bisru, as was a prisoner, one of the most important men in this group, a man called Dalla. A new lineage house, *tharu*, was built, probably by the Haweliya lineage. The new *caudri*, Meda, the younger brother of the former *caudri*, requested that, under each step leading up to this lineage house, one of the heads be placed. When certain villagers decided to kill Dalla, Meda stepped in, saying enough people had already died. He gave the prisoner one rupee and a turban and let him go. Dalla returned to his village, Singhar, where he was ill received. People criticized him for coming back alive, freed by the enemy. So Dalla left for the village where his married daughter lived, near Firozpur Jhirka. He spent a month there. One day, when he asked his grandson to prepare his hookah, he heard him answer: 'How long are you going to make trouble for us?' Dalla departed from his son-in-law's house. He returned to Bisru, handed his dagger to Meda and told him: 'Kill me because no one wants me, neither my *bhāī* in Singhar nor my daughter.' Meda replied: 'If no one will take you in, I will, I have a place for you to live and I will take care of you.' He led him to a site where Dalla built a house and a new village which took the name Dallapas. This village was absorbed into the territory of Bisseriya.

The informants who link this village to Badgujar refer to the territory that this former *nepalya* clan has recently claimed. For the others, Badgujar *got* is not a *pal*, and therefore, does not have a territory; and Dallapas, founded thanks to the Demrot living in a section of Bisseriya territory, is part of this *thamba*, even though it does not now regard itself as belonging.

As an agnatic kin unit, Bisseriya *thamba* includes all members of the subclan residing in the territory of the same name, but also other descendants of the same founding ancestor who live in other places. For instance, some Demrot originally from Bisseriya now live in the village of Saroli, which is part of Bajja *thamba*, Chirklot *pal*. They continue to claim, not only their title of Demrot, but also their affiliation to Bisseriya, even though, in terms of territory, they are part of Bajja and not their original *thamba*. Thus the two meanings of the word *thamba*, territorial unit and kin unit, do not always coincide, and context alone allows one to distinguish between them. We will see the importance of this unit in marriage alliances.

THE *GOT-NEPALYA*: A CLAN WITHOUT A TERRITORY

Unlike the *got-palya*, the *got-nepalya* does not have a territory and a political dimension, only a lineage and a residential dimension. Because of this it does not have *thamba* units.[10] The descendants of the founding ancestor of these *got* formed a series of lineages which are dispersed among the different villages. Two types of case need to be distinguished:

• The village was founded by a descendant of the ancestor of the *got-nepalya* and is inhabited uniquely by lineages descended from this ancestor and which prevail (that is, possess pre-eminent rights on the land) in this locality. This locality is part of the territory of a *got-palya thamba*. We have given the example of Dallapas, founded by a lineage from Badgujar *got*, but territorially a part of Bisseriya *thamba*; let me also mention the case of the different villages of Gorwal *got-nepalya* like Malab, Bhadas, Nagina, Badri, and Neemli connected to Meoliya *thamba* in Derwal *pal*.

• The village is inhabited by lineages arising from a *got-nepalya* and a locally dominant *got-palya*. In this case, residential dominance is shared among the different Meo agnatic groups. But at the level of the *thamba*, it is the *got-palya* which determines the type of solidarity in the event of conflict between territorial sections.

A distinction must be made between territorial and residential principles: a village connected with a *got-nepalya* is not a relevant political unit in Meo relations. As part of the *thamba* of a *got-palya*, it must follow the political alliances of the latter, even if it means fighting its own agnates living in villages in the opposing *thamba*. Residential dominance is a separate matter, because it is defined by a connection with the land and therefore, between the castes associated with the village.[11]

THE MEO VILLAGE AND ITS LINEAGE SUBDIVISIONS

In the Mewat region one finds Meo villages, Thakur villages and Jat villages. Each of these, called *gaon*, has a number of castes. The dominant caste, the one which has a pre-eminent right over the land, gives the village its identity. In some villages, several high-caste lineages—Meo (Muslims), Thakur (Hindus), and Jat (Hindus)—share the lands and form dominant castes. But villages in which the Meo are the only dominant caste outnumber the rest.

We will take several different cases to illustrate the composition of Meo villages.

The one-*got-palya* village

Bisru, the site of our fieldwork, is a big village of nearly 5000 inhabitants, built on a hill. This is where Bisseriya *thamba* (Demrot *pal*) originates. Bisru's

Meo are divided into three big lineages founded by separate descendants of the village's founding ancestor and dispersed into three quarters. These lineages, termed *thok* or *mohalla*, are: Uparla, Dhaja, and Haweliya. The name of the first lineage means 'those of the upper quarter'. The informants say that the name refers to the divisions of the Meo part of the village into three lineages occupying three quarters[12] called: Uparla–Bicharla–Nicharla: 'those of the upper quarter', 'those of the middle quarter', and 'those of the lower quarter'. This geographical division exists in Bisru, even if it is not always expressed directly in all lineage names. The lineage house, *tharu*, in Dhaja is said to stand in the middle of the village. This opposition between upper and lower mediated by the middle does not mean that the spatial occupation actually coincides, or that there is any difference of status among the three lineages. Figure 3.4 depicts the structure of a typical *got-palya* village.

If the number three recurs time and again when informants talk about Bisru's lineages or quarters, the reality on the ground is far more complex. There is a fourth, independent, lineage, Sapera; and the Dhaja lineage is actually made up of four segments which do not descend from a common ancestor. We thus arrive at a total of seven lineages. Each of the seven units can claim a certain degree of autonomy in dealing with internal conflicts in the lineage panchayat, or 'council'.

Bisru		
Thok (lineages)		
Uparla (Sapera)	Dhaja (Dhand, Gand, Kampaniya, Dandiya)	Haweliya

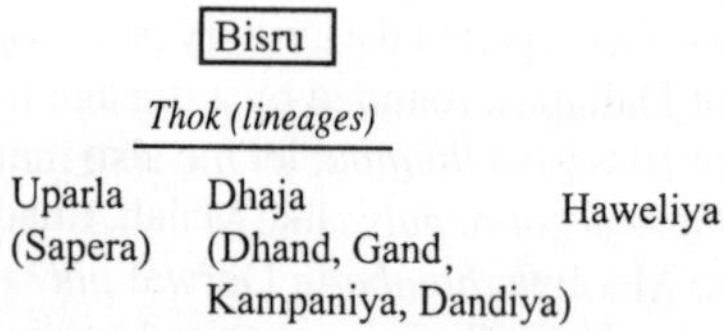

Figure 3.4: Structure of a typical got-palya *village*

Nevertheless, informants say that Sapera should be counted with Uparla and that Dhaja's various segments make up a single *thok*. This combination of lineages into three agnatic units is not simply a device. The existence of three lineage houses (*tharu*), that of Uparla, of Dhaja, and of Haweliya, in which the panchayats are usually held, points to such a grouping. For instance, Uparla lineage invites Sapera to its councils, and the four Dhaja segments are convened together in their lineage house. Furthermore, when an Uparla boy gets engaged, it is customary for the bride's agnatic relatives to make various presents to the future bridegroom and to his lineage. It is not unusual for Sapera households to be taken into account when reckoning the gifts each family is to receive, as though they were an integral part of Uparla. But on all these occasions, reference to the three-part division always depends on the goodwill of the parties involved. Amalgamation is imperative only during the festival of Muharram, for the procession of the *tajiā*, the construction representing the martyr's mausoleum. The procession is supposed to set out from the central lineage house (Dhaja), proceed to the upper house (Uparla), and then go on to the lower one (Haweliya), before finally submerging the *tajiā* in one of the ponds located on the outskirts of the residential zone. Here we have a representation of space with 'three' lineage houses 'plus one', the pond.

Other *got* too have lineage segments living in Bisru. Their ancestor is believed to have settled there after having married a girl from a Demrot lineage. These lineage segments have neither a lineage house nor a lineage council, however, but are dependent on a Demrot lineage to which they are attached. For instance, a lineage segment of Naï *got* lives in the Uparla lineage quarter following a marriage;[13] it uses the latter's lineage house and its panchayat, even when the conflict is confined to the segment. While it keeps its *got* identity, this segment is also part and parcel of the Uparla lineage. In this big village of Bisru, the Demrot lineages hold almost exclusive sway. In this sense, Bisru is a one-*got* village.

I will now give an example of other villages, stressing not their lineage subdivisions, analogous to those of Bisru (the figure of 'three' lineages appears regularly, even though it cannot be generalized), but their composition in terms of *got*.

The one-*got nepalya* village

The village of Dallapas is inhabited by lineages stemming from Badgujar *got-nepalya*. This is, therefore, a Badgujar village, even though it stands in the Bisseriya territory and is politically dominated by the latter. The dominant *got* unit here differs depending on whether one is referring to the residential or the territorial level. It is the residential unit which gives the village its identity. But from the territorial standpoint, this village is a satellite of Bisseriya, although things are beginning to change with the constitution of a Badgujar territory.

Two cases of multi-*got* villages

The village of Naï, which stands in Palam *pote thamba*, Chirklot *pal*, is made up of seven Chirklot lineages and one lineage from Sukeriya *got-nepalya*. The ancestor of this last group is said to have married a woman from one of the Naï Chirklot groups and to have gone to live with his father-in-law. Over time, his descendants came to constitute a Sukeriya lineage. Like each of the Chirklot lineages in the village, this lineage has its own lineage house, its own council, and even takes part in the village panchayat on the same footing as the Chirklot lineages. This is, therefore, different from the case of Bisru, where the representatives of other *got* than Demrot have no autonomy. Here we have a good example of a multi-*got* village.

The fourth example is slightly different from the other three. Saroli village was founded by a Demrot lineage from Bisseriya *thamba* and was formerly attached to its territory. Over time, members of Chirklot overran the Saroli territory and its vicinity. At present the village of Saroli is incorporated into Bajja *thamba* of Chirklot *pal*. The Demrot lineage still living there keeps its autonomy by maintaining a lineage house and a council separate from that of the Chirklot lineage. But it was forced to recognize the latter's dominance

Group of houses belonging to close kinsmen, with grain silo and outdoor kitchen

An old-fashioned house (wattle and thatch)

A tharu, *lineage house in the village of Bisru*

over the subclan territory. Saroli is a multi-*got* village, but it is different from Naï. It is made up of lineages stemming from two *got-palya* with adjoining territories, one having finally gained a lead over the other in obtaining the attachment of the village to the *thamba*.

These four examples do not exhaust the different internal configurations of the Meo community living in a village. They do, however, show that village residential identity and local subclan territorial identity do not wholly coincide.

Lineage subdivisions

Each lineage is divided into a number of lineage segments or lines, which are also called *thok* or *khandan* and which occupy part of a quarter (designated by the same term). Each line is made up of several restricted or extended families called *kumba*, who occupy a house, or *ghar*.[14] We will not study these kinship units in detail here, as it would add nothing to our analysis of the relationship between kin groups and territory.

Table 3.2 sums up our analysis of territorial, residential, and agnatic segmentations and the relationship between in the Mewat region.

Table 3.2: Summary of the territorial, residential, and agnatic segmentations

Segmentation levels	Territory and agnatic kin		Agnatic kin alone
1	*Pal* Territorial units	*Got-palya* Clan	*Got-nepalya* Clan
2	*Thamba* Territorial unit section	*Thamba* Subclan	
	Residence and agnatic kin		Residence and agnatic kin
3	*Gaon* Village, lineages		*Gaon* Village, lineages
4	*Thok* Quarter, lineages		*Thok* Quarter, lineages
5	*Thok* or *Khandan* Subquarter, line		*Thok* or *Khandan* Subquarter, line
6	*Ghar* House	*Kumba* Family	*Ghar* House / *Kumba* Family

Two of the units are based on territory: the *pal* and the *thamba*. The village and its subdivisions are essentially residential units. The distinction between *got-palya* and *got-nepalya* operates from the standpoint of territory but not residence. The *thamba* as a territorial unit is more clear-cut than the higher *pal* level. Its relationship with the lower level is marked by the distinction between the original village and its satellites.

SEGMENTATION AND POLITICAL STRUCTURE

We will restrict ourselves to a few indications about the political relations that go with territorial and residential organization. Segmentary-type conflicts occur at the level of certain neighbouring *pal* and closely related *thamba*. Any aggression on one side triggers a reciprocal aggression. Violence between these units is endemic and sporadic. I will present various examples of such conflicts.

A conflict between *pal*

The villages of Bisru and Pausar, Demrot *pal*, were on very bad terms with the village of Kot, Chirklot *pal*, located a few kilometres away. Randhir, *caudri* of Bisru knew that a violent clash was inevitable and decided to be prepared. He urged the people of Pausar to secure the support of the Jat village of Rawat. This was done in the following way: the men of the two villages exchanged turbans and became each other's *bhāī*. Randhir set out for Kot with the aim of impressing the men of Chirklot. He took with him his best marksmen, who put on a demonstration. The headman of Kot calmed down for a while, but then decided to attack Pausar. He asked Randhir's help. Randhir replied: 'I cannot, for Pausar is my mother'.[15] He received the reply: 'Pausar is no longer your mother, she has gone away with another husband.' So Randhir set out for Pausar with his men to side with them against Kot. The battle opposed, on one side, Bisru and the members of its subclan plus Pausar and its subclan supported by the village of Rawat and, on the other side, Kot and the men of its subclan plus several Jat villages (in conflict with Rawat). Many were killed on both sides. Sometime later, the men of Kot attacked Bisru but were forced to retreat. Endemic hostility persisted between Demrot and Chirklot for a long time.

In this example, it was not the totality of the two *pal*, but territorial sections associated with subclans which opposed each other. That being said, people talked about the conflict in terms of *pal*. Here two remarks limiting segmentary opposition seem to me to be in order:

• The feuding groups are territorial neighbours. It is significant that people refuse to take or give wives between adjoining units. Bisru and Pausar and their respective subclans do not exchange women with Kot and its subclan. As a rule, marriages are contracted far away, and one does not wage war on one's allies by marriage.

• There is no process of mediation which would put an end to conflict between territorial groups. At best, some members of the hostile groups see to it that the violence does not get out of hand. These are either members of the same *got* who are dispersed between the two territories, or members of *got-palya* that are on good terms with both sides.

A conflict between a *pal* and a *thamba*

There were two married sisters: one lived in a village of Uttawar *thamba* (Chirklot *pal*) and the other in the village of Bisru (Demrot *pal*). The second committed adultery with one of her sister's husband's brothers. The agnates of the cuckolded husband decided to punish the guilty lovers. One day they came upon them in the village of Bisru and cut their noses.[16] Uttawar *thamba* wanted to take revenge on the Demrot *pal thamba*. The conflict between the *pal* was rekindled. The men of Bajja *thamba* (Chirklot *pal*) warned Bisseriya of the impending threat. They advised them, whatever they did, not to venture into Chirklot territory and to be on their guard. They did this, we were told, because they were fighting with Uttabar *thamba* and so took advantage of the situation to show their hostility to this group. But our informant added that, if a Demrot man had ventured into Chirklot territory and had been set upon by Uttawar men, no Bajja man would have been allowed to protect him. A while later, the men of the two *pal* involved sought to resolve the discord. Compensation was paid by the agnates of the wronged husband to Uttawar *thamba*, which renounced vengeance. Bajja *thamba* was asked not to interfere in such conflicts in the future (that is, not to take action against the members of its own *pal*). This agreement does not mean that peace has been restored between the parties involved. Sooner or later feuding will once again break out between the *pal* and between the two *thamba* of Chirklot *pal*.

This conflict is slightly different from the preceding one. It shows how the endemic hostility between the two *pal* can flare up on different occasions. And we see how *pal* solidarity is demolished when *thamba* from the same territorial unit clash. Bajja's intervention was aimed at Uttawar, with which differences were far from being settled.

These two instances of conflict show that there is indeed a tendency for segments to oppose each other—*pal* against *pal* at the higher level, and *thamba* against *thamba* at the lower. But these oppositions do not always manifest themselves according to this logic. It seems that the *pal* are not frequently mobilized whereas solidarity between *thamba* is more evident, more systematic.

Conflicts within the *thamba* and its subdivisions

These conflicts are not the affair of segments. It is the panchayat, the council with which the *thamba*, village, or lineage is affiliated, which is charged with settling the quarrel. The Meo acknowledge that relations between agnates, especially within a quarter between members of the same lineage, are always very tense. The disputes are often caused by problems of land, quarrels over an inheritance or territorial boundaries. It is not unusual for quarrelling agnates to insult each other and sometimes to break off relations. But the council is convened only if violence has actually broken out or threatens to do so. The process is no different from that described many times for other Indian communities. Each party exposes its grievances, an attempt is made at conciliation, and if this does not work, the members of the council look for a solution. Sometimes this takes several meetings. But once the decision has been taken, it must be applied. Anyone violating the decision is severely sanctioned: he is excluded de facto from all matters concerning the lineage, the village, or the *thamba*. In such conflicts, the distinction between *got-palya* and *got-nepalya* is not relevant.

Conflicts within a lineage

I will give two examples of conflicts between agnates, one of which had dramatic consequences.

In lineage A, segment a1 was on bad terms with the other segments of the group. The men and women of a1 were always quarrelling with their neighbours and agnates. One day, some silverware was stolen from a man from segment a2, who claimed to have recognized a young man from a1 as the thief. The matter went beyond simple insults. The council of lineage A was convened. X, the oldest man in a1, denied that anyone from his group would have committed such a theft. But the victim maintained his accusation. After a long discussion, it was decided that a member of a1 would come on Friday, after morning prayers, and swear on the Koran that his group was not responsible for the theft. X delegated his son Y to take the oath. But the following day, a fire destroyed a barn in the quarter. In the rush to put out the fire, a child, the son of Y, struck his head against a stone and died in the hours that followed. This tragedy hit the village hard. For the Meo in that quarter, Y and his father had sworn falsely and been punished by heaven. Everyone spoke of the child's qualities, an innocent victim of the crime of the adults of a1. The whole quarter took an active part in the funeral. The members of a1 were not called back before the meeting because they had been tragically punished by the gods. After a brief mourning period, quarrelling between a1 and the rest of the lineage resumed.

Another less dramatic conflict gives us the opportunity to see the council function in more detail.

One day, a quarrel broke out between two women from closely related agnatic lines; one stabbed the other in the head with a knife. The wounded woman was taken to a dispensary and cared for. Her husband and her children were furious and threatened to assault not only the guilty woman but also her family. Tempers frayed and the situation grew bitter. The elders of the three other families in the lineage intervened, but to no avail. It was therefore decided to convene the council. As people were angry, the two parties refused any attempt at conciliation. Their agnates threatened to exclude them from the group if they persisted. At last an agreement was reached. The guilty woman's husband paid compensation to the husband of the victim. Both parties were warned that a more severe sanction awaited them if they quarrelled again.

Generally speaking, the sanction against those who refuse to obey the decisions of the panchayat is applied according to two principal modes: either the other men refuse to smoke the hookah with the culprit—such refusal being considered a form of exclusion—or they decide not to speak to him or help him until he has changed his attitude. For example, here is the story of two brothers who quarrelled over an inheritance. After a dispute, one decided to complain to the police, in spite of all attempts at conciliation. He refused to appear before the council. The panchayat decided that no one in the quarter was to speak to him as long as he persisted in wanting to take the matter to court. After a few days, the man changed his mind. But he had to pay a fine to the council for having defied its authority.

The presence of a tendency for segments to oppose each other at the levels of the *pal* and the *thamba*, and the absence of any such tendency in the lower-level units confirms, for the political sphere, the difference drawn above between territorial structure and residential structure.

Men smoking a hookah

Headmen: The authority of the *caudri*

The *caudri*, or 'headman', exists at two territorial levels: the *pal* and the *thamba*. *Got-nepalya* are not supposed to have *caudri* because they do not have a territory. The *caudri* of the *pal* is usually chosen from the oldest village in the territory. As he is called upon to act less and less often, few people in the territorial unit remember his name or the village he comes from.

The *caudri* of the *thamba* is always chosen from the dominant subclan's village of origin, and more specifically from a particular line, called the eldest, at least in principle. As this section of the territory is an unbroken area and smaller than the *pal*, the names of the successive headmen are more easily retained and their actions are remembered.

The *caudri* is appointed for life and cannot be dismissed. In former times he would carry out the orders of the panchayat, of the *pal* council, or of the *thamba* council, leading the men into battle against other *thamba* or seeing that council decisions were carried out in matters of internal justice. Whenever there was a ceremony, he would be given a place of choice and he was the first to be served in dinners. Today he no longer leads men into battle and plays little role in administering justice for the *pal* or the *thamba*. Alternatively, he still enjoys ceremonial precedence. People consult the *thamba* headman because he is supposed to be the most knowledgeable about the traditions and his advice is valued. Their attitude towards him is that which one would adopt towards an elder. *Thamba* members respect him, listen to him, follow his advice insofar as it does not go against their own interests. As elsewhere in India, though, this kind of traditional authority is dying out.

For both levels of headman, succession follows the rule of primogeniture The eldest son takes his father's place. The council of the *pal* or the *thamba* ratifies the new appointment, but if it is not satisfied with the pretender to the title or if several brothers present themselves as the legitimate heir of the preceding *caudri*, the council can, after deliberation, choose its own candidate or even suspend any decision pending an agreement.

History of the *caudri* of Bisseriya *thamba*

Caudri Ahmed, from Haweliya lineage, headed not only his subclan's territory but also a number of villages in the vicinity, to which he lent his protection in exchange for a tax. The representative of the Mughal emperor in Firozpur Jhirka, Nawab Shamsuddin, asked Ahmed to turn over 50 per cent of this tax, but in vain. So he decided to attack Bisru, but he was unable to gain entry and was forced to turn back. He incited the men of the village of Singhar (inhabited by lineages from Badgujar *got*), with whom Ahmed was on bad terms, to kill him. A short time later, Ahmed learned that some Englishmen were coming to Punhana (a little town 6 km from Bisru). He decided to pay them a visit in order to learn their intentions concerning the Mewat region. As he passed the cemetery (*kabristan*) of his lineage, he saw his younger brother, Meda, sitting beside a fakir, and spoke to him in these terms: 'Why are you sitting there with that *gund* [a pejorative term used for very low-status wandering fakirs]?' The fakir felt humiliated, and he cursed Ahmed.[17] The latter arrived in Punhana and went to a sort of caravanserai where he thought he would find the Englishmen, and waited for them there. The men from Singhar, who had laid this trap, killed Ahmed as he slept and cut off a piece of his corpse, which they sent back to his house. The people of Bisseriya *thamba* sought out Meda, Ahmed's young brother, rather than Ahmed's eldest son, and asked him to be their new *caudri*. Meda answered that he would accept this charge only when he had avenged his brother. Which he did some time later.[18]

Here is an example of the *caudri*'s younger brother being preferred over his less capable and less-esteemed eldest son. The two brothers were very close, and the elder had included the younger in all his undertakings. The council decided to offer him the office, a decision which had later repercussions. Two *caudris* were chosen in succession from the younger Meda's line. When the third was to be appointed, dissent arose between two of the candidates: the eldest son of the deceased headman, and therefore from Meda's younger line, and a descendant of Ahmed's elder line, who demanded the return of the office of headman to his group. The dispute grew bitter, and the council was unable to make a choice, since neither of the two candidates seemed more fit than the other to occupy the office. The decision was suspended for several years, and an interim *caudri* was chosen from among the sages of the Uparla lineage, pending the appointment of the real *thamba* headman. In the end, the deceased headman's eldest son was appointed when the candidate from the eldest line dropped his claim. While they stress the rule of primogeniture, the Meo also accept its waiver.

For the Meo, there is no such thing as a *pal* or a *thamba* without a headman, even if the title has become purely honorary. The existence of a territory implies the presence of a man invested with authority. The two orders are inseparable. The *caudri*'s authority does not give him or his line any special status, however. All clans and their subdivisions are equal. And the *caudri*'s precedence over the other members of his *pal* or his *thamba* does not alter this principle. As the eldest, the headman is first among equals, and he acts on behalf of the council and only with its consent.[19] In reality, the council has always had—and still has—a preponderant role.

HEADMEN, TERRITORY, AND KINSHIP

Two points are worth mentioning: there is no overarching *caudri* for the region of Mewat and the institution of headman was not set up by an outside royal authority and is not subservient to one.[20] These two aspects are linked, as is shown by a myth about Balot *pal*, collected by the geographer Abdulaziz.

The village of origin of this *pal* is Garh Dhamina, near Delhi, which is adjacent to, but just outside, the Mewat region. The village headman, a man named Koka Rana, made an alliance with the emperor of Delhi and, with his help, established his power over the entire Mewat region, subjecting all rebellious territories. He placed members of his own clan in strategic positions to oversee the population. When the Meo found themselves no longer able to carry on their traditional activity as bandits, the twelve other *pal* decided to rid themselves of this tyrant and to destroy Garh Dhamina. But as the village lay outside the Mewat region and they had to cross hostile territory to get there, they needed a ruse. They donned their best apparel and split up into fifty-two *barāt* groups (a group made up of the bridegroom's paternal kin, who accompany him when he goes to escort his young bride to the wedding ceremony). They were thus able to approach the enemy village without arousing suspicion. The Meo attacked the village in numbers and destroyed the fifty-two wells, the fifty-two panchayat lineage houses and the fifty-two altars. The people of Balot were forced to disperse. Today they have only villages and no territory, even if they are still termed a *pal*.

This story teems with information. The *caudri* of a *pal* wants to be the leader of all the Meo. To accomplish this, he imposes his own power and gets it legitimized by an outside authority. His village is located just outside the Mewat area. It is as though the only imaginable way for a man on the inside to dominate a region was to place his capital outside so as to surround and occupy the land. The opposition would come from the twelve other *pal*. This deliberate act on the part of a man and his *pal* was a challenge to the traditional mythico-historical order. As we saw, legend does not acknowledge the pre-eminence of any one of the thirteen *pal*, and, furthermore, the principle of twelve 'plus one' does not imply any idea of closure. No *pal*, therefore, can be both a part and the whole. The political ambitions of the Balot man were countered and crushed. Nevertheless, while Balot found itself without a territory in the end, it remains a *pal*. We are back at the beginning with the thirteen *pal*, each with a *caudri*.

To get back to this situation, the twelve *pal* do not oppose Balot directly; as rebel territorial units, they have recourse to a particularly significant trick: they make fifty-two *barāt* composed of as many agnatic groups, converge on the tyrant's village, enter and destroy it by demolishing the signs of his authority: the wells, the panchayat, the altars, each of which numbers fifty-two. Fifty-two, it must be remembered, is also the number of *got*, the agnatic kin groups. Thus the Balot headman not only set himself apart from the twelve other *pal* by proclaiming himself both the part and the whole in territorial and political terms, he also attempted to show his political might by diverting the symbolic value of the figure fifty-two away from its traditional use. It is this traditional use which the twelve other *pal* restore by their action.

But there is more to come, and a look at the figures will show us the way. I have already said that the real number of territorial or residential units does not correspond to the number fixed by tradition. We have seen that the number of eleven or twenty-one villages per *thamba* is by no means a limit; just as the figure of three lineages divided into three quarters of a village rarely fits with reality. These different figures show that uneven numbers are a sign of prosperity.[21] But the thirteen *pal*, or territorial units, are the most significant example. They carry a name, and people explicitly state that their number is composed of twelve 'plus one', the latter not being simply added on. Finally, this figure of thirteen territorial units is closely associated with that of fifty-two *got* or patrilineal clans. It is hard to tell whether this second figure refers to two times twenty-six or to four times thirteen. In passing, we can note the difference with respect to one of the cash gifts which is made up of fifty-one rupees. The story emphasizes that the return to the thirteen *pal* of the myth must be accomplished through a particular manifestation: that of the fifty-two *got*.

We have seen that the agnatic kinsmen gave their expression to the fact of territoriality while going beyond it. In this context, the fifty-two *got*, the agnatic reference groups, represent a whole encompassing a subordinate element, the territory, but they are also a sign of openness. We can thus say that the even numbers (twelve on the one hand and fifty-two on the other) are both the sign of a closure, of a death of the relationship, and a sign of wholeness,[22] although it must be stressed that the principle of closure is never confirmed at the territorial level, and that the principle of totality applies to the domain of agnatic kindred, confirming its permanence and domination.

Furthermore, while the story indicates that the members of the twelve *pal* disguised themselves as fifty-two *barāt* parties, it is groups of agnates who go in procession to fetch the bride. The tyrant's village is identified with the village of a bride. In other words, the mention of the *barāt* refers, not only to the agnatic groups, but also to marriage. The totality of the fifty-two patrilineal clans encompassing the thirteen territorial units cannot be closed. It opens on to this 'plus one' which constitutes the marital union. The rest of this book will be devoted to this theme.

APPENDIX

Myths collected by Dr Abdulaziz

The five Yadav clans claim to have the same origin, and two of them, Chirklot and Punglot, recognize each other as children of the same mother, and never intermarry. The five ancestors of these clans once lived together in the hills. They were bandits and attacked caravans and peasants. These complained to the governors of the region. The five ancestors were besieged by the king's men, who guarded the five paths leading to the hillside village. Feeling themselves in danger, each of the ancestors donned a different costume and, one at a time, left by a different way.

The first disguised himself as a wandering entertainer playing a little drum called a *damru*. He went to live on a hill near Rajgarh and built a fort that was called Kajhota. This was the first ancestor of Demrot *pal*, whose name comes from the instrument which enabled him to escape. Kajhota is also considered to be the Demrot's village of origin, even though it lies abandoned today.

The second dressed up as a snake charmer and left the house. His descendants were the Punglot, *pung* being the local name for the snake charmer's small flute.

The third one, brother of the second, left disguised as a seller of string bags, called *chirka*, and his descendants were the Chirklot. The two brothers established themselves in the same village, Neemli, from which the two clans originate.

The fourth left dressed as a barber, and his descendants were the Naï (barbers).

The fifth disguised himself as a grass cutter, and his descendants were called the Dulot, the name being derived from *dub*, a local term for a kind of grass.

For the other clans, I will cite the following myths:

Landawat: Following a quarrel, one group was almost entirely exterminated by another. Only one woman, who was pregnant, escaped the massacre. She fled and gave birth to a son in the forest. She left the newborn child under a bush. A Mirasī (from the caste of bards) found him, and took him home and raised him. He named him Saliyur Bhurt. When the child grew up, he established himself in a village that he called Baghora, and he was the ancestor of the

Landawat. The other name of this *got-pal* is Baghoriya. The Landawat have a special relationship with the Mirasī, whom they call *dādā*, paternal grandfathers. They seat them, as their elders, at the so-called head of the charpay (a rope bed used for sleeping and to seat visitors).

Derwal: The first village of this *got-pal* is Lalhor. Two brothers used to cultivate fields there. The first harvested cereals and was the ancestor of the Derwal. The second grew a kind of plant, *tomri*, from which he made a snake charmer's flute. Then he, as well as his descendants called Nath, took to the life of wandering entertainers. To this day, the Derwal and the snake charmers maintain fraternal relations owing to their shared origin.

Notes

1. Aggarwal (1971: 25–7) collected an identical version with the same figures. He also says that 'at a funeral feast a person may invite all "757" villages of his *pal*' (ibid.: 26).
2. The different *got-palya* are grouped by origin into five great Rājpūt units from which they claim to have come:

    (a) Tomar: Balot, Derwal, Landawat, Ratawat; (b) Yadav: Chirklot, Demrot, Dulot, Punglot, Naï; (c) Kachhwa: Dehngal, Singhal; (d) Rathor: Kelasa; and (e) Chauhan: Pahat.

    Other myths about those *pal* exist, some of which are common to the Rājpūt groups and others specific to one clan or another. We give some of these, collected by our assistant Abdulaziz, in the annex at the end of this chapter.
3. By way of comparison, it is interesting to recall that, according to one myth, the distribution of the territories of the Swat Pathan region among the different Pakhtun warrior clans was carried out by a saint (Barth 1959: 9–10).
4. Malamoud pointed out, in conjunction with the Sanskrit texts, the importance of the 'plus one', which is not of the same order as the other numbers to which it is added. In particular, he emphasized the different contexts in which 'three plus one' is not a simple addition of like terms. Without attempting to make a term-for-term comparison, I would like to note that we find a similar logic among the Meo, even if the numbers are not the same. Their 'plus one' makes an odd number, whereas Malamoud's examples add up to four, an even number. The symbolism of numbers in the Meo culture would be worth analysing in greater detail. The figure twelve is probably a composition of four and three, while the figure fifty-two is most likely a composition of 'twelve plus one' times four. Malamoud's figure of four would find its meaning in this context. But our analysis is still in its first stages, and the hypothesis demands a somewhat closer look at the facts (1989: 137–61).
5. Among the Nuer, the distinction between *dil*, 'aristocratic', and *rul*, 'foreigner' is also made between the clans and the subdivisions which give their name to the tribes and their territorial sections, and the members of the other clans living in the territory where their own clan is not dominant. The difference between the two kinds of unit within the same territory is not a matter of status but above

all one of 'prestige' and 'influence' (Evans-Pritchard 1940: 203–15; Dumont 1971a: 55–73).

6. Abdulaziz, the Meo geographer with whom we worked, has collected from Jagga Brahmins the names of the now-abandoned villages of origin of the different *got-palya*: Kajhota for the Demrot, Sohari for the Ratawat, Burja for the Kelasa, Nîkach for the Naï, Baghora for the Landawat, Nihon for the Dulot, Garh for the Pahat, Neemli for the Chirklot and the Punglot, Lilhor for the Derwal, Raisina for the Dehngal, Bhundsi for the Singhal, and Garh Dhamina for the Balot (Abdulaziz, n.d.: 4–17). Very few Meo know the names of these sites, and even fewer the name of each one's founding ancestor.

7. When informants were asked the name of the ancestor of Bisseriya *thamba*, some said they did not know. Others said they asked the Jagga Brahmins and gave us a name. Yet we obtained a number of names, and it is hard to tell which one is the true ancestor or if there really is a true ancestor. Since the Jagga Brammins have refused to discuss this with us up to now, it is not easy to give a firm answer.

8. It is sometimes said that, when they arrived in the *thamba*'s village of origin, the founding ancestor of the subclan and of the territorial section was accompanied by Brahmin families (different from the Jagga). These received a pre-eminent right over certain lands; the rest, the vast bulk of the village lands, are owned by the descendants of the founding ancestor of the Meo subclan.

9. See pp. 97–8 for the first part of this story.

10. Apart from the exceptions mentioned above, I recall here the example of Balyan *got*, which claims one territory and three *thamba*: Dhojiya, Mangariya, and Nogaya.

11. Ch. 1; pp. 23–7, the *jajmānī* system.

12. The terms for the quarters are the same as those used for the lineages.

13. The grandfather of the household heads is said to have come to live in his wife's Uparla quarter. The ban on marrying a woman living in one's own village resulted in Uparla and this segment of Naï *got* ceasing to intermarry. According to one informant, the members of this segment are the *bhānjā*, children of *bahin*, of the village. This is the only case in which the viewpoint of not a specific Ego but a residential unit is used to determine a kin tie.

14. The *khandan* (lines) of Uparla (founding ancestor: Dadda Piru): Elchi; Isar; Mahajan; Bhopat.

15. It must be remembered that Bisru's founding ancestor came from Pausar. But that does not explain why Randhir calls Pausar its mother rather than its father.

16. Actually this involves slitting one of the nostrils so that the edges of the cut will never heal together. The person thus punished will wear the infamy of his guilt forever.

17. As has been said, the fakir is a funeral priest. This incident should perhaps be seen as an omen of the *caudri*'s death and his succession by his younger brother.

18. For the outcome, see p. 87, the story of the founding of Dallapas village.

19. It also seems—this is a hypothesis that needs checking—that the headman is the necessary link between, on the one hand, his clan or dominant subclan and, on the other hand, the villages stemming from the other clans, from the *got-nepalya* in his territory. We should recall here the example of Dallapas, a Bisseriya *thamba* village, but inhabited and dominated by Badgujar *got*. The

story, briefly mentioned above, tells that a Bisseriya *thamba caudri* established the founding ancestor of Dallapas village. In other words, this village, which does not belong to the dominant *got*, was integrated into the *thamba* through the intermediacy of the *caudri*.
20. The Meo say that their *caudri*s were not inaugurated by the kings of Alwar or Bharatpur or by the Mughal emperor of Delhi, and were not their vassals.
21. This can also be seen in the cash gifts which always correspond to an odd number 'plus one', in order to keep the relationship alive.
22. Another context indicates that completeness is both a sign of death and a reference to a totality. When the Meo built our house, we noticed that there was a stone missing in the steps leading up to the roof. When asked about this, our informants replied that completeness is the work of God, not of men. That was why one never totally finishes a house. It is necessary to leave something incomplete (this can be in various places) as though the site were still open and the work was still going on. Subsequently, we were able to confirm that the same was true in the other houses and that this was not merely a justification or a rationalization after the fact. Since the construction of any house is accompanied by rites designed to promote the prosperity of the family who will live there as well as an unbroken succession of generations, imperfection appears as a ritual sign of fecundity, while perfection is characteristic of divine transcendence and must be kept separate from human activity.

The marriage alliance

Before analysing the asymmetric marriage alliance practised by the Meo, I feel it would be useful to say why and in what sense I have chosen to use this term, borrowed from Dumont. This author distinguishes between the general and the restricted theories defined by Lévi-Strauss in *The Elementary Structures of Kinship*. The second term refers to societies in which marital choice is governed by 'a certain kind of positive rules, since these societies uniformly prescribe or prefer marriage between persons who fall into the anthropological category of cross-cousins' (1971a: 91). Dumont thus designates the restricted theory as the 'marriage-alliance theory' (ibid.: 91).

The general theory starts from the prohibition on incest as a universal fact and regards it as 'the negative expression of a law of exchange, the partial expression of a universal principle of reciprocity, the necessary counterpart of the institution of social ties between families' (ibid.: 92).

A number of objections have been made to this general theory; in particular to the idea that men exchange women. But for Dumont:

> A more radical objection bears on the explanatory value of the notions of 'exchange' and 'reciprocity'. ... It is true that the author can apply these notions to the modern, individualistic view of things only if he confronts two agents whose relationship may appear fairly arbitrary: the individual subject, ego, and across from him the agent comprised of the rest of the people in the society under consideration (with the exception of a few close relatives) (ibid.: 93).

In other words, whereas the restricted theory favours relationships, the general theory of *The Elementary Structures of Kinship* marks the primacy of the subjects, the partners for whom exchange, which implies reciprocity, is eventually functional. L. Dumont suggests a way to avoid this danger:

> We may perhaps be able to get around these difficulties by departing slightly from the letter of *The Elementary Structures* and saying that the prohibition of incest attests that an incompatibility, and therefore, a complementarity between consanguinity and affinity, is always present to some degree and that those societies practicing cross-cousin marriage exhibit it in its most logical and complete form (ibid.).[1]

Dumont is prudent and advances what is merely a working hypothesis for linking the general and the restricted theories (note the use of 'perhaps' and 'to some degree'). But he becomes more affirmative when he speaks about cross-cousin marriage with the idea of 'an opposition in its most logical and complete form'. This is clearly a second formulation of the marriage alliance in the guise of a *'distinctive* [my emphasis] opposition between consanguinity and affinity' (ibid.).

The question then is whether the marriage alliance theory supposes a close and necessary link between the two statements: the positive marriage rule and the opposition between consanguinity and affinity. To answer this, we must examine the two phenomena further.

THE POSITIVE RULE FOR MARITAL CHOICE

Not every positive rule of this order necessarily leads to the marriage alliance. Dumont rightly points out that the preference for marrying the patrilateral parallel-cousin does not come under this heading (1971a: 23). To speak of a marriage alliance, the necessary (but clearly not sufficient) condition is the prohibition of marriage with the anthropological category of parallel-cousins and the presence of discrete exogamous units. These units or one of their more restricted segments can constitute marriage units properly speaking, which enter into relations with others.

Secondly, the positive rule can be of two kinds: to use Lévi-Strauss's terms, we will distinguish between marital choice by class or groups (*cf.* dual organizations or marriage classes among the Kariera or the Aranda) and choice in terms of individuals (a given category of cross-cousins). Dumont becomes more specific:

... we will make a distinction between the global or holistic view in which the whole society appears as being organized into groups connected by a determined rule of intermarriage—as in dual organization—and what we will call the individual or local point of view in which the rules relate to a particular subject, as in cross-cousin marriage (ibid.: 98).

Dumont's clarification has its importance. Whereas for Lévi-Strauss the two kinds of determination are regarded as 'so many examples of a recurring fundamental structure' (1967: 158–9), for Dumont, the two viewpoints do not have the same structural outcome. Contrary to the local point of view, the global viewpoint implies a cycle of intermarriages which links all groups to each other in a well-defined manner. That is why Dumont introduces the notion of holism. But the expression seems too strong to me. If the local viewpoint does not necessarily introduce an idea of cycle, there may not also be, from the global viewpoint of the groups, similar facts, in other words, intermarriage ties between units which do not necessarily imply an idea of closure? We will come back to this question.

Thirdly, the marriage rule supposes the repetition of the same kind of marital union over several successive generations, hence the transgenerational character of the marriage alliance.

Finally, these different points are explicitly stated by the societies under consideration and are not induced by the anthropologist. They are neither empirical findings nor statistical models. The positive marriage rules are part of the representations these societies have of themselves. Yet they also make it possible to elaborate different marriage-alliance models (marriage between bilateral cross-cousins, with the matrilateral cross-cousin or the patrilateral cousin).

The interest of the marriage alliance is that it can be compared: it identifies that which is common or similar, from a structural or formal point of view, in societies where these rules prevail and only there. Beyond the various applications of a positive rule for marital choice, one can, of course, speak of recurrence of the same structure, as Lévi-Strauss writes. But how can we assess the variations from one society to another which anthropologists have been reporting since Leach and Needham? We have indicated the difference between determination by class and individual determination. There are others, too, notably when it comes to asymmetric marriage: the question of the partners' status (isogamy, hypergamy, hypogamy), closed or open exchange cycles, and so forth. Are these secondary features or should we, on the contrary, highlight the differences by noting that they are a function of other aspects of kinship? The question is an important one: what status should the anthropologist assign to formal models, and more specifically to the marriage alliance from a comparative point of view?

THE MARRIAGE RULE AND THE CONSANGUINITY/AFFINITY OPPOSITION

At first sight, the distinctive opposition between consanguinity and affinity seems to be merely a way of formulating the distinction between those with whom or into whose group one may not marry and who fall into the category of consanguines, and those with whom or into whose group one may marry and who are affines. Either this distinction is a convenient way for the anthropologist to express the marriage alliance—but it adds nothing to the rule—or it must exist in the society under consideration which divides kin into these two categories. The second term of the alternative would suggest that the positive rule and its implications do not suffice to be able to speak of marriage alliance, and that it is necessary in addition that the local kin distinctions and more generally the kinship terminology express it as well. But this hypothesis (which Dumont formulates with caution) is too restrictive. It postulates that the marriage alliance is meaningful only if the marriage rule concurs with other kin distinctions, only if it is the expression, as it were, of kinship in general in the societies in question. It would reduce the concept of marriage alliance to a locally defined model of kinship, but at the same time, would block out the comparative perspective. For in order to measure differences, we must begin with similarities, failing which we succumb once again to the kind of relativism that nullifies any attempt at anthropology. What about societies which have an asymmetric marriage rule but no distinctive opposition between consanguinity and affinity? Shall we say that they do not practise marriage alliance? In this case, each society would have to have its own concepts to qualify this type of marriage, and each kinship system would consequently be absolutely different from all others. But if we grant the marriage-alliance model built on positive rules described above, a certain relevance as a partial expression of kinship and of a paradigm shared by several societies, the differences in the ways the model is actualized and its relation to the other aspects of kinship will become significant.

Or to put it another way, there is no use in talking about marriage alliance if we do not recognize a sort of subsystem which takes its meaning from both its internal relationships and from its relation to a wider set of kin. The comparison is now no longer confined to the level of the marriage alliance, but extends to the relationship between marriage alliance and the other aspects of kinship connected with it.[2] It is now a question of the connection between the partial whole constituted by the model built on the marriage rule and a broader configuration which takes account, not only of the terminology, but of the matrimonial prestations as well.[3]

MARRIAGE ALLIANCE AND INDIA

To state the question in more concrete terms, I will say, following Dumont, that, in south India, marriage alliance is closely linked with the opposition between consanguinity and affinity, and that the diachronic dimension of marriage is expressed terminologically by the transgenerational transmission of affinity (1975a: 47–83). Afterwards, it will be shown that, in the north, among the Meo, marriage alliance is linked to the diachronic dimension of the hierarchical opposition between metasiblingship at the global level and affinity at the subordinate level. In this context, marriage is both an expression of this metasiblingship and an expression of affinity. Unlike the case of south India, a distinction must be made between the concepts of marriage and affinity. The same kind of problem arises if one looks at the relationship between marriage alliance and matrimonial prestations. Whereas in south India these are articulated with the consanguinity/affinity opposition, for the Meo, one must again take into consideration, on the one hand, metasiblingship in its two manifestations (the 'non-differentiated' aspect of the global level and the brother–sister chains at the subordinate level) and, on the other hand, the relative distinction between consanguinity and affinity. Taking a more global view, among the Pramalai Kallar and the Dravidian groups of south India the marriage alliance is expressed in the relationship between brothers-in-law, while among the Meo, it supposes relating two brother–sister pairs linked by marriage.

I contend that the concept of marriage alliance is of interest only if it is perceived, on the one hand, as a model and, on the other, as a subsystem of a broader system of kinship which includes both the terminology and the ceremonial prestations. It is through the comparison between the Pramalai Kallar and the Meo that we will approach a more global understanding of marriage in India.[4] This chapter will therefore study the forms of marriage alliance practised by the Meo and then go on to see how kinship terminology becomes meaningful in this context. The next chapter will be reserved for the details surrounding the matrimonial prestations, which are themselves embedded in the broader set of marriage rites and more generally life-cycle rites.

PROHIBITED MARRIAGES

The Meo have two kinds of exogamous units: the *got* and the village. The first is the largest agnatic group, the clan; and the second is the local or residential unit sometimes composed of lineages from different *got*. According to some informants, the *thamba* as a territorial unit is also exogamous. Thus, the lineage segment of *got* Naï which moved to Bisru following a marriage with a Demrot lineage can no longer take wives from its new village or from the different villages of Bisseriya *thamba*. But this is not a general case: a lineage from Sukeriya *got* living in the village of Naï, which belongs to Palam *pote thamba* (Chirklot *pal*), does not marry with the different Chirklot lineages in the village, but it is allowed to marry Chirklot women from other villages in Palam *pote thamba*.

The rest of the marriage prohibitions apply to individuals: one may not marry any of one's patrilateral parallel or cross-cousins or one's first-degree matrilateral cross-cousin; and one may not marry anyone from one's mother's village of origin.

Generally speaking, the marriage alliance in any given society is considered exclusively from either a global or a local point of view, to use L. Dumont's vocabulary. Among the Meo, both viewpoints exist at the same time, but they do not have the same meaning or the same implications; we will study them one after the other.

ASYMMETRIC MARRIAGE FROM THE GLOBAL VIEWPOINT

The exogamous units of reference are the *thamba* as kin units for the *got-palya*, and the lineages living in the villages for the *got-nepalya*. Bisseriya is a *thamba* of the Demrot *pal*. When it comes to kinship, Bisseriya includes not only the Demrot living in the *thamba* but also the other lines which originally came from this *thamba* and are now living in another territory. Thus for instance the Demrot lineage in the village of Saroli, located in the territory of Bajja *thamba* (Chirklot *pal*), follows the marriage alliances of its original *thamba*, Bisseriya. All Bisseriya Demrot must contract the same alliances.

Each *got-nepalya* is divided among several villages founded by the descendants of the ancestor of the *got*. Each one of these villages is identified with the original lineages of this *got*, even if the lineages of other *got* have subsequently settled in them. For instance, five villages (Malab, Bhadas, Nagina, Badri, and Neemli) are considered as Gorwal *got* villages; likewise, six villages (Matepur, Chhaisa, Baupur, Hunchpari, Angrawali, and Gangora) are regarded as villages belonging to Sukeriya *got*. All the village lineages of a clan have the same alliances. Even if a lineage segment moves to another village, it continues to follow the alliances of its original village. Thus the Sukeriya *got* lineage in the village of Naï (Palam *pote thamba*, Chirklot *pal*) contracts the same alliances as its village of origin, Gangora.

In speaking of these agnatic groups, subdivisions of the *got*, as intermarriage units, we are merely following the Meo themselves. The members of these units distinguish:
- those to whom they give their daughters,
- those from whom they receive their wives, and
- those with whom it is forbidden to marry.[5]

There are various cases of prohibition of intermarriage between clans or subclans. Two *got* recognizing each other as having a common ancestor forbid all intermarriage. Thus according to a myth, Dehngal and Singhal both descend from children of Sita and therefore may not intermarry. Other units refuse to intermarry without saying when and why this prohibition was established. Between Bisseriya *thamba* and the different Chirklot *thamba* (with the exception of Palam *pote*), there is a prohibition on marriage and no one knows why. The informants from Bisru call the members of the different Chirklot *thamba* (except one) *bhāī*, and regard them as consanguineous *bhāī* with whom marriage is forbidden. Relations between the latter are far from peaceful and sometimes take the form of violent clashes. The same is true between these *bhāī* in neighbouring clans, as shown in the preceding chapter.[6]

Without actually looking for a relation of cause and effect, a connection can be made between prohibition on intermarriage and political enmity. The tension prevailing between agnates and between consanguineous *bhāī* contrasts with the warmth of relations between affines. Like many rural Indians, the Meo like to travel and they visit their affines for more or less extended periods of time whenever the occasion presents itself, and sometimes with no particular reason at all. But they avoid calling on their 'quasi-agnatic' *bhāī* without a compelling reason and they never stay long.

To situate these alliances, we will take the example of Bisru and Bisseriya (Figure 4.1). The Demrot in this *thamba* take wives from all the *thamba* of Denghal, but they do not give them their daughters. Alternatively, they make a distinction between the two Derwal *thamba*: Taï, who gives them girls, and Meoli, to whom they give their daughters. The same goes for the *thamba* of Balyan: only Nogaya receives daughters from them, while Mangariya and

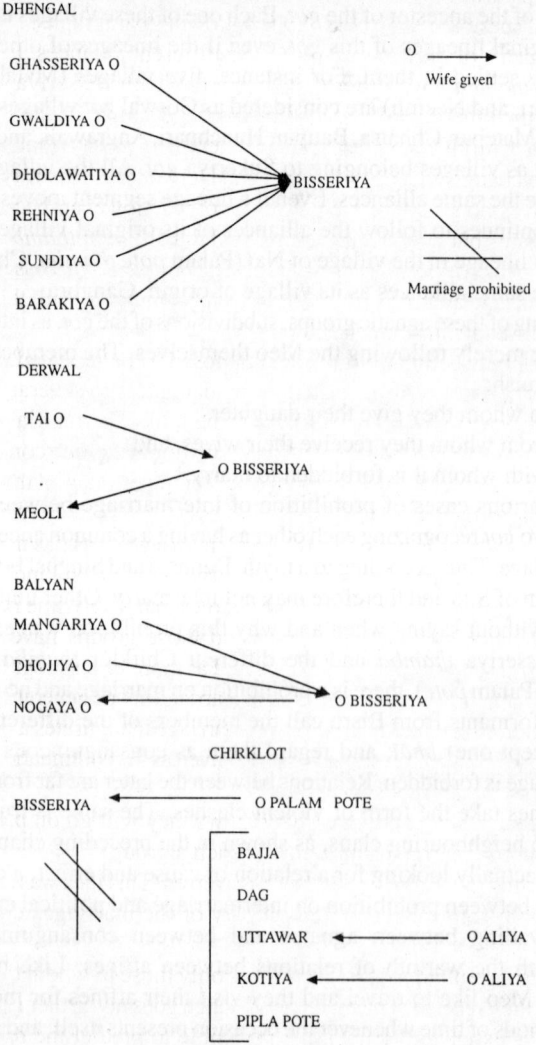

Figure 4.1: *Permission and prohibition of intermarriage between clans*

Dhojiya give them daughters. Finally, Bisseriya receives women from Palam *pote thamba*, in Chirklot, but neither gives to or takes from any other *thamba* in this *pal*. On the other hand, a neighbouring Demrot *thamba*, Aliya, gives its daughters to two *thamba* in Chirklot. It is interesting to note that Bisseriya and Aliya were presented to us as two separate *thamba* because of the difference in their choice of matrimonial allies.

Several features of the marriage alliances at the group level need further explanation. These are explained in the following paragraphs.

The segments of the same *got* can have different alliances. For instance, two Derwal *thamba* have different alliance ties with Bisseriya, one giving women and the other taking them (see also the example of the two Demrot *thamba* with Chirklot). Some would be tempted to say that women are effectively exchanged between Demrot and Derwal *got*. This way of looking at things makes no sense for the parties involved, however, because *got* are exogamous units but not marriage units, and the different *thamba* of one *got* are often unaware of each other's alliances. The people of Bisseriya do not know the marriage alliances of the other Demrot *thamba*, with the exception of Aliya, whose territory touches theirs.[7]

Marriages between these units are supposed to be repeated, and indeed they are. Each group gives its sisters or its daughters to several groups and receives women from other units of the same rank. The marriages can stop in one generation and be resumed in the next without anyone considering the alliance to have been broken off. It does not seem pertinent in this context to speak of preferential or prescribed marriages.

For the Meo, marriage alliance between marriage units has no beginning. To our knowledge, there is no story of the origin of a given kind of marriage between two groups. Each marriage unit knows that, from time immemorial, these groups have given them women and those groups have taken their women. Marriages have only to be repeated at more or less regular intervals to confirm the alliance. Sometimes a single marriage in one generation is enough to serve as a reminder. In other words, no marriage inaugurates a new alliance relationship between groups. Every union is given as the continuation of another contracted a generation or two earlier.

The alliance has no end; everyone knows they will go on practising the same asymmetric marriages in such and such a group.

The direction of the alliance cannot be reversed. This idea was categorically rejected by our informants and our survey of the marriages confirmed as much.

Each marriage unit looks to and knows only those to whom they give and from whom they receive. The marriage alliance goes no further in the manner of a transitive extension. Thus it is impossible to predict the relationship a group will entertain with their wife-giver's giver; it can give women or take them. And vice versa, the wife-taker of a group's taker can be either its wife-giver or its wife-taker. We have examples of both cases. One of Bisseriya's takers is Mangariya, whose taker is Dholawatiya; the latter gives to Bisseriya. Palam *pote* has as a taker Sukeriya, one of whose takers is Bisseriya, who itself takes wives from Palam *pote* (Figure 4.2). There is no chain of marriage alliances, and even less any idea of a closed circle of intermarriages, as generalized exchange suggested. This is in apparent contradiction with the terminology—did we not see that the *sālā* of ego's *sālā* is his *sālā*—therefore, that the wife-giver's giver again falls into the category of wife-giver? In reality, the Meo reason differently. The *sālā* of the *sālā* is for ego a *sālā* only in the absence of a marriage link between them. If ego is directly linked with him, it is this relationship which prevails over the one he can establish through his primary affine.

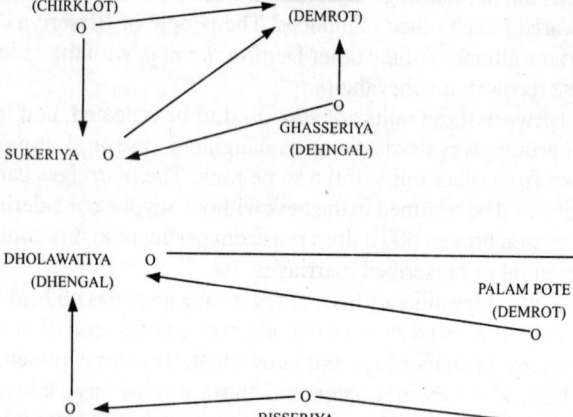

Figure 4.2: Alliance between thamba

There is no difference of status between the marriage units. It is never said that the wife-takers are superior or inferior to the wife-givers. The *thamba* of the *got-palya* and the village lineages of the *got-nepalya* are all equal. From the global standpoint, asymmetric marriage is isogamous.

It is not necessarily the marriage units which actually decide this or that marriage, and they do not always take part in the negotiations and the ceremonies involved. The marital choice is made, not by the *thamba* or the village lineages, but by the family and its lineages, who are the principal parties concerned by the prestations and counter-prestations that accompany any marriage. That is why I say that these are reference units, in the sense that every matrimonial union must respect the rule of asymmetric alliance between these groups, and not the empirical marriage units.

To sum up: the unilineal descent principle, which structures territorial and local units by means of the subclans (*thamba*) or the village lineages (*thok*), requires as its complement marriage. The Meo community is not only a whole made up of the thirteen *pal* and the fifty-two *got*; it is also—and just as importantly—a set of units linked by agnation and marriage. The global point of view of marriage alliance does not result in a cycle linking all marriage units into a circular chain, but in the definition of three categories of kin groups recognized by each unit: agnates or quasi-agnates, wife-takers, and wife-givers.[8]

PREFERENTIAL MARRIAGE FROM THE LOCAL OR INDIVIDUAL VIEWPOINT

Marriage is just as significant from the local or individual point of view, though in an altogether different way from the global viewpoint. Here we are dealing with matrimonial unions between families. From the diachronic standpoint, these marriages define family lines and, as we will see further on, at least three lines must be taken into consideration: two on the wife-taker's side and one on the giver's. I recall here the principal rules which apply at this level:

• A man may not marry any of his patrilateral parallel or cross-cousins or his first-degree matrilateral cross-cousin.

• A man may not marry a woman from his mother's village, but his patrilateral parallel cousin and his son may. Alternatively, a man is allowed to marry a woman from the same *thamba* as his mother.

These prohibitions do not mean that there is no marriage preference at this level, though.[9] To locate this preference, let me quote the following saying: *phuphi ke sath bhatiji*: 'the paternal aunt with her brother's daughter'. This means that a woman will try to bring her brother's daughter into her own husband's village, or failing that, a girl from her natal lineage, not for her own son but for one of his agnates; this marriage is highly prized and sought after. This paternal aunt will carry out the negotiations, for she knows both her brother's daughter and the boys in her husband's village; she is therefore, well suited to judge who will make the best husband for her niece.[10]

This allows us to establish the diagram shown in Figure 4.3. We have taken two agnatic *bhāī* in village A, their descendants, and their marriages. One of

116   Kinship and Rituals among the Meo of Northern India

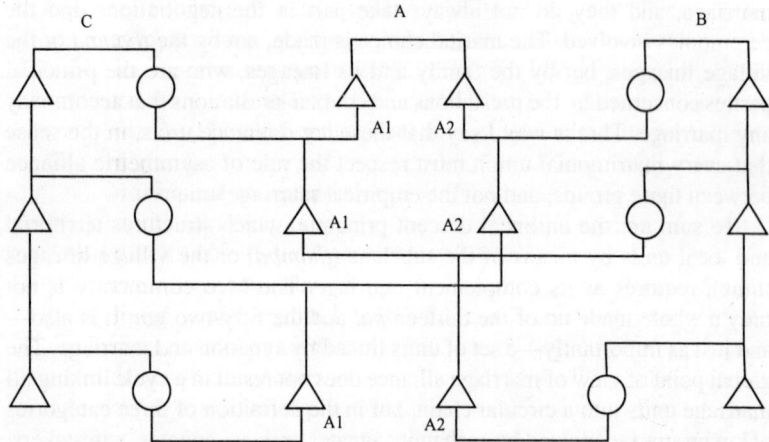

Figure 4.3: *Preferential marriage in diachrony*

the agnates marries a woman from village B, and the other a woman from village C or village B' from the same *thamba* as B, which does not affect the diagram in any way. As the terminology has told us, C and B become as consanguineous *bhāī* if they were not already. Through this marriage, two separate lines can be distinguished: A1 and A2. A man reproduces the marriage of his paternal uncle and paternal grandfather, but not that of his own father.

Several features of this type of marriage must be underscored:

• First, each wife-giver line (whether B or C) is linked to two wife-taker lines (A1 and A2). The two sides are thus asymmetrical. In other words, B or C gives women to A generation after generation, and A divides them among its lines. We can look at this another way. The diagram shows a line in B or C. In fact, the paternal aunt can choose either the daughter of her *saga bhāī*, her 'real' brother, or the daughter of another *bhāī* from the same lineage. The distinction between direct and collateral lines does not come into play on the 'giver' side, for B or C. Alternatively, there can be no confusion between lines on the 'taker' side A.

• Second, from the standpoint of the diachronic aspect of marriage, the distinction between direct and collateral lines over two successive generations produces the same effect as the alternation of generations in the same line, as Figure 4.3 shows. Another interest of this diagram is that it shows how the alternation of generations articulates with asymmetric marriage with the matrilateral cross-cousin (without the first-degree cousin being considered one with whom marriage is permitted) and not necessarily with marriage with the patrilateral cross-cousin (forbidden among the Meo), with which we are accustomed to associate it. Furthermore, unlike the latter type of marriage, the direction of the unions is not reversed.

Can one speak of marriage alliance from a local standpoint? The existence of a preferential rule and the repetition of the marriage over several generations allow us to say yes. This formula can be compared to the semi-complex structures studied by Héritier (1981: 73–131). The difference between the same-sex sibling relationship and the brother–sister relationship, whose importance in this kind of structure she stressed, appears clearly in the Meo case. Furthermore, despite the relative extension of the prohibition, the preferential marriage is repeated 'as nearby as possible' (ibid.: 109). It must nevertheless be noted that, among the Meo, the fact that unions are unidirectional makes any return impossible, even after several generations. One does not find here any circular form (Héritier's *bouclage*) of alliance, whose importance Héritier underscored in this type of structure. This is probably due to the presence of the asymmetric alliance between the groups. One is thus led systematically to situate the two points of view with respect to each other.

CONTRASTS AND SIMILARITIES BETWEEN THE TWO POINTS OF VIEW ON THE MARRIAGE ALLIANCE

These two points of view on the marriage alliance are not homologous. To be sure, Figure 4.3 establishes certain analogies between the global view and the local view, and there is a certain continuity between the marital choice expressed in terms of the group and the same choice expressed in individual terms. But there are differences, too.

Every marriage is reckoned from the global viewpoint of the groups (*thamba* or sets of village lineages) perpetuating the alliance. In this context, every matrimonial union must be considered at this level. From the local point of view, the marriage alliance as we have constructed it is preferential. Other marriages are contracted without being conceptualized after this local model.

The marriage alliance seen from the local point of view is constructed over three generations, but rarely more. It has a beginning and an end, unlike the alliance seen from the global viewpoint. In other words, the distinction between direct and collateral lines and the alternation between generations remain localized and have no permanent character.

Finally and above all, unlike the alliance between groups, every matrimonial union expressed in inter-individual terms, whether or not it obeys the preferential rule, implies superiority of the man's side over the woman's. The *behnoï* is thus said to be superior to his *sālā*. Here we are no longer dealing with isogamy. But is this hypergamy as we are used to thinking of it in the case of marriage in north India? The question is not a simple one and it demands examination.

MARRIAGE ALLIANCE, 'HYPERGAMY', AND RITUAL FUNCTION

Dumont contrasted two formulas: one valid throughout south India, supposing status equality between the bride and the groom (particularly in the case of the principal marriage) and therefore isogamy; the other, more often practised in the north, accepting a 'slight difference in the status of the bride's family with respect to that of the groom' (again in the case of the principal marriage) (1996a: 152). In the second case, hypergamy (whether mandatory or optional) must be broken down into three points: (a) the difference in status prior to the marriage or as established by the marriage is neutralized from the diachronic standpoint so that the children of this union have the same status as their father; (b) the woman is lower than the man; and finally (c) the girl's marriage is regarded as a 'gift of the maiden', this specific gift (in the image of the gifts made by high- or middle-caste people to the higher-status Brahmins) being accompanied by other gifts of goods which are just as unidirectional (ibid.: 153). More generally, hypergamy introduces a major feature of the caste system into kinship, status, and prevents any kinship system functioning autonomously with respect to caste (1966b: 116).

It is not my intention to discuss whether or not this analysis is founded for north India, but rather to show why the notion of hypergamy is not applicable to the Meo. I will not go back over the neutralization of the status difference or the woman's inferiority with respect to the man; instead I will stress the nature of the asymmetry between the two sides of the marriage and the 'gift of the maiden', the principal sign of this asymmetry. The last point will be the centre of the analysis of the marriage rites, so I will simply allude to it here and detail the first point.

First, the contrast pointed out by Dumont establishes a sort of alternative: isogamy in south India, mandatory or optional hypergamy in the north. Yet the Meo practise isogamy, therefore, status equivalence, from the global point of view on the marriage alliance, between the wife-takers and the wife-givers, and at the same time superiority of the groom's family over the bride's if the marriage is considered from the individual or local point of view. We, therefore, cannot content ourselves with the alternative defined above.

Furthermore, there is no difference before the marriage between the taker families and the giver families. One does not marry 'up'; marriage instates the superiority of the wife-takers, which is not the same thing.[11] This superiority is affirmed by the ritual without enabling us to speak of any permanent difference of status between the two families. Outside the strictly ritual framework, nothing distinguishes the two sides.[12]

The 'gift of the maiden', which Dumont regards as an important sign of hypergamy, underscores the superiority of the *behnoï* over his *sālā*. It is not a question simply of marking the difference between the two sides of the marriage, but of establishing an asymmetry between the chains of relatives. The *behnoï* will of course be shown respect by his *sālā*. But it is his wife, that woman 'given' in marriage, who will be the principal officiant in the rites which bring together the two sides. She will return to her brother's house for the circumcision of his son and for the marriage of his children. She will hold a place equivalent to that of a Brahmin priest in these rites and will receive fees for the ritual services she performs. All these points will be discussed in detail in the next chapter. Suffice it to note here that the superiority of the *behnoï* over his *sālā* is inseparable from that of the married sister (the *bahin*, closely associated with the *behnoï*, her husband) over her brother, her *bhāī*. Marriage in this case is inseparable from the brother–sister relationship. Once more we encounter a fundamental feature of the kinship system, namely that the *behnoï/sālā* opposition is an integral part of the broader opposition between the chains of opposite-sex metasiblings and the chains distinguishing affines and same-sex siblings.

Marriage alliance and kinship vocabulary

Kinship vocabulary is situated at the interpersonal level and not at that of inter-group relations. When confronted with the preferential marriage at the inter-individual level, it seems at first sight that there is no homology between these two aspects of kinship. From the standpoint of terminology, every marriage at some point installs a relationship between a man who takes a wife, a *behnoï*, and another who gives his sister, a *sālā*. But in the following generation, all their children are each other's *bhāī*, without distinction between consanguines and affines. In other words, for a particular ego, his father's *sālā* is his own *māmā*, and the latter's children are his *bhāī*, like his real brothers or the children of his father's brothers. The kinship vocabulary thus does not confirm the marriage alliance; it seems even to contradict it.

In reality, things are not that simple. The earlier analysis of this vocabulary showed the hierarchical relationship between *bhāī* and *sālā*, which is merely the expression of the relationship opposing, on the one hand, metasiblingship at the global level, and on the other, the relative distinction between consanguines and affines. This relationship must be resituated in the diachronic dimension of the alliance.

Indeed, the son of my *māmā* is my *bhāī*, and he will not give me his sister in marriage, but can give her to one of my agnates. Following this union, he will no longer be my *bhāī*, but will become the *sālā* of my agnate, and therefore, my *sālā* as well. It is thus from the category of *bhāī* that its opposite is taken, the category of *sālā*. This distinction can in fact be generalized to all generations.

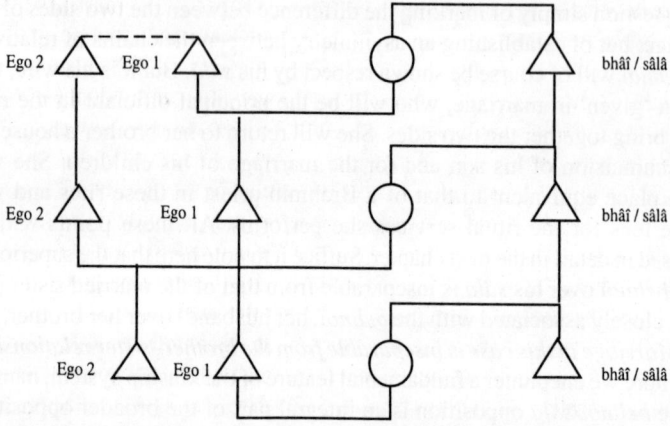

Figure 4.4: Marriage alliance and kinship terminology

The *māmā* of a male ego is the *sālā* of his father, who therefore, also regards him as a *bhāī*. In this fashion we can work our way back up the generations. The hierarchical opposition between *bhāī* and *sālā* has neither beginning nor end.[13] Each generation thus refers back to a sort of relationship which could be termed 'original' between metasibling *bhāī* in order to establish within itself a distinction between consanguineous *bhāī* and affinal *sālā*. The hierarchical opposition of the basic cell has a transgenerational dimension and is articulated with the marriage alliance (Figure 4.4).

Let us now turn to the relationship between a *behnoï* and a *sālā*. From the terminological standpoint, the *behnoï* belongs to a chain of opposite-sex metasiblings while the *sālā* is part of a chain which distinguishes between a pair of same-sex siblings and affines. *The superiority of the first over the second in marriage fits perfectly with the hierarchical opposition in the terminology between the two kinds of chain.* This explains why, for a male speaker, it is indispensable that his sister marry, not only so that he may have a brother-in-law, but in order to establish a relationship with the couple formed by his sister and his brother-in-law. Once again, we find the transformation of the sister-as-'gift' into the principal officiant in the rites for her brother.

In this context, the superiority of the *behnoï* over the *sālā* is not automatically passed on from one generation to the next. As I have said, the children of the *behnoï* and the *sālā* are metasibling *bhāī* and *bahin* to each other. A new marriage re-establishes the distinction between *behnoï* and *sālā*. In each generation, it is necessary to come back to metasiblingship at the global level, and thus to the image of the 'non-differentiated' whole, to be able once again to create the necessary distinctions and identify the asymmetry between the two sides of the marriage.

We are now ready to make a more systematic comparison of marriage alliance and kinship vocabulary. The global point of view and the local point of view on marriage are not simply in a relationship of inclusion, they also stand in a hierarchical relationship of encompassment. Every inter-individual preferential marriage is reckoned as perpetuating the marriage alliance between groups, but the converse is not true. This is another way of saying that the marriage, taken at the level of the groups involved (subclan or set of village lineages) is the union of reference, while the marriage at the inter-individual level (between families) is the preferential union. Isogamy is the permanent form of relationship within which each particular union constructs, for the duration of a generation, the ritual superiority of one of the sides over the other.

The kinship vocabulary applies only to the inter-individual level, and no direct link can be made between the kin terms and the global viewpoint of the marriage alliance. Therefore, the comparison cannot be made element by element. The structural homology must be grasped at the level of the principles organizing marriage and the kinship vocabulary. Just as isogamy encompasses the asymmetry between the two sides of the marriage, higher-level metasiblingship, which recognizes only non-differentiated *bhāī* and *bahin*, encompasses the asymmetry between the chain of opposite-sex metasiblings and the chain distinguishing same-sex siblings and affines. This homology that we have just outlined will assume its full meaning when we analyse the marriage rites.

Notes

1. In his book, *Dravidien et Kariera*, Dumont repeatedly stresses the close connection between marriage alliance and transgenerational affinity: 'Rather than speaking of cousin marriage, we prefer "marriage alliance". Better still, these systems could be characterized by the fact that they place great value on kinship by marriage or affinity, and for this reason give it a diachronic or transgenerational dimension' (1975a: 5). Further on, speaking of the marriage rule which is not 'a by-product of other institutions such as descent or residence' (ibid.: 48), the author emphasizes: '... the outcome of the rule is that it causes affinity to be transmitted from one generation to the next, rather like the transmission of membership in an exogamous group. Owing to the rule, marriage acquires a diachronic dimension, it becomes an institution which transcends the generations and which I will call "marriage alliance" or simply "alliance"' (ibid.: 48).
2. Comparisons between societies with marriage alliance and those without this rule will have to be based on other criteria, other principles. This means that there is not one single axis of comparison but several, depending on the societies and the level of analysis.
3. Lévi-Strauss himself points out that the exchange of women is part of a system of total exchange of goods, privileges, rights, and obligations (1967: 148–9).

But this perspective on exchange, which he owes to Mauss, does not appear in the rest of his book.

4. A systematic comparison of the two communities will be attempted in the concluding chapter of the present work.
5. Each *thamba* or lineage recognizes the existence of other similar units with which it does not entertain any of the three relations defined above. These are usually very remote groups. When members of these groups meet, they do not dwell on the absence of relations, but instead try to establish the existence of some kin tie through a third party. In this case, it is the person encountered—and not his group—who will be qualified using the many possibilities of the kinship terminology. If I can establish that the stranger is the *sālā* or the (consanguineous) *bhāī* of my *sālā*, he will be my *sālā*; if he is the *behnoï* of my *sālā*, he will be my (consanguineous) *bhāī* (see the rules of terminology).
6. See Chapter 3, pp. 93–4, the conflicts between Bisseriya *thamba* (Demrot *pal*) and Kotiya *thamba* (Chirklot *pal*).
7. While working on kinship in an area of Punjab, Hershman reported analogous findings: '... it is not dispersed clans who are linked in immutable wife-giving or wife-receiving relationships which cannot be reversed; it is only localized segments of them. Thus for example, if one dispersed clan X is divided between villages A and B and if a second dispersed clan Y is divided between villages C and D, whereas the marriage relationship between A and C may be one of wife-giver, it is possible that the relationship between B and D may be one of wife-taker. Therefore it is the localized clan segments which are the units which stand in irreversible marriage alliance relationships to one another and not the dispersed clan as a whole' (1981: 229).
8. The wife-givers and the wife-takers do not have distinctive names as is the case among the Kachin studied by Leach (1954).
9. Dumont and Parry indicate, for the north Indian societies they studied (Gorakhpur for one and Kangra for the other), that extension of the prohibitions does not mean that the marriages cannot be repeated generation after generation: 'In other words, the rules of exogamy exclude repetition only in the direct line of descent, and there is nothing to prevent one from marrying with the same people as one's collateral lineage kin' (Parry 1979: 287); 'To put it otherwise, we may sum up the two Sarjupari rule by stating that it is permissible to repeat intermarriage between local descent groups provided that the direction of intermarriage is not reversed and that the repetition is not between the same households' (Dumont 1966b: 105).
10. This saying also indicates that a marriage preference subsists in the same group generation after generation, and we thus once again find the global aspect of intermarriage, that between groups.
11. Hershman makes a distinction between two meanings of the term hypergamy: 'The term "hypergamy" has been employed in two distinctly different ways in the literature: firstly, it has been used in a general sense to refer to any system of marriage where the wife-taker is regarded, in some sense, as "superior" to the wife-giver; and secondly, it has been used more strictly only to describe a system of hierarchically ranking intermarrying groups ... where those who occupy a

higher status receive women in marriage from those more lowly ranked. The critical point in drawing the distinction between these two usages is whether it is an individual marriage which creates the inequality, or whether that inequality is part of an ongoing structural relationship which has an existence independent of any single marriage but which is reinforced by it' (1981: 227–8). This seems to me an essential distinction, but can the term hypergamy then be used in both cases without creating confusion?

In his analysis of the Rājpūt of Kangra, Parry lends no importance to this distinction, and that makes his interpretation difficult to accept: 'It is at first sight tempting to distinguish between a system of "prescriptive" hypergamy in which it is mandatory to give one's daughter "up" and a system of "preferential" hypergamy which merely recommends one to do so. But this distinction is difficult to sustain. Although in the second case a daughter can legitimately be married to an equal, the marriage itself may create an inequality between the wife-givers and the wife-receivers so that after the event every marriage is conceptualized as hypergamous' (1979: 196). How can one say that marriage creates a difference of status between the two sides and at the same time maintains the opposite, that the difference of status results in one kind of marriage or the other?

12. Hershman, writing on the Punjabi community he studied, makes observations analogous to our own: 'The son-in-law or sister-husband occupies a position of great honour in relation to all his wife's kinsmen in a degree relative to their genealogical proximity to her, but this honour is something which accrues to him personally and is not shared by all his kinsmen. Therefore, it is my argument that it is only within specific ritual contexts that two kin groups, whether lineages or kindreds, may be seen to be aligned in hierarchical status, but this ritual inequality at least in present-day Punjab has no further implications for ongoing relations of political inequality between the two' (1981: 199).

13. It would, therefore, be erroneous to think that the distinction between *bhāī* and *sālā*, between consanguines and affines in one generation, refers to a consanguineous relationship in the generations above which would, therefore, have an encompassing value.

Marriage ceremonies: Ritual prestations

The protagonists of the marriage ceremonies are the bride and the groom, the two families concerned by the union and their respective lineages. On either side, two figures intervene and play essential roles: the mother's brother (the groom's or the bride's maternal uncle) and the father's sister (the groom's or the bride's paternal aunt), who on this occasion is called the *sahvāsanī*.[1] The first must bring gifts to his sister, to the bride or the groom and to their agnatic kin. The second is in charge of the festivities and the performance of the principal marriage rites, thus relegating the mothers of the two spouses to a relatively secondary role.

The marriage involves three stages:

• The betrothal or *sagāī* takes place at the home of the boy; the girl's people come with the gifts which will mark the engagement of the two families.

• The wedding ceremonies proper, or *biāh*, go on over a span of a month or so. They begin simultaneously at the home of the groom, called on this occasion *nausā*, and at the home of the bride, or *nausī*. They come to a close in the bride's village, when the groom, accompanied by his male agnates, comes to receive the gift (*dān*) of the dowry (*dahej*) followed by the gift of his new wife, whom he will take back to his own village. Three days later the young woman returns to her natal village for approximately a year.

• The ceremonies accompanying the woman's definitive departure for her husband's village, or *gaunā*.[2]

I first describe the different moments of the marriage ritual. Then I will analyse the prestations and counter-prestations exchanged within each side of the marriage and then between the two sides. Finally, I will situate the ritual roles of the maternal uncle and the paternal aunt of the groom and the bride. From there, I will go on to show how marriages are linked from generation to generation through the life-cycle rites. The last two points will enable us to understand how the opposite-sex metasibling chain and the opposition between consanguines and affines acquire their meaning and how the brother–sister link and the marriage alliance are connected.

The choice of the marriage partner is made by the parents; however, the agnatic kin in their lineage and their village as well as other people[3] may give their opinion and even influence the decision. The size of the dowry and the expenditures to which the father of the bride must agree give rise to extensive discussions. Persons known for their negotiating skills—usually barbers and sometimes certain agnatic kinsmen of the families concerned—are charged with reaching an agreement suitable to both families. The expenditures entailed in a wedding are considerable; some families, it is said, have to borrow heavily from members of the merchant caste, the *baniyā*, to meet their obligations. As in many other parts of the north, child-marriage is allowed but rarely practised today. Generally speaking, the future couple has no say in their parents' decision and are obliged to accept it; they do not know each other and are not supposed to try to meet before the wedding.

DESCRIPTION OF THE RITES

THE ENGAGEMENT

The betrothal or *sagāī*

A delegation of the bride's agnatic kinsmen, led by her paternal uncle (her father is not allowed to go with them) and by a barber, calls on the boy's parents. They are received by the boy's father, in his home. The boy's father's agnates are invited to the reception. The barbers of the bride's family prepare the ceremonial food, *pakkā*, *sakranai* (rice boiled with white sugar and liberally doused with clarified butter just before serving). At dusk, everyone clusters, in one room, around the delegation. One of the delegates, usually the barber, presents the gifts in kind meant for the groom and the various cash presents for him as well, to the members of his lineage and to certain figures from his village.[4] Then a meal is served: the members of the delegation eat first, and then the host's agnates are served. The visitors spend the night at the lineage house and leave for home the next morning. These gifts presented in public by the girl's people to the boy's family seal the betrothal.

The next step is for the girl's parents, who will incur the greatest expenses, to set the wedding date. This can take several months. Traditionally, a Brahmin astrologer used to be consulted as the only one who could determine the auspicious day,[5] but this practice has fallen out of use now.

The 'wedding announcement' or *lagan*

The barber chosen by the bride's group (formerly, services of Brahmins were also used) is charged with conveying to the groom's parents the latter announcing the date of the wedding, when the groom accompanied by his male agnates, will come for his bride. The barber is given a meal and a small sum of money before leaving again. A few days later, he returns with the *tel* (mustard oil which will be used for the groom's ritual bath) and again receives a gift.

THE WEDDING PREPARATIONS

The preparations take several days and are carried out in the groom's village as well as in that of the bride. They begin with the arrival in the two villages of the *sahvāsanī*, the bride's or groom's father's married sister. Sometimes, several married sisters will come to lend a hand with the preparations, but only the *eldest* is regarded as the true *sahvāsanī*; the others must obey her. Other girls, usually the bride's and the groom's real or classificatory sisters, come to help out. All these women take part in the preparations, particularly in the whitewashing of the house and the preparation of the meals. During the rites, they sing, accompanied by the young women of the village.

With the help of other women and the barber, the *sahvāsanī* directs and organizes the *batnā* (purificatory bath) and the *banvarā* (procession in the direction of the *jaṅgle* or forest). For the sake of simplicity, I will describe the rites as they are performed for the groom.

Batnā

This rite takes place in the house of the boy's family. The groom is bathed and is anointed with the mustard oil, *tel*, that has been sent by the parents of the bride. The *sahvāsanī* is assisted here by the barber and the *bhābī*, usually the boy's eldest brother's wife. After having bathed in water, the young man stands on a board (*patrā*) and the barber rubs him with the mustard oil: first his hands and arms (starting on the right), then his face, shoulders, chest and back, and finally the lower body. The boy then dons a new set of clothes. The *sahvāsanī* ties a yellow thread, *kangnā* around his right wrist and places the *sehrā* (crown with threads hanging down which hide the face) on his head.[6] After which she performs the first *arti*, on the doorstep of the house: this ritual gesture consists of passing around the groom's head, in a clockwise movement, a tray holding a lighted candle, one or two paisa (roughly equivalent to pennies), some rice, the herb known as *dub*, and a copper pitcher (*lotā*) half-filled with water.

The ceremony as practised in the Meo village of Chavandi Kalan, in Rajasthan, differs slightly (Aggarwal 1971: 182). Seven women (four must be married women from the villlage, called the village *bahū*, or 'daughter(s)-in-law', and three as yet unmarried *bahin*) are invited to carry out the ritual bathing of the groom. The *sahvāsanī* ties the *kangnā* around the right wrist of each woman. That evening, the same seven women anoint the groom's feet, knees, shoulders, and forehead with a mixture of mustard oil and turmeric. These gestures are repeated seven times by each of the women. After which they sprinkle water in the four directions. The *bhābī* rubs the groom's body with the oil. Then the seven women bathe him while pinching him. The *bhābī* places the crown, *sehrā*, on his head. And he puts on a new set of clothes.

In both variants of the *batnā* ceremony, the *sahvāsanī* plays a crucial role. But, whereas in Bisru, she participates directly, in Chavandi Kalan, she directs the village women like so many assistants after having tied the yellow thread around their wrist.[7]

Banvarā[8]

After the purificatory bath, the groom, dressed in his new clothes, wearing the crown and carrying the cane (*butā*), two insignia of royalty, sets out in 'procession in the direction of the forest (*jañgle*)', which begins at the far edge of the residential zone. He is led by two young companions, one on either side, and accompanied by his paternal aunt, the *sahvāsanī*, and by a barber carrying the copper tray with the lighted candle, a few grains of rice, and the copper pitcher half-filled with water. His 'sisters', *bahin*, bring up the rear, singing. As the procession passes in front of each house, the inhabitants of the quarter step up and drop a paisa or two into the pitcher after having first circled them around the groom's head. When they come to the end of the residential zone, the *sahvāsanī* once more performs the *arti*. The procession then returns to the groom's house and begins the same ritual a second time. When the *banvarā* is over, the groom can remove the *sehrā* and take off his new clothes.

The *batnā* and the *banvarā* are repeated several days in succession both for the boy as well as for the girl, until the boy's departure for the village of the girl, and for the girl, until she leaves with her new husband.

After the first performance of the *batnā* and the *banvarā*, the groom must observe certain rules (the same apply to the bride). These are:

- He can no longer leave the village residential zone unaccompanied without the danger of being attacked by *bhūt*, wandering evil spirits (to which we will return later), who can possess him, drive him mad, or even kill him. If he goes into the fields, a friend of his age must go with him.
- He must also keep within reach his cane (*butā*) or sword (*talwar*), attributes of his royal status and which protect him from the *bhūt*.
- He stops all work.
- He is forbidden to sleep on the rope bed (charpay) but must instead sleep on the floor.
- He abstains from meat and all spicy or bitter foods, and must eat only purely vegetarian fare cooked in butter and sweetened.

Batnā and *banvarā* are rites of separation. Before their performance, the bride and the groom were no different from other people. Afterwards, each in his or her village is raised above their ordinary condition, like a king and a queen. This transformation, worked by the bath and the anointment and which can be regarded as a consecration, places the couple in a state of purity which makes them vulnerable to dangers from evil spirit and at the same time, owing to the prohibitions, secures them protection from such dangers.

The mother's brother's gifts: The *bhāt*

The day before the wedding, the maternal uncle, accompanied by certain agnatic kinsmen, comes to the village of his nephew or his niece to present the *bhāt*.

He must arrive only after the completion of at least the first ritual bath and procession. His brother-in-law waits for him on the outskirts of the village and takes him to the men's part of the house (*banglā*), while his wife prepares for the ceremony. This is what traditionally used to happen: on the doorstep of the house, the sister, carrying the copper pitcher (*lotā*) on her head, would wait for her brother; her husband would be standing behind her holding a copper tray bearing some rice and the herb known as *dub*. The brother would drop some money into the pitcher, greet his sister, and place on the tray the gifts he had brought for his nephew (or his niece), his sister, his brother-in-law, his sister's husband's sister, and her brother-in-law's parents. He would also give one rupee for each household in the lineage and one for each member of the village 'council' (panchayat). He would then be invited into the house where he and his agnates would be given a meal. The pitcher is no longer used. And it is now the sister who holds the tray and receives the gifts, while her husband stands behind her.

Cak pūjā or 'the ritual worship of the (potter's) wheel'

These ceremonies over, the mother of the boy (or the girl) must fetch the new pots for the house from the potter (*kumhar*). She is accompanied by the married women of the village and the barber's wife. Traditionally, when they got to the potter, the mother would draw around the edge of his wheel (*cak*), with the turmeric (*haldi*) she would have brought, five swastikas, representing the god Ganesh. Nowadays the potter performs this rite himself. The women who have come with the mother sing songs mocking the virility of the village men. Then gifts of rice, wheat, mustard seed, and gur (unrefined brown-coloured

Cak pūjā: New pots are carried back to the house

sugar) are given the potter as *neg*, a fee for his services as a ritual specialist. The women then take away the pots. There are three kinds: a big pot, called *matka*, regarded as a male object; a smaller pot, *ghariya*, set on top of the first and regarded as female; and finally, a small male pot, *tekna*, which is carried in the hand. The symbolic representation of the couple and its offspring was explicitly expressed by our informants.

Payment of the *nota*

A day or two before the wedding, the gifts called *nota*[9] are presented to the fathers of the groom and the bride by their respective *bhāī*. These cash gifts are divided into two equal parts: one-half is considered to be the repayment of an earlier gift made by the present recipient, and the other half as a gift to be returned to the present donor at a later date. For instance, if someone gives Rs 51, a sum of Rs 25 is given to reimburse an earlier gift and the balance Rs 25 will be returned at some time when rites are performed at the home of the donor. It is important that accounts are never closed, that the relationship can go on, and the 'one more' is the sign of the present moment.[10] The *bhāī* present are not only those from the agnatic group—lineage or clan—they include all those who classify as consanguineous *bhāī*. Affines do not take part. Each gift is recorded in a notebook together with the giver's name. The sum given will be used to repay the debts incurred by the father of the boy or the girl in organizing the festivities, or to complete the dowry (in the girl's case).

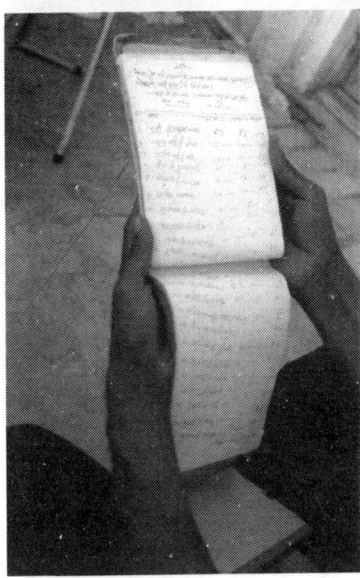

Recording the nota *gifts*

THE WEDDING

The wedding begins on the pre-established day. It takes place in several stages.

The bridegroom's *salam* and the departure of the *barāt*

Early in the morning, the young bridegroom takes off his old clothes and dons a new set.[11] He can hold the cane (*butā*) in his hand or place it beside himself. He prepares to set out to bring his future wife. At this point he receives from the women, his *bahin* and his *bhābī* (sisters-in-law), cash gifts or other items. This ceremony is called the *salam* or '*bida*', the 'farewell'.

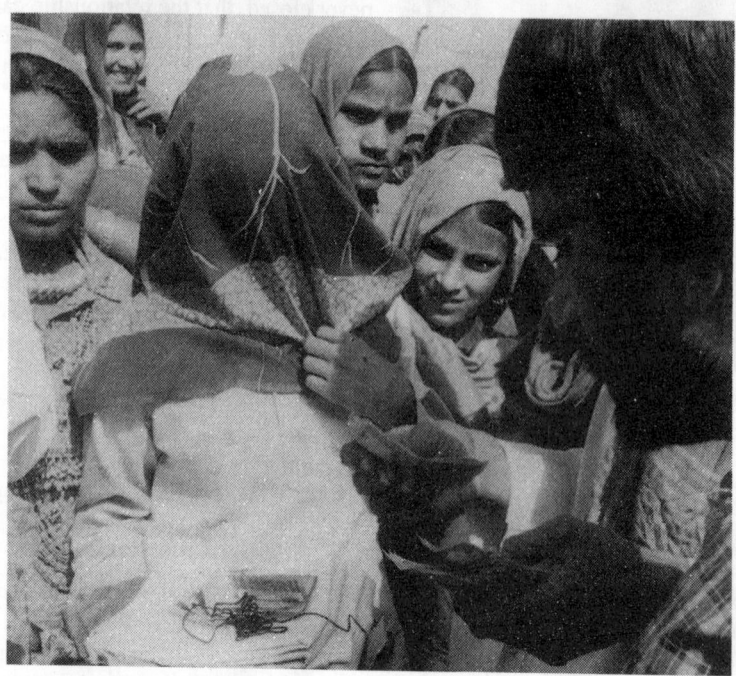

Giving the bhāṭ

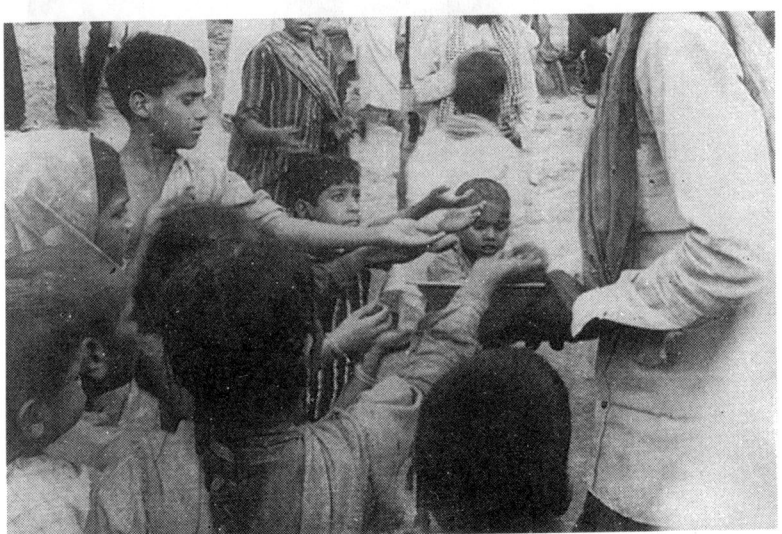

Distributing the guṛ *to the children*

The groom receives the departure gifts or ṣalam

Marriage ceremonies: Ritual prestations 133

The candidates for circumcision are adorned like bridegrooms and receive the salam *gifts*

The women sing before the departure of the barāt

Traditionally the groom used to go around to the different households of his lineage to signal his departure and to receive the *salam* or *bida* gifts. Today this rite takes place in the young man's family courtyard. He sits on the bed, charpay, wearing the insignia of his sovereignty. At his side, on the lower part of the bed, regarded as the younger part, sits the barber, an empty basket covered with a cloth on the ground at his feet. One of the groom's close agnates hands out pieces of *guṛ* to the children present.[12] This sweet, of which the Meo are very fond, is usually given to the children before the start of any important rite so that it will take place in an auspicious climate. Then comes the 'farewell' ceremony. The *sahvāsanī* presides and presents the first gift. The young man's *bhābī* outlines his eyes with khol and gives him a small sum of money. Then the other women (the young man's sisters or the married women from the village) file by, present their gift and bless him. Each woman is also supposed to pour a handful of wheat into the barber's basket.

The gorva *fee paid to the eldest member of the* barāt

Meanwhile the men prepare the departure of the *barāt*, the party which is to accompany the groom. The boy's father is supposed to stay behind and is represented by his own father or his brother, the eldest one if possible. He urges his male agnates to go with the young man, asking each household in his lineage to send at least one if not several of its members. The women stay in the village. Traditionally, many members of the *barāt* used to ride in an ox cart: the groom sat in a four-wheeled cart covered with a canopy called a *rath*, while his companions followed in the two-wheeled cart called a *bhelī*. The Meo are familiar with various episodes of the Mahabharata and maintain that the *rath* is the kind of cart used by the Pandava warriors when they fought their Kaurava cousins at the battle of Kurukshetra. In this context, then, the 'sovereign' husband is elevated to the rank of these mythic heroes. Today the trip to the girl's village is made by car for the groom (and two or three of his friends) and by bus or truck for the rest of the *barāt*.

The ceremonies at the bride's home

The *barāt* arrives in the bride's village, where it will spend from one to three days.[13] The eldest male in the girl's lineage makes a cash gift called *gorva* to the eldest man in the groom's party. After which the *barāt* enters the village amid taunts from the women (the bride's classificatory sisters and paternal aunts), who sing songs mocking their guests. The latter are not supposed to reply, but should feign indifference even when the women tease them about their virility.

Nikah

All the men of both parties make their way to the mosque for the *nikah*, the marriage contract, the only Muslim institution to figure in the ceremonies. The men sit in the mosque and pray, while one of the bride's kinsmen leaves to ascertain her assent. When the bride's positive response is announced and the groom's is given, the *mullah* pronounces the *nikah*. Dried dates (*chwara*) are distributed all around in an uproar which strikes a sharp contrast with the preceding gravity. Then everyone leaves the mosque.

The ceremonial food prepared by the barbers for a Meo wedding

Barothī

The ceremony described here is no longer performed on a regular basis. The groom and the older men of the *barāt* make their way in procession to the bride's house. The bride's *sahvāsanī* is perched on a tall stool on the doorstep of the house, a copper pitcher half-filled with water on her head, blocking the groom's way. She will let him by only when the eldest member of the *barāt* has dropped a few rupees into the pitcher. This gives rise to a comic scene which amuses everyone. The *sahvāsanī* is on a high seat, and the oldest member of the *barāt*, even if he is very tall, has trouble getting the coins into the pitcher. His agnatic kinsmen have to lift him up. Once more the women make fun of the *barāt* party. Once this mocking rite is over, the groom enters the house and receives from his future father-in-law twice the sum given the *sahvāsanī*.

Tokri-ka-neg (*fee for the basket*)
The eldest member of the *barāt* presents the gifts for the bride, usually lengths of cloth, perfume, and jewellery. These are the only gifts of any importance to go from the boy's side to that of the girl. The eldest member of the *barāt* then distributes cash gifts (called *badhar*) to the castes serving the bride's family (in particular the barber, the water-carrier, the bard, etc.).

Samdhī *pūjā*
The eldest member of the *barāt* is the object of yet another mocking rite called *samdhī* pūjā 'ritual worship of the *samdhī*', performed by the mother of the bride. The two people involved are related as *samdhī–samdhan*, as co-in-laws. We will return to this rite which marks an important point in the ceremonies.

The ceremonial meal
After this rite, a meal is served to all the guests, in a courtyard arranged for the occasion. The different groups of Meo guests do not eat together. The *barāt* party is served first, then comes the turn of the bride's maternal uncle and those who accompanied him with the *bhāṭ*.[14] Guests from the village (members of the various lineages) eat last. The leftovers are distributed to the service castes. The meal is prepared by the barbers and served in earthenware

The ceremonial food given to the barāt *by the groom's family*

vessels called *bhublā*. These are used only once, then thrown in a corner outside the tent. They will be taken away and destroyed by the women or the men of the *bhangī* caste or 'sweepers'.[15]

Payment of dahej

The dowry is usually composed of various everyday objects (bedstead, table, chairs, dishes, electric fan, bicycle, etc.), jewellery (silver bangles and necklaces—sometimes worth several thousands of rupees, for the young bride), and a sum of money.[16] In principle, the groom is the recipient of these gifts and may dispose them of as he wishes. But it often happens that his father or his elder brother reserves certain objects for himself or uses them to make up the dowry for their daughter.

In the course of our fieldwork, we found cases in which it was the groom's father who provided the girl's dowry and not the other way round. In this case, it is said that 'the girl was sold', *larki bicta*. Here a marriage according to the rules is opposed to another, reduced to a sort of business transaction, converting the girl to a commodity. This shows that it is hard to speak of the dowry in economic terms. To 'sell' a woman is a disgrace, but it is done when a girl's parents are poor. That said, when it comes to the rites, everything must be done as though the dowry was going from the girl's side to the boy's.

A few hours before the *barāt* leaves to accompany the couple back to the boy's village, the dowry is displayed in the courtyard, where the guests are received in presence of all the men attending the festivities. The groom sits, usually on the bed, surrounded by the *dahej*, while the older men of the *barāt* party receive the jewellery and money from older men on the girl's side. It is at this point, and then only, that the size of the dowry can be contested. As a rule the groom's kinsmen demand more. And some spirited haggling may ensue until the two parties come to an agreement. After which the father of the bride or one of his representatives gives each member of the *barāt* one rupee. The groom's party then bids farewell, loads the dowry onto the bus, and leaves.

The salam *and the couple's departure*

While the dowry is on display, the village women perform the *salam* to the bride, who has put on her ceremonial dress and all her jewellery. The groom comes in to get his young wife. He is treated to a small ceremony by his *barsas* (his wife's elder 'sisters') and his *sālī* (his wife's younger 'sisters', generally unmarried). The first give him their blessing while the second pinch and tease him without his being allowed to react. The bride then readies herself for the departure. She receives one last gift (a few rupees), from her maternal uncle, and then leaves the house with her husband to be installed in the cart, *rath* (nowadays in a car). Throughout this ceremony, the bride weeps and manifests her reluctance to leave the house of her father, her mother, and her brothers.[17] Beyond the conventional aspect of these tears, it must

The groom surrounded by furniture and other objects which make up the dowry (dān-dahej)

A short bargaining session over the jewellery and money in the dowry (the groom's side always demands more than is given)

Wife's 'sisters' mock and pinch the groom

not be forgotten that, once in her husband's village, the young bride will have a lower social position than what she enjoyed in her natal village.

As they are about to leave, the *sahvāsanī* bars the road and prevents the cart from leaving the village. The eldest member of the *barāt* gives her a sum of money so that she will step aside and allow the couple to pass. This ceremony is called *bahaura*.

The couple's arrival in the groom's village

When they arrive in the groom's village, the couple is given a noisy welcome by the women, who crowd around the young bride and escort her to her new home.

The bride laments

Sometimes, as the boy's village comes into view, a race breaks out among the young men in the *barāt* party. The first to reach the groom's house to announce the return of the *barāt* is supposed to receive a gift from the boy's

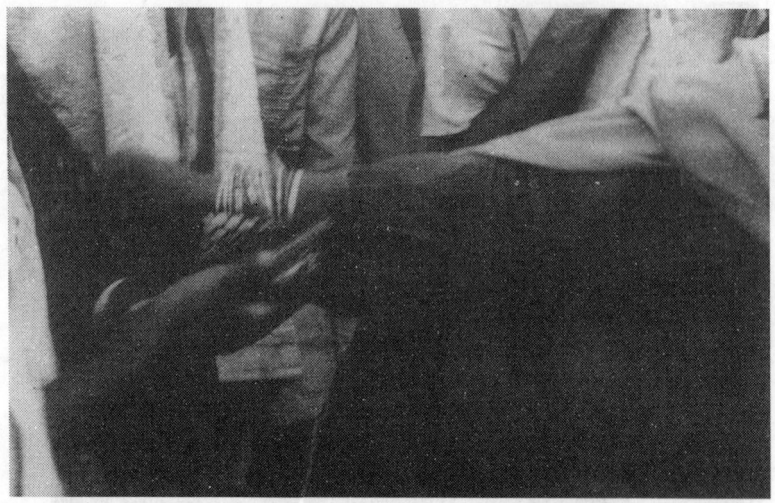
Detail of the gifts from the wife's 'sisters'

father. The race and the gift are regarded as auspicious for the couple's future. The race, therefore, gives rise to a great deal of excitement.

The *sahvāsanī* awaits the couple at the door of the groom's house. She places a board over the threshold, on which the bride and the groom each set their left foot. The *sahvāsanī* then performs the *arti* on the couple. One of the groom's younger brothers sits on his knee and says to him: *bhāī, bhāī, gur mero or choro terro*, 'Brother, brother, the gur for me and the boy for you', then he does the same with the bride, replacing *bhāī* with *bhābī*.

After this ceremony comes the *munh dekhna*, or literally 'to see the face', at the groom's home. The groom's sisters and the wives of his agnates call on the bride and give a sum of money to 'lift the veil and see her face'. Three days later the bride returns to her parents and does not come to live definitively with her husband until a year later.

The *gauna* or the bride's definitive 'departure' for her husband's village

The *gaunā* ceremonies are fairly summary. The husband, accompanied by a few agnates, goes to his wife's village to bring her back to his home. He is received and fêted by his parents-in-law and their agnatic kin, with whom he spends from one to three days. When the time comes for him to leave, he receives the *salam* gifts from his *sālī* (sisters-in-law), who tease him, as well as gifts (lengths of cloth) for his parents and his sisters. Each of his agnates present receives one rupee from the father of the bride. Once again she weeps and laments as she leaves the village.[18]

It is usually only after the *gaunā* that the marriage is consummated. Some Meo say that the young couple may have intercourse during the three days the bride spends in her future home following the wedding. Others maintain that this is not possible, for if the young woman were pregnant and decided not to return to her husband's house, the situation might cause serious friction.

ANALYSIS OF THE RITES

The marriage rites we have seen are the outward manifestation of caste interdependence—which takes us back to the *jajmānī* system studied in Chapter 1—and deploy kinship relations proper to the Meo community. It is this second aspect which we will now examine.

As far as kin ties are concerned, the wedding can commence only if the paternal aunt and the maternal uncle have both fulfilled their ritual obligations during the preparatory phases. Only then can the prestations within each side and those directed to the other side take place. If we look more closely at the ritual sequences, we see that the marriage being celebrated supposes not only that of the parents but that too of at least the paternal aunt. This means that every wedding will have consequences for future rituals: after the prestations and the formation of the couple, children will be born, their father's married sister will come and officiate for their marriage and their mother's brother will bring them ceremonial gifts. In short, for each side the preparatory phases of a marriage grow out of the preceding weddings, and the present wedding will be prolonged in the marriage rites of the couple's children. Even if, on the occasion of a given marriage, the complementary roles of the paternal aunt and the maternal uncle precede the rest of the gifts and counter-gifts, there is in reality no absolute beginning. *The analysis can account for the marriage rites only if it takes into consideration the sequences they form with successive generations. The diachronic aspect is an essential component of this kind of ceremonies.*

We will first take an analytical approach to the prestations and counter-prestations and the ritual roles of the maternal uncles and the paternal aunts. Then we will come back to a more synthetic view of the rites, with a more complete diachronic diagram.

THE SYSTEM OF CEREMONIAL PRESTATIONS

The exchange of prestations in the marriage ceremonies takes two very different forms: some are carried out between agnatic or quasi-agnatic kin, and the bulk of the rest, between affines.

Reciprocal prestations between consanguines

The main gift calling for a counter-gift (on some other ritual occasion) between consanguineous *bhāī* is the *nota*. The term means literally 'invitation'. The Meo use it in the following way: someone who organizes a celebration or a ceremony can invite someone else in person or can send a messenger; the person gives the invited guest a small sum of money (Re 1), called *nota*. To accept this means that one is committed to respond to the invitation.[19] Here the rank of the persons involved is irrelevant: they can be from different castes, or agnates, or affines.

But in the marriage ceremonies or for a circumcision, the *nota* means something else. The gift comes principally from the agnatic kindred, but also from *bhāī* with whom marriage is forbidden: these are the consanguineous relatives from other villages and the members of other village castes considered to be equivalent to consanguineous *bhāī*. The ceremony ending the mourning period, called *fatiya* (on the fortieth day after the death), occasions an analogous gift from both kinds of *bhāī*.[20] This gift between consanguineous *bhāī* is always split into two halves: one regarded as a counter-gift for an earlier gift made to the guest (on the occasion of a marriage, a circumcision, or the end of mourning) and the other as a gift which will have to be repaid by the same guest at a later date (on the same occasions). Reciprocity between agnates or quasi-agnates is a special form of debt, and this system of gift and counter-gift always opens on to the future.

At each marriage and more generally on the occasion of the principal life-cycle rites, the amount of the *nota* received indicates to one and all the extent of one's network of consanguineal ties. It marks a transition between the earlier debts repaid by one's consanguines—principally agnatic kin— and new debts which the receiver will have to reimburse sooner or later.

A gift received by a man can be repaid by him or by his son to either the donor or to one of his descendants. For instance, at the end of mourning, the deceased's agnates who received a gift from him in the past now repay the *nota* to the son, thus creating with the latter the same relationship as they had with the father. Through this type of prestations, the ties of consanguinity are inscribed not only in the present, but down through the generations to come.[21]

Other prestations are made between agnates which call for counter-prestations. Each family in the groom's lineage provides him with a meal and gives him a few kilograms of grain for the young women who will sing at the wedding. The same ceremony takes place on the bride's side. The family of the boy or girl who has received this meal must in return offer an equivalent meal to the different families of his or her lineage when they celebrate a wedding or a circumcision. In the different *salam*, the gifts are made to the groom or the bride by women (sisters or married women in the lineage). These women represent the different families of the agnatic group. The brothers or the husbands of these women expect to receive an analogous counter-gift from the recipients (again through the women) when they celebrate a marriage in their own household. In the case of the gifts given to the groom by his future wife's agnatic *bahin*, it is the duty of her family to give in turn, not of the family of her husband.[22]

All these gifts and services should be also understood as a contribution by the agnatic and other consanguineous kin to the expenditures of the families involved in the marriage and as a way of recognizing the existence of the new couple.

Unidirectional gifts between affines

The gifts exchanged between the two sides of the marriage are more diversified and more complex. For the most part, they flow from the wife's side to that of the husband, from an inferior who gives a woman to a superior son-in-law who receives her. Nevertheless, some less valuable gifts go in the opposite direction. We will study these two forms of unidirectional gifts one after the other.

Gifts from the girl's side to the boy's

We will begin with the gifts made for the *sagāī* (betrothal) at the home of the boy. These are meant not only for the groom and his family but for his agnates and for the representatives of his village as well. Table 5.1 lists the gifts given at two *sagāī*. The donor is the father of the bride.

Table 5.1: Gifts given at two *sagāī*

Recipient	First sagāī (amount in Rs)	Second sagāī (amount in Rs)
The groom	1,500	1221
Groom's paternal grandfather and grandmother	151 + 151	
Groom's father and mother	51 + 51	5 + 5
Groom's paternal uncles and their wives	21 + 21 (each couple)	5 + 5 (each couple)
Groom's paternal aunt	11	5
The 67 households in his lineage Rs 1 per household	67	67
The different service castes of the lineage:		
• barber (*naī*)	11	1
• bard (*mirasī*)	11	1
• water-carrier (*sakkā*)	5	1
• sweeper (*bhangī*)	1	1
The nine members of the panchayat	9	9

To this must be added the sums given by the girl's side to his *bahin* who is already married: five in the first case, seven in the second.[23] The largest amounts are the gifts made to the groom and then those to his close agnates. Gifts are also made in both the cases to the lineage (in fact to the different households) and to the village (represented by the panchayat).[24]

At the time of the wedding, the unidirectional gifts which go to the same side, are presented in the girl's village when the groom comes with his agnates to fetch his wife. The principal gifts are that of the bride: the *kanyādān* ('gift of the maiden'), to which we will return later and that of the *dān-dahej*, the dowry. The latter is given to the groom, but the eldest member of the *barāt*, usually the groom's paternal uncle, receives gifts at various times. In addition, each member of the *barāt* also receives a symbolic gift of one rupee or more, reminiscent of the gift made to each household in the groom's lineage at the time of the *sagāī*. We once again find, at the time of the wedding, the same gifts are given to the groom, his family, and his lineage (Table 5.2).[25]

The gifts from the boy's side to the girl's
The gifts made by the boy's side to the girl's are addressed to women: the wife, her mother, or her paternal aunt. We will study first the gifts made to the new wife, then the rest.

The gifts to the bride
These are made at two points: when the *barāt* comes to the girl's house and when the bride arrives in her husband's village. In the first case, the gift is called the *tokri-ka-neg*, 'fee for the basket', which basket contains lengths of cloth, perfumes, and other small presents sent by the boy's parents and transmitted by the eldest member of the *barāt*. Nothing is given in return. Here the girl's future parents-in-law participate by their gifts in the constitution of the couple. The Meo stress that these gifts are worth much less than the principal gift of the dowry, paid by the parents of the girl. The asymmetry between the two sides of the marriage is thus underscored. But these presents are given to the girl following the *barothī* rite. We will see later how the *barothī–tokri-ka-neg* tandem should be interpreted as analogous to the *bhāṭ* and how to understand the mocking which takes place at that time.

In addition, the *munh dekhna* is given to the bride for the privilege of lifting the veil and seeing her face. This is the first time her husband's agnatic kinswomen and the married women in his lineage see her, and it is a way of marking the beginning of their relationship with her. These gifts complete those made by the same women to the groom at the time of the *salam*, when he set out for his bride's village.[26]

Gifts with larger counter-gifts in return
The prestations which flow from the boy's side to that of the girl are the *barothī*, made to the bride's paternal aunt, and the *samdhī pūjā*, which the

Table 5.2: Gifts exchanged between the two sides at marriage

Occasion and location	Girl's side	Nature and direction of gift	Boy's side
1. Betrothal at the boy's house			
(a) *sagāī* gifts	girl's father ====	money ===>	groom, various agnatic kinsmen, village panchayat, service castes
2. Wedding			
2.1 Girl's house			
(a) *Gorva*: given upon arrival of *barāt*	lineage elder ====	money ===>	eldest member of *barāt*
(b) *Barothī*	*sahvāsanī* <===	small fee ===	eldest member of *barāt*
	girl's father ====	double fee ===>	groom
(c) *Tokri-ka-neg*: gift in kind (clothes, perfume) brought by the *barāt*	bride <===	clothes, perfume ====	boy's parents
(d) *Badhar*	barber and other service castes <===	cash ====	eldest man
(e) *Samdhī* pūjā	*samdhan* <===	cash ====	*samdhī*
	girl's father ====	return of twice the sum ===>	eldest member of *barāt**
(f) *Dahej* ceremony	father ====	*dahej* ===>	groom and his family
	father ====	Re 1/ person ===>	members of *barāt*
(g) *Bida* or *salam*	*bahin* and *bhābī* of bride ====	small cash fee ===>	groom
(h) *Bahaura*	*sahvāsanī* <===	small cash fee ====	eldest member of *barāt*
2.2 Groom's house			
(i) *Munh dekhna* ('to see the face')**	bride <===	money ====	*bahin* and *bhābī* of groom

*See 'The birth of *samdhī* pūjā' on p. 158.
**Here the bride is placed on the groom's side, that is why this gift resembles the *salam*.

eldest member of the *barāt* gives to the bride's mother. In both cases, twice the amount must be returned. This indicates that there can be no reciprocity between the two sides of the marriage, or more accurately, that the system of prestations and counter-prestations must preserve the asymmetry between the two sides, which underscores the superiority of the boy's side over that of the girl.

If we now compare the reciprocal and the unidirectional gifts, we note that the second are larger and more diversified than the first. Relations between agnatic or consanguineous kin are dyadic: one gives only to a family from which one expects something in return. Alternatively, relations between affines involve various kin in addition to the two families concerned: both the groom's close agnates—in particular the paternal aunt—and his distant agnates receive gifts. As the sequences unfold, the unidirectional *sagāī*, or engagement gifts, announce the future ties of affinity. At the time of the wedding itself, the gift giving begins with the reciprocal prestations, which indicate the timeless aspect of the ties between consanguines; then the affinal ties are established by the unidirectional gifts. In other words, affinity cannot be shown before first affirming consanguinity. Reciprocity between consanguineous *bhāī* marks a relationship of equality; the unidirectional gifts between affines indicate the superiority of the boy's side over that of the girl.[27] But things are even more complex, and the distinction between consanguinity and affinity is encompassed by the metasiblingship ties. To understand this last statement, we must consider the roles of the mother's brother and the father's sister.

THE GIFT OF THE *BHĀT* BY THE MOTHER'S BROTHER

In India, the unidirectional gifts given at the time of the marriage normally entail others when the couple has children. Among the Meo, the wife's brother brings to the village of his *behnoï*, brother-in-law, the *cūcak*, a set of presents (lengths of cloth, cash) for the birth of the first son,[28] then the *bhāṭ* for the boy's circumcision,[29] and again the *bhāṭ* when the couple's children marry. His gifts do not continue beyond this generation, though, and it is the maternal uncles of the children born of the new couples who take over.

Bhāṭ means literally 'boiled rice', but also 'present, service, gift'.[30] If one combines the two meanings, one arrives at the idea that, through this kind of prestations, one nourishes, feeds. The same notion is present in the term *cūcak*. The gifts which make up these two modes of giving should be relatively large, sometimes worth several thousand rupees. They are for the sister, her husband, their children (essentially the boy or the girl for whom the ceremony is being held), the husband's parents and brothers and the sister (usually the eldest), the *sahvāsanī*. Each household in the brother-in-law's lineage and each member of the village council receives one rupee. At first sight, these gifts seem to be an extension of and analogous to the unidirectional prestations which characterized the marriage of the children's mother. But there are two major differences: in this case it is the brother of this mother who brings the gifts and not her father (or a representative), and it is the sister (the same one who was given with the dowry) who receives the gifts with her husband. In order to understand these differences, we need to go back to the gifts exchanged between the two sides of the marriage and pause over the most important point in the wedding: the gift of the bride.

In my analysis of the prestations, I singled out the one which in north India is customarily called *kanyādān*, 'gift of the maiden'. Her importance in the ritual sequence must be stressed. Among the Meo as in other communities, the *dān*, which we translate as 'gift', includes not only the *dān-dahej*, the gift of the dowry, but also that of the girl. As Parry remarked (1986: 453–73), the *dān* is a unilateral gift with nothing in return, no reciprocity.[31] This gift of the maiden must be that of a virgin, purified, and decked in all her jewellery. The woman who is 'given' is not an object, no more than the cow given to a Brahmin is a mere animal. She has a sacred quality about her and, in a certain fashion, a divine spark.[32] This gift to the husband is the equivalent of the gift made to the Brahmin priest (Dumont 1966a: 153; English trans. 1970: 117) and places the recipient on a superior plane to the donor.[33]

Must we say that the gift of the maiden results in her complete transfer from her natal group to that of her husband? Parry does not express his opinion on the *kanyādān* directly, but he does indicate that, generally speaking, the gift is neither a loan nor a security. He goes on to say: 'It is alienated in an absolute way, and the very definition of the gift is that it involves the complete extinction of the donor's proprietary rights in favor of the recipient' (1986: 461). Parry brings the question of the gift down to a legal problem: he speaks of an alienated good, of a transfer of proprietary rights. In my opinion this singularly reduces the scope of this kind of gift and raises the problem of the notion of property, in the sense here of private property.[34]

The question posed by this analysis is the following: Does the girl given in *kanyādān* cease to be a member of her natal group and become a member of her husband's group? A priori, that is exactly what happens: the bride weeps because she is going to leave her family where she was coddled and enter the family of her husband, where she will be under the orders of her mother- and sister-in-law, before gaining a respected position in her husband's village with the marriage of her children. But the gift of the

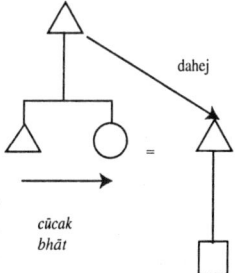

Figure 5.1: *Gifts given by the father and the brother*

maiden goes beyond the mere juridical framework of the transfer of ownership of a piece of property. The woman in *kanyādān* is the principal sign of the relationship between donor and recipient, and, in reality, she remains affiliated to her original lineage while becoming associated with that of her husband (Figure 5.1).[35]

In the context of the marriage, the gifts of the father of the bride are given to a son-in-law, an *asnāw*, as well as to his agnatic kin, all of whom are affines for the donor. In the generation below, the situation is entirely different. To be sure, the ceremonies are performed for the children of a couple, and the gifts can be seen as going from a maternal uncle to his nephews and nieces. But as the terminological analysis showed, this maternal uncle is first of all the mother's brother,[36] and the nephews and nieces are sister's children. He gives the *cūcak* and then the *bhāṭ* to his sister, his *bahin*, to his brother-in-law, his *behnoï*, to his brother-in-law's sister, who is also his *bahin*, and so forth. We are no longer in an affinal setting, but in a relationship with which we are by now very familiar, that of metasiblingship, which transcends the consanguinity/affinity distinction. The chain of relatives established is more important than the respective interests of the two sides. The woman is not simply the object given; together with her husband, she is the subject who receives gifts from her brother.[37] Let us remember that, traditionally, she stood before the front door of the house, the pitcher on her head, with her husband a step or two behind her holding the tray on which the gifts would be deposited. Today, the pitcher has disappeared and the tray is held by the sister, her husband simply standing behind her. The unity of the husband–wife couple is affirmed before the brother, who gives the presents. The sequence *dahej–cūcak–bhāṭ* is thus indeed the continuation of the unidirectional gifts, but its sociological significance in terms of kinship has changed: from opposition between agnation and affinity, it has shifted to the affirmation of metasiblingship.

In short, *kanyādān* should not be separated from its outcome, its ultimate form: the *cūcak* and *bhāṭ* gifts. In this context, the woman given does not cease being a sister to her brother; in fact she becomes the sister *into which marriage has made her* and, as the principal recipient of the gifts from this brother, she plays a principal role in her husband's family. But her role does not end there. In her home village, the married sister acquires a pre-eminent position as principal officiant in the life-cycle rites of her own brother's children. This will be shown in the next part of our analysis.

RITUAL SERVICES PERFORMED BY THE *SAHVĀSANI*, THE FATHER'S MARRIED SISTER

In effect, this married sister[38] comes home to officiate in her natal lineage on different occasions. First of all, at the birth of her brother's children, and particularly of the first son, she is supposed to perform an important purification rite for the mother and child. I will briefly describe the context of her intervention.

Childbirth and the period following it are marked by impurity of the mother and the child.[39] For three days, the mother does not leave the bed, does not touch the floor of the house, and keeps her clothes contaminated by the pollution of childbirth. The child is cleaned off, wrapped in a length of cloth by the midwife and, for the first three days, is given only water sweetened with guṛ to drink.[40] On the third day, the mother and the child bathe and put on new clothes; the old ones are destroyed or given to the low castes. At this time, the father's married sister comes to wash the breast of her sister-in-law and draw off the first milk. It is only then that the newborn child is allowed to suckle. The couple gives the sister *neg*, a ritual fee. The role of the married sister is not so much to remove the impurity as to install the mother–child relationship in the realm of purity. Furthermore, her first ritual act for her brother demonstrates not only her purificatory function but also her role as complement to the mother in the child's survival.[41] The *chatiko* (literally 'sixth day') ceremony is when the first locks of hair are cut by the barber and the new child is given a name.[42] This second elimination of defilement and the introduction of the child into society by giving it a name is also marked by the intervention of the married sisters of the father and the grandfather. These women bring the child shirts and bonnets (*kurta-topi*), which he will wear for his first year at least.[43] These clothes will protect him during this initial phase of growth.

Earlier, I mentioned the homology between the circumcision and the marriage rites. In both cases, the married sister is the *sahvāsanī*, the chief officiant in the rites, assisted by the barber. For her ritual services, she also receives *neg* from her brother. In both sets of rites, the *sahvāsanī*'s function is first of all to purify: she cleans and whitewashes her brother's house and she presides over her nephew's or her niece's ritual bath. Later she leads the *banvarā* procession and performs the *arti*. Thus she raises the future spouse above his or her condition to that of purified king or queen, obliged to respect certain taboos: eat only vegetarian foods, *pakkā*; never leave the village unaccompanied so as not to be attacked by the *bhūṭ*, evil, impure spirits who roam the *jañgle*. It is, therefore, not enough to be purified and elevated to the condition of king or queen; it is also necessary to respect the prohibitions associated with this ritual consecration. These enable one to avoid any contact with pollution and to ward off those dangerous spirits which drive people mad and can even kill.

In all these circumstances, the *sahvāsanī* can be seen as the paternal aunt who acts on behalf of her nieces and nephews. But she is first and foremost the father's sister, and it is in her brother's house and for his children that she acts. *The ties between two successive generations can be understood only* through the ties of metasiblingship which link the mother's brother and the father's married sister.

This raises three questions: How does the married sister's function as ritual officiant compare with the same functions in the caste system? Why does the ban specify that the future groom or bride may not leave the residential zone alone but must be accompanied by a friend? What is the meaning of the *arti* which follows the purificatory bath?

The brother–sister tie, equivalent to the Brahmin–Kshatriya relationship

During the marriage rites, members of several castes, notably the barbers, provide ritual services in exchange for a fee, *neg*. They are always members of lower castes but, on the occasion of a ceremony, they are elevated, as it were, above their normal station. Nevertheless, even in these circumstances, they are still lower than the Meo for whom they officiate. The married sister can in no way be assimilated to this group. Nothing begins until she arrives. Both her brother and her sister-in-law are supposed to obey her and follow her instructions, as are the members of the service castes. It should be noted that the barber—who ranks close to the high castes and who is regarded as nearly high caste—is supposed to assist her in the many ceremonies and acts as cook only under her orders. Finally, the function of the married sister is not so much to remove impurity as it is to bring purity to her brother's house and to consecrate the future spouse by elevating him to the status of king. *In these circumstances, she occupies a position with respect to her brother which is comparable to that of the Brahmin with respect to the warrior, Kshatriya.* The ritual dignity accruing to the members of the other castes which provide their services makes sense only with reference to the *sahvāsanī*, who holds the highest function in the rites, that of priestess. From this standpoint, the *neg* received by this married sister is the equivalent of the ritual fee, the *dakṣiṇa* given to the Brahmin for carrying out the function of officiant, of sacrificer (Malamoud 1976).

Bhūṭ and *hamzad*

In answer to the question on the prohibitions associated with *bhūṭ*, I will briefly say what they are. The term is not specific to the Meo or the other Muslims. As a rule, in India it designates persons who have committed suicide or have died a violent death (by murder or by accident) without having fulfilled their destiny, and in particular without having completed the rites they had undertaken. To this first definition of *bhūṭ*, I will add a second which seems to be peculiar to the Meo. For the Meo, every birth is double: the human child has a twin called *hamzad* (a Persian term, literally, 'born with') which is a bodiless being. For forty days, this twin attempts to suckle at its mother's breast.[44]

She must uncover only one of her breasts at a time so as to feed the human child and starve the *hamzad* to death. If the latter were ever to survive owing to a lapse of the mother's vigilance, sooner or later it would attack its human twin, steal his 'soul', *atma* or *ruhu*, and change him into a *bhūṭ*. Thus one becomes a *bhūṭ* only through the action of one's double. If the groom (or the bride) must be accompanied by a young friend, a sort of human double, whenever they go into the forest, is this not in order to prevent the *hamzad* double from keeping the person company—and therefore attacking them?

Arti

This term is used in two ways: it designates the tracing of a circle with a tray bearing a lighted candle in front of an idol or a person or persons, here the groom or the newly-weds.[45] This rite is performed at the end of the *batnā* (ritual bath), in front of the house entrance. It is also the high point of the *banvarā*, when the procession reaches the outskirts of the residential zone, the beginning of the *jañgle*—the cultivated fields and the forest. And finally, it is the ritual gesture performed by the groom's *sahvāsanī* when the couple arrives and before they step into their new home.[46] All of this seems to indicate that the *arti* is associated with places which separate or connect. The fact that this rite is performed by a woman, the groom's father's married sister, has its importance, as the analysis of the following myth will show.

When we asked our chief informant about the significance of the *arti*, he answered with the myth of Mirased Hussain.

The king of Taragar (Ajmer region in Rajasthan), Chawka Ben, had erected a great palace on a hilltop. Every day he would burn more than 300 kilograms of cotton soaked in oil. The smoke could be seen from a great distance, as far away as the Arabian Sea. The king of the latter region, Mirased Hussain, asked one of his subjects to go and recognize the country where this light was coming from. The emissary, named Rosansa Darwish, arrived in Taragar. He sat down at the foot of the hill. After a while, some women passed by who brought yogurt (*dahi*) to the palace every day. He asked one of them to sell him some. The woman replied that, if he would agree to pay more than one piece of gold for each pot, which was what the king of Taragar gave, she would sell him some. The emissary agreed but on condition that he could taste the yogurt to see if it was sweet. But the yogurt turned out to be sour, and the emissary, furious, slapped the woman across the face.

The woman went to tell her misadventure to the king, who ordered the culprit to be seized and to receive a punishment which reflected his sin. The emissary of the Muslim king had his finger cut off. But the finger began jumping around in front of him. The man told it to calm down and swore he would avenge it before *Id ul-Fitr* (the major Muslim festival), adding that many men were going to die.

He went back to his king, Mirased Hussain, and told him his troubles. The king was furious and decided to set out for Taragar and make war on Chawka Ben. But he was to be married, and the *batnā* rites were barely over; and so his mother asked him not to leave because it was dangerous to interrupt the ceremonies in this way. The king would not listen to her and decided to carry on regardless. So the mother went to see her son's horse, Duldul, and told him to bring his master's head back to her before the battle began.

Mirased Hussain arrived with his army in front of Taragar. The horse did as he had promised, and took his master's head back to the king's mother, and then returned. The headless king began his war. Single-handedly he exterminated Chawka Ben's entire army, and his horse, with one sweep of his tail, destroyed the hill on which the palace stood. The old women of Taragar were worried and decided to take action. One of them performed *arti* before the king and his horse, and both fell down dead.

From this highly complex myth, we will retain one crucial point directly connected with our analysis of the rites: having left to wage war against his mother's will, while his own marriage rites had just begun, the young Muslim king is forced to hand over his head to his horse, who takes it to the king's mother.[47] In the mind of our informant, the might of this decapitated man becomes boundless. But it is the strength of a warrior turned *bhūṭ*, an evil spirit. Whereas the initial marriage rites had elevated him to the condition of purified king, his departure from his kingdom and his violence change him into an impure, dangerous king. And only the *arti* performed by an old woman can kill him and stop the massacre. In such a context, this ritual gesture prevails over the warrior's strength. It saves the inhabitants of the kingdom of Taragar from the deadly danger represented by the wandering spirits.

There are notable differences between the myth and the rite. In the rites, the purificatory baths and the *arti* are closely associated and ensure the protection of the groom-king; in the myth, the king does not complete the rites that have begun and undergoes the *arti* after he has become a king-*bhūṭ*. Instead of protecting him, this ritual gesture now kills him, thereby saving the kingdom of Taragar.

But in the myth as in the rite, the *bhūṭ* and the ritual action of the *arti* are associated. The *arti* protects the groom-king from the *bhūṭ*, provided he respects certain taboos.[48] In the myth, the *arti* neutralizes the harmful effects of proximity between the sovereign and the impure evil spirits. And in both scenarios this ritual act demonstrates the superiority of a woman officiant over whoever possesses violent power in its dangerous form: the king-*bhūṭ*, or in its purified form: the groom-king. The ruler of Taragar is powerless to resist Mirased Hussain, the king-*bhūṭ*. The groom cannot single-handedly perform the rites which raise him to the status of sovereign. The old woman in the myth and the *sahvāsanī* thus occupy the same ritual position, which makes them superior to the holders of royal authority. Once again we encounter an opposition equivalent to that between the priest and the warrior.

Affinity and metasiblingship

It is now possible to gain a clearer understanding of the transformation ensuing on a couple's marriage. The preparatory phases of the marriage elevate the groom and the bride to the status of king and queen. But in the wedding itself, when the girl's father hands her over as a 'gift' to her husband, he places the latter in a position equivalent to that of a Brahmin priest who receives a 'gift' for which nothing is expected in return. The affinal relationship establishes an asymmetry between the wife-takers, regarded as superior, and the lowered wife-givers. After the marriage, however, it is no longer the husband, but his wife who will occupy this priestly function.

The woman, whom we will call A, object of the gift, becomes, after the birth of her children a, the main recipient of the gifts—*cūcak* and *bhāṭ*—given by her brother B (Figure 5.2).

But not only does this married woman A receive the ceremonial gifts given by her own brother B, she will also become the chief officiant in his household for the circumcision of his sons or the marriage of his children b. For these ritual services, she will receive a fee, *neg*. It must be kept in mind that she does not come as the wife of an affine, but as the sister into which

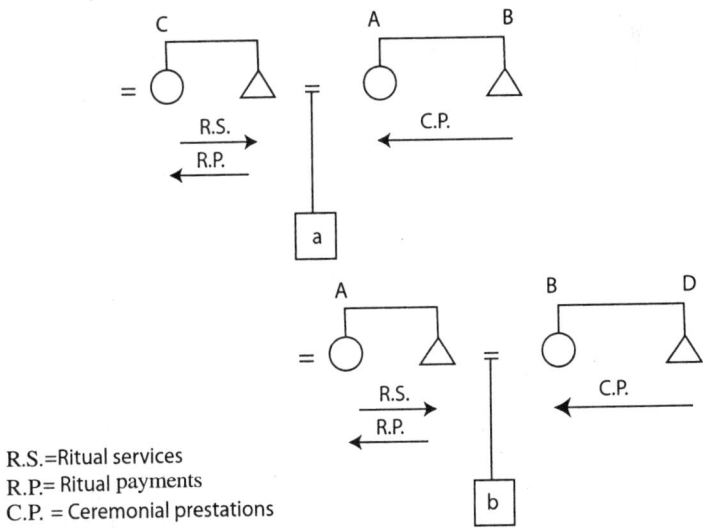

R.S.=Ritual services
R.P.= Ritual payments
C.P. = Ceremonial prestations

Figure 5.2: Complementarity between ritual services and ceremonial prestations

marriage has made her. She officiates in the home of her *bhāī*, more specifically of her 'own' brother, and of her sister-in-law.

The relationship between the brother B and his sister A unfolds in a diachronic process and involves, on different occasions, the children of A or those of B. But one has only to look at each of these occasions to see that the brother B–sister A relationship cannot be taken in isolation. Brother B does not make gifts to his sister A and to her children a alone, he must also make gifts to his second *bahin* C: his sister's husband's sister. This woman C is herself the officiant in the ceremonies for children a. If one regards A as the officiant for her brother B, her ritual work is completed by the ceremonial gifts from her second *bhāī*, D, her brother's wife's brother.

To sum up, every time a brother–sister relationship appears, it is imbedded in the opposite-sex metasibling chain, the double brother–sister pair linked

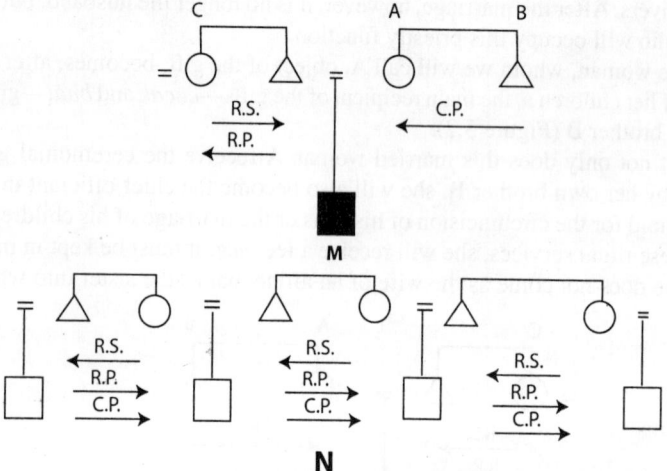

Figure 5.3: Synchronic sequence of ritual services and ceremonial prestations

by a marriage (*cf.* part M of Figure 5.3; part N of the same figure shows how these different chains of relatives can be linked).

We see appearing in this metasiblingship chain, the complementary actions of the maternal uncle, or more accurately the mother's brother, who, with the *bhāt* in particular, 'nourishes' the couple formed by his sister and her husband as well as their children, and that of the paternal aunt, or more accurately the father's sister, who purifies, protects, and thereby ensures her brother's descendants a new lease on life. In these ritual actions, the asymmetric relationships between affinal brothers-in-law recede into the background, while the opposite-sex metasibling chain moves to the fore. In short, the transformation of the married sister and, with her, the importance of the brother–sister tie can be understood only in terms of the shift from the opposition between consanguinity and affinity (with the constitution of the couple) to opposite-sex metasiblingship (when the couple has children).

But this analysis is still insufficient to characterize the form taken by metasiblingship in the rites, or the relations between this kind of link and affinity. There are two important points which should be stressed:
- The rites lead us to differentiate between the brother–sister vector and the sister–brother vector, which the terminology regards as equivalents. When a brother looks at his sister, her husband, and so on, he sees people who are superior to him; when a sister looks at her brother and his wife, she sees a couple that is inferior to her and who owes her ritual gifts and fees. This difference in status is conferred by the rite itself.
- But a distinction needs to be made between a married sister's superiority over her brother in the context of metasiblingship and that of the wife-takers over the wife-givers in the context of affinity. So what does the double brother–sister pair linked by a marriage add to the relationship between brothers-in-law (*behnoï–sālā*) or sisters-in-law (*nanad–bhābī*)?

At the time of the wedding, the unidirectional gifts indicate the affinal ties between the two sides of the marriage and the superiority of the wife-takers over the wife-givers. These gifts continue in a special form with the *cūcak* and the *bhāṭ*, but, as we have stressed, while the father of the girl gives her at the same time as he gives the dowry, his son, who takes over from him, gives gifts and ceremonial fees to his own sister, to her husband, to her husband's sister, to their children, and to other members of the household. However, these gifts and fees do not allow one to distinguish clearly between metasiblingship and affinity.

When the opposite-sex metasibling chain appears in a rite, the unidirectional gifts made by the brother to the couple formed by his sister and his brother-in-law complement and complete the ritual services that the married sister, chief officiant in the ceremonies, has performed for this same couple and for which she receives a fee. The superiority of the married sister over the brother is shown, on the one hand, by the fees she receives and, on the other, by the ritual services she performs.[49] The first form of asymmetric relationship is analogous to the affinal ties, the second is proper to metasiblingship.

The ritual services performed by the married sister thus shift the affinal ties over to the side of metasiblingship and give a different meaning to the ceremonial gifts given by the maternal uncle. They produce something like a new birth (in addition to the biological birth ensured by the parents), a new life in the same way as initiation does for the twice-born at the caste level.[50]

This brings us to one of the major propositions of my analysis, namely that the opposite-sex metasibling chain sets up a triad: the wife's brother, who brings the gifts; the husband's married sister, who performs the ritual service; and the couple marrying their child and for whom the other two are acting. This triad

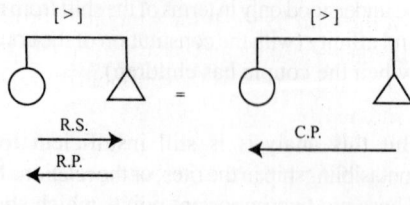

[>] : ritual superiority

Figure 5.4: Asymmetrical relations between the two brother–sister chains

can be understood as the articulation of two dyadic relationships *of two married brother–sister chains of relatives which are at once alike, different, complementary, and ranked: alike because they designate the same* bhāī–bahin *relationship; different because the first is marked by unidirectional gifts which 'nourish' and the second by a ritual work which ensures a new lease on life; complementary because every marriage requires gifts and ritual work; and finally, ranked because the ritual work of the second married sister is characteristic of metasiblingship while encompassing, on the one hand, the unidirectional gifts made by the brother to the first sister and, on the other hand, those which are made in the context of affinity by the wife-givers to the wife-takers* (Figure 5.4).

Marriage in its diachronic dimension

As we near the end of this analysis of the prestations and ritual roles entailed in marriage, a remark is called for. When I began by examining the affinal ties as they were transformed into relations of metasiblingship, I presented what was still only a partial view of the marriage rites and their effects. The affinal tie between two families comes into being during the actual wedding, after the consecration of the groom by his father's married sister and after the giving

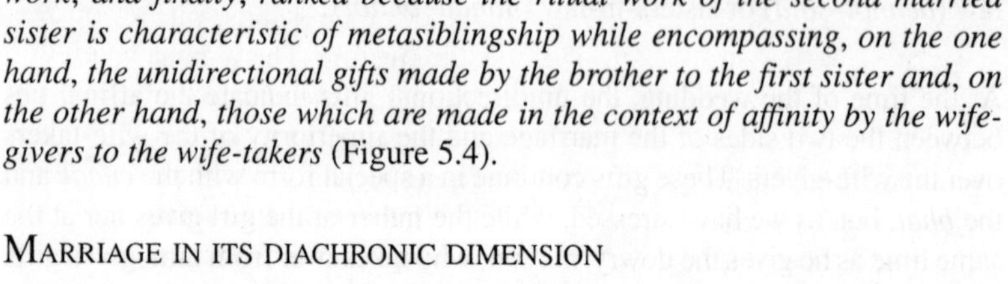

Figure 5.5: Metasiblingship chain in diachrony

of the *bhāṭ* by the bride's mother's brother. In other words, metasiblingship precedes affinity and continues in other guises. Having broken down the set of ceremonies into their principal dimensions, I will now present a global and necessarily diachronic view of marriage.

Figure 5.5 shows the ritual linkage entailed by marriage over three generations. It is within this sequence of links that it will be easier to situate two rites which take place during the wedding: the *barothī* and the *samdhī pūjā*, which precede both the ceremonial meal and the payment of the *dahej* by the father of the bride. In both ceremonies, the eldest member of the *barāt* meets with derision.

Barothī as a mocking *bhāṭ*

The *sahvāsanī*, it will be remembered, stands before the entrance to the house, bearing a copper pitcher on her head,[51] and allows the eldest member of the *barāt* to pass only if he can manage to drop a silver coin into the pot. After which the man enters the house and presents the gifts (*tokri-ka-neg*) for the bride. The analogies with the *bhāṭ* ceremony are striking: the site of the ceremony—a threshold—before which a woman stands, pitcher on head, the gifts. But the differences are just as interesting. The woman receiving is not the sister of the man giving. We know that, in the *bhāṭ*, the married sister, who receives the gifts, is considered to be superior to her brother. Yet we have said that, during the wedding itself, the groom's side is treated as being superior to the bride's. The *barothī* thus seems to indicate a relative inversion, since it is as though the eldest member of the *barāt* were acknowledging the superiority of the bride's paternal aunt and not asserting his own superiority and that of the groom who accompanies him. The gifts made to the bride are *neg*, ritual fees. In all likelihood, this means that the man's side is acknowledging the transformation of the bride by her *sahvāsanī*. In this particular context, the bride is accorded the same status as the groom (they are queen and king); the relative character of the inversion in this rite somewhat tempers the wife-takers' superiority over the wife-givers. The asymmetry between the two sides at the affinal level is set against a background of symmetry. An analogous idea appears in the *samdhī pūjā* rite.

But there are two final facts which need to be understood: Why is this rite accompanied by mocking? And why do the sisters and the paternal aunts of the bride make fun of the wife-takers on this occasion and, more generally, for as long as the *barāt* is in the village? In answer to the first question, we should note that the boy's side is not supposed to react, even when it is made fun of. The *sahvāsanī* receives a small sum of money as a ritual fee, but the girl's father must in turn give the groom twice that amount, thus re-establishing the normal direction of flow in the asymmetric relationship between the two sides of the marriage. The teasing itself thus becomes laughable, and the inversion must not lead to any misapprehensions as to the superiority of the boy's side in the wedding. The teasing is addressed to a superior who, at the time of the *barothī*, pretends to be inferior and gives presents (small ones), thus playing the role which normally falls to the wife-giver.

The second question is more complex and goes beyond the scope of the *barothī*. While they are in the bride's village, the *barāt* party behave in a condescending manner to show the superiority of the wife-takers. But the women's teasing reminds them that, in the bride's village, the superiority they enjoy is only temporary and that only these women can occupy the highest function in the family, that of ritual officiant, and have a right to be shown the respect due to their position.

The wedding *samdhī* pūjā

This rite takes place between the *barothī* and the meal followed by the payment of the dowry, or *dahej*. *Samdhī* and *samdhan* are reciprocal terms used between two sets of kin, those of the son-in-law and those of the daughter-in-law. The agnatic *bhāī* of a *samdhī* is also a *samdhī*. The agnatic *bahin* of the *samdhan* is a *samdhan* as well (Figure 5.6).

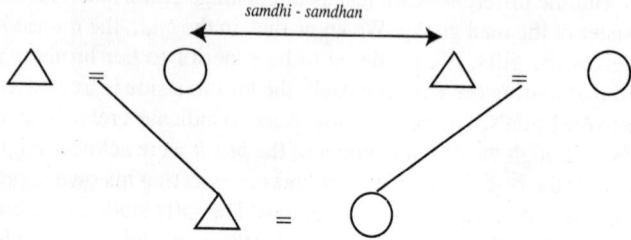

Figure 5.6: Reciprocal terms in affinity

These reciprocal affinal kin terms do not indicate the direction of the marriage, unlike *sālā*, *nanad*, and so on. A *samdhan* covers her face in the presence of her *samdhī*, but makes fun of him, particularly during rites, without his being supposed to answer back. She thus apparently adopts contradictory attitudes: distance through the veiling and proximity through the derision. The relationship between two *samdhī* or between two *samdhan* is not marked. There is thus an asymmetry in the relation between the *samdhī*, a man, and the *samdhan*, a woman, which at the same time implies a symmetry on another level between the two sides, since the relations between the *samdhī* (boy's father) and the *samdhan* (girl's mother) is perfectly identical to that between the *samdhī* (girl's father) and the *samdhan* (boy's mother).

In the *samdhī* pūjā rite, the eldest man in the *barāt* stands in for the groom's father. Taking advantage of a moment when he is not paying attention—for instance while he is smoking the hookah, with other men in the courtyard—the *samdhan* slips up and places on his head an *indi* (a decoratively braided rope crown usually used for carrying a waterpot on the head) and the copper pitcher (*lotā*), then she presses her hand, which she has blackened with coal, on his back. Her *samdhī* then gives her a sum of money which her husband will pay back twofold. This ceremony is carried out amid general laughter, and the women of the village once again make fun of the guests. When this rite is over, the ceremonial meal is set before the members of the *barāt*, then the *dahej* is given to the groom by the girl's father.

This rite seals the affinal tie between the two families involved in the marriage. The same rite is performed in an equivalent but inverse manner at the birth of the couple's first boy-child.

The birth *samdhī* pūjā

The child's maternal uncle, who is supposed to bring the gifts known as *cūcak*, arrives with several agnates, notably one of his father's elder or younger brothers or, if this is not possible, one of his father's agnatic *bhāī*. The newborn child's paternal grandmother performs the same *samdhī* pūjā on the person standing in for the maternal grandfather, just as she did at the wedding. There is one difference, however. The *samdhī* pretends to be about to give a large sum of money, but he merely shows it, and it is the child's paternal grandfather who actually gives her a small fee. After this rite, the child's maternal uncle gives the *cūcak*, and the guests are invited to sit down to a meal.

The samdhan, *after the* samdhī *pūjā performed on the anthropologist*

The *samdhī* pūjā is the only rite in which a man has a copper pitcher placed on his head. In the other ceremonies, it is borne by a woman, notably by the married sister when her brother brings the *bhāt*. Here the man is in a way feminized and, as in the *barothī*, the accompanying derision marks both the bounds of the transformation and the transitory character of this affinal tie with respect to metasiblingship.[52]

Returning to Figure 5.5, we note that the *samdhī* pūjā extracts the two sets of kin from the opposite-sex metasibling chains and creates a link between them so that they participate in the creation of a new couple or a new family. The equivalence of the couple's parents, expressed by the reciprocal affinal kin terms, relativizes, here as in the *barothī*, the superiority of the wife-taker over the wife-giver. From the standpoint of caste endogamy, it neutralizes the differences introduced by the marriage and allows the children the same status as their two parents. The first *samdhī* pūjā, which follows the appearance of metasiblingship, prepares the way for the affinal tie, for the gift of the maiden and the dowry by the father of the bride; the second, which puts an end to the affinal relationship, precedes the payment of the *cūcak* and prepares the way for the opposite-sex sibling relationship, for a whole new series of gifts, services, and ritual fees which are part of a new chain of two brother–sister pairs linked by a marriage.[53] Through its two ritual manifestations, the *samdhī–samdhan* relationship serves as a relay for the opposite-sex metasibling chains located in two generations.

The samdhan *hides and mocks her* samdhī *while her husband looks on amused*

In this sequence of links, the *samdhī–samdhan* relationship characterizes the affinal tie as being at the same time asymmetric and symmetric, or more accurately, as being asymmetric against a backdrop of symmetry. Alternatively, the brother–married sister metasibling link is always unidirectional and can never be reversed.

The opposite-sex metasibling chain in its diachronic dimension

The brother who brought the *cūcak* and then the *bhāṭ* for his sister's children has no obligation to the following generation, that of his great nephews and nieces. He gives way to their maternal uncle. Likewise, his sister acts as *sahvāsanī* for her brother's children only, not for his grandchildren. She will be replaced by her niece, her brother's daughter.[54]

Three remarks are called for here:
• From the point of view of a man a, for the ceremonies concerning his own children, his sister takes over from his paternal aunt X as *sahvāsanī*. From the point of view of his wife b, again for the ceremonies concerning

her children, her brother takes over from her maternal uncle Y (Figure 5.7).
• From the point of view of the man and from one generation to the next, the *bhāt* should come from different families, lineages, and even villages, since a man cannot marry someone from his mother's village. There need not be a kin tie between the giver of the *bhāt* in one generation and the giver in the following generation. On the other hand, a niece always takes over from her paternal aunt as *sahvāsanī* for her brother's children. The saying *phūphī ke sath bhatījī*, 'the paternal aunt with her niece' (her brother's daughter) is not only significant when it comes to the marriage alliance, it also appears as a form of ritual transmission of role between the women of an agnatic line. This implies a series of brother-married-sister chains of relations, which harks back to a feature of the terminology, namely that descent (in this case unilineal) acquires its full meaning through the opposite-sex metasibling chain (Figure 5.8 M).
• From the point of view of the woman, and from one generation to the next, the uterine nephew takes over from his maternal uncle to bring the *bhāt*. The successive *sahvāsanī*, on the other hand, are not related to each other: a woman's paternal aunt and the woman's husband's sister are not blood relatives; they come from different lineages (Figure 5.8 N).

There is a big gap between parts M and N of Figure 5.8: owing to the patrilineal descent system, the paternal aunt and her niece come from the same agnatic group (Figure 5.8 M), while the maternal uncle and his uterine nephew (Figure 5.8 N) can only belong to two different groups, like a mother and her daughter. In the right-hand part of Figure 5.8 M, an agnatic line is formed by the succession of generations, while the left-hand part of the same figure shows a series of brother–sister pairs from different lineages. This is understandable if one remembers that a man cannot take a wife from his mother's village. In Figure 5.8 N, the two lineages from which the two families linked by marriage come change from one generation to the next.[55]

That said, it is important to note the predominance of the opposite-sex metasibling chain in the succession of generations. The affinal ties which appear on the occasion of each marital union cannot be repeated between two families; they are not transgenerational here, as they are in south India. Ultimately, they are a relay between these metasibling chains located in different generations. Likewise, the unilineal descent reckoning in Figure 5.8 M becomes meaningful only through and for the transmission of the brother–sister relationship from one generation to the next.

INDIVIDUALIZING AND RELATIONAL ASPECTS OF MEO RITES

Marriage rites can be interpreted as rites of passage.[56] For the principal actors, the bride and the groom, there is a period which institutes a break with their

162 *Kinship and Rituals among the Meo of Northern India*

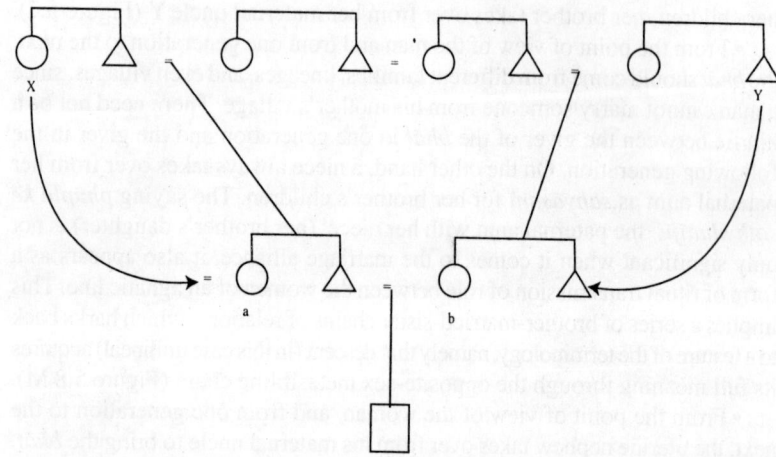

Figure 5.7: *Diachronic sequence of ritual roles*

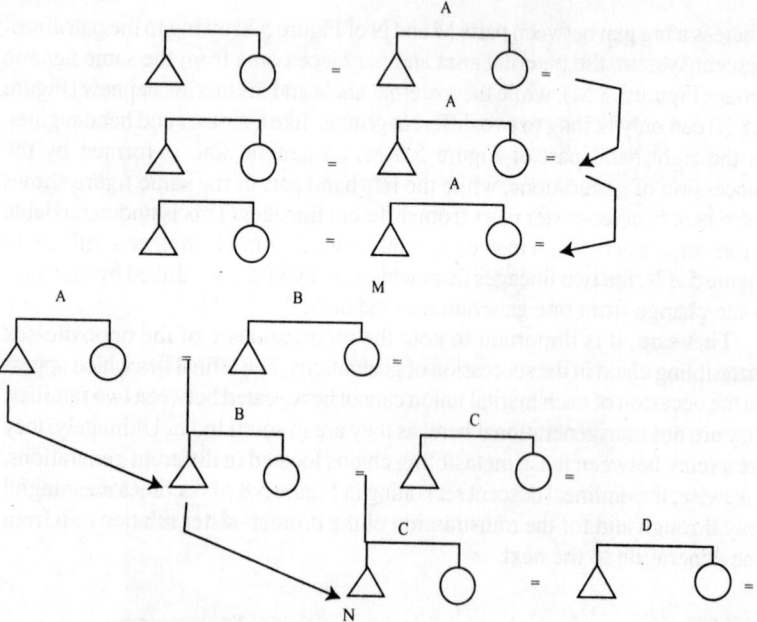

Figure 5.8: *Successive marriages and ritual roles*

unmarried state, marked by preparatory rites (baths, processions); a period of marginality or liminality during which they are not supposed to do any work and must adhere to a set of very strict taboos before entering into their new social state as husband and wife, constituting a couple called to found a home and a family. The children of this couple will follow a ritual path (birth, circumcision, marriage), a long series of rites of passage which will change them and lead them in turn to create a new family cell. Since we are in a patrilineal system, the son will take over from his father and carry on the agnatic line. The rites of passage enable one to understand and to articulate the destiny of the social persons, the organization of the family, and the perpetuation of the agnatic groups.

But the life-cycle rites, and particularly the marriage rites, are not merely rites of passage. Rites of passage privilege the viewpoint and the finalities of the entities, the social subjects (the individual, the initiate, the family, etc.). The married state entails more than responsibilities to one's household and with regard to one's children. The wife must also assume her role as married sister and officiate back in her natal village for her brother, who in turn has ceremonial obligations towards her. That means that no household or family is constituted of itself alone or can live turned in upon itself. As in the caste system, interdependence is the essential feature of the Meo kinship system. The couple does not exist, has no reality if it is not joined by the wife's brother and the husband's married sister. This chain of relatives can be extended beyond the two brother–sister pairs, since the married sister who comes to officiate for her brother receives from him, when her own children marry, ceremonial gifts after her husband's sister has performed the preparatory rites. Therefore, no household, no family is completely autonomous.[57] The importance we give to the ties between two brother–sister pairs linked by a marriage leads us to see that the maternal uncle and the paternal aunt are just as essential, if not more so, to their nieces and nephews as their parents are.

Furthermore, as I have shown at length, the sequence of life-cycle rites does more than simply help constitute agnatic lines within a lineage. Each generation reproduces, with new individuals, this opposite-sex metasibling chain which operated in the preceding generation. We saw how, to this end, the preparations for a given marriage bring to a close the interventions of the paternal aunt and the maternal uncle of the bride and the groom, how at the time of the wedding, not only two families are defined which will enter into a 'wife-taker'-'wife-giver' relationship of affinity, but also two equivalent *samdhī–samdhan* couples, and finally how, after the birth of children, a new chain of opposite-sex metasiblings will replace the affinal ties and develop until these children too marry.[58]

The preparatory phases of a marriage are not the true beginning, but spring from other rites of which they are the conclusion. The unending thread running through the Meo life-cycle rites unreels from the opposite-sex metasibling chain. In this context there is no true beginning or end.[59] Here too we see the difficulty of analysing these rites as simple rites of passage.

In addition, if affinity is a relay between two metasibling chains, the preparatory phases of the marriage[60] are even more important than the wedding because they bring into play that which constitutes the core of the Meo kinship system: the chain of two brother–sister pairs linked by a marriage. This chain—and here we come to a crucial proposition—must be understood in the light of the complementary but also of the hierarchical relationship between, on the one hand, the ritual services (entailing in turn ritual fees) and, on the other, the ceremonial gifts. In my analysis, I have evoked a comparison between the married sister and the Brahmin priest. The emphasis on the ritual services–fees tandem also suggests a comparison between the brother–married sister tie and the relationship developed in the texts between sacrifier (one who offers the sacrifice and for whose benefit the ritual is done) and sacrificer (the priest who performs the ritual). In both cases, there is, on the one hand, an officiant who performs the ritual gestures and, on the other, those for whom these gestures are performed and, above all, in both cases there is payment of a ritual fee (*neg* in the Meo case, and *dakṣiṇa*, in the case of the Vedic sacrifice).[61]

MARRIAGE ALLIANCE AND CHAINS OF METASIBLINGS

The two ways of understanding the saying 'the paternal aunt with her niece' can be combined here (Figure 5.9).

The two women marry into the same lineage but into different lines (B1 and B2), and the niece takes over her aunt's role as *sahvāsanī*.[62] Apparently, the transmission of the relationship of superiority between a married sister

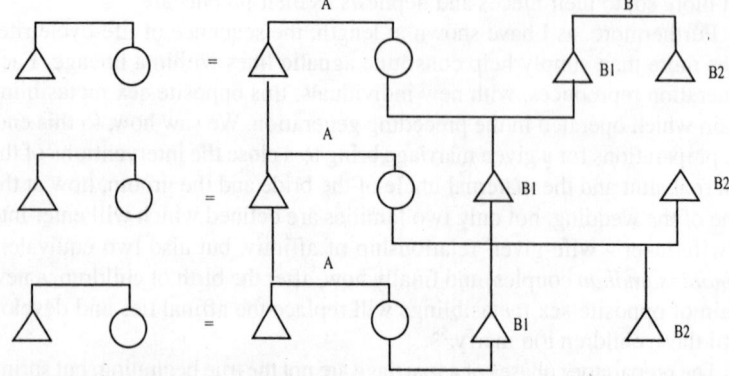

Figure 5.9: Paternal aunt with her niece

and her brother combines with that between wife-taker B and wife-giver A. This would seem to produce a form of hypergamy, a sort of 'female line' stemming from a lineage A married into a lineage B, and one could combine the transgenerational superiority of the married sister over her brother with that of the wife-taker over the wife-giver. This is a tempting picture, but one we cannot retain.

From the local standpoint, this is a preferential marriage alliance. It has a beginning and an end, unlike the chain of metasiblings, which supposes a system of permanent transgenerational ties. The important point is the married status of the successive *sahvāsanī*, not where they have married. Repetition of the metasibling chain is necessary to the rite, whereas repetition of the preferential marriage is not a necessity of the marriage alliance.

In the end, the two essential dimensions of Meo kinship having a transgenerational character are the marriage alliance from the global viewpoint and the opposite-sex metasibling chain in the rites.

In the marriage alliance, the isogamy between wife-taker and wife-giver encompasses the superiority of the groom's family over that of the bride; this hierarchical formulation has its counterpart in the terminology, in the relation between the basic equality of the *bhāī* and the *bahin*, metasiblings on the non-differentiated higher level, and the relative superiority, at the affinal level, of the *behnoï*, the sister's husband, over the *sālā*, the wife's brother. In the rite, the pre-eminence of the married sister over her brother, of the ritual work over the ceremonial gifts, relativizes the importance of the

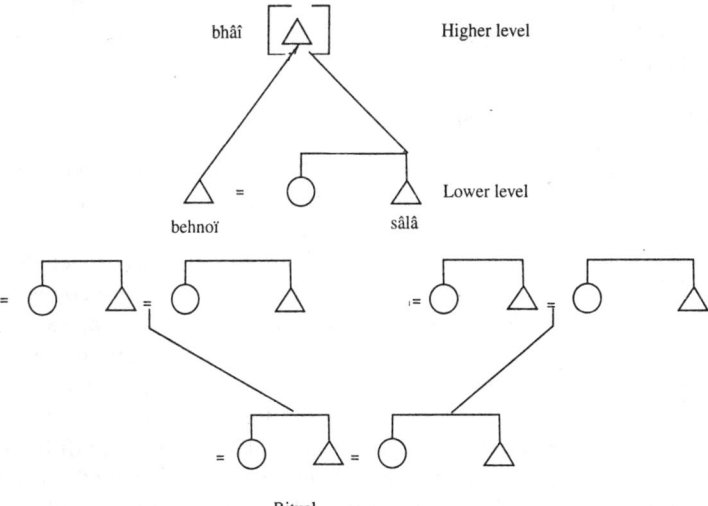

Figure 5.10: Marriage configurations

affinal ties between the two families linked by this marriage (Figure 5.10).

In either case, affinity is subordinate, and metasiblingship is the encompassing form of both dimensions of kinship. But in the marriage alliance, it is the equality of the *bhāī* and the *bahin* in the higher-level, 'non-differentiated' chain of metasiblings which expresses the equality of the two allied groups, while in the rite, it is the directional *bahin–bhāī* vector which manifests itself in the married sister's superiority over her brother.

It must be said that the rite shows no trace of the status equality between the two sides except in the affinal *samdhī–samdhan* relationship, which is a transitory point, a point of passage between the two opposite-sex metasibling chains. But that is not all. Isogamy and 'non-differentiated' metasiblingship at the higher level are, on the one hand, a backdrop which serves to sum up, as it were, the Meo kinship system and, on the other hand, a kind of screen onto which are projected the ritual ties which drive the life of the Meo community. Each generation re-establishes the equality between *bhāī* and *bahin* before going on, at the ritual level, to extract the unidirectional vector, the pre-eminence of the *bahin*, the married sister, over the *bhāī*, her brother. Or to put it the other way, between brother and sister, there is a sameness (as between brother–brother or sister–sister, or any members of the same generation) and at the same time an absolute difference expressed by the marriage rites. These are meaningful not only because they create affinal ties between brothers-in-law or establish the alliance, but also because they represent the privileged means of perpetuating the twofold nature of the brother–sister tie. I will return to this subject in the concluding chapter.

CONCLUSION

Kinship, caste, and *varna*

We have emphasized that the married sister, the *sahvāsanī*, holds a position in the kinship system equivalent to that of the Brahmin priest in the caste system. Like him, she receives ritual gifts and fees from those for whom she officiates. Kinship is thus not at first sight an autonomous domain since it includes a major feature of caste: status. Does this mean that there is a simple continuity between the two dimensions of social relations? The matter is complex. First of all, we noted that asymmetric marriage alliance between groups did not suppose a difference of status between wife-taker and wife-giver. Isogamy[63] refers back to the complementarity between the two sides and not to a hierarchical ranking. Next, the married sister is the object of a gift before becoming a subject who officiates. We saw how the superiority of the affinal wife-takers is prolonged by a superiority of the sister as marriage had made her. In other words, in each generation, it is the life-cycle rites which reveal the superiority of one side of the marriage over the other and of the married sister over her brother. Hierarchical caste differences are permanent and embedded in the morphology of society; and, while it is essential for the rites to actualize them and set them in motion, the rites do not create these differences.

To understand this discontinuity between the Brahmin's position and that of the married sister, we must go back to the definition of status. In the caste system, status is indicated by a separation (importance of birth, endogamy, ban on commensality) as well as by an interdependence (complementarity between pure and impure, between ritual services and fees). In the Meo kinship system, this separation of status is subordinated to interdependence. One does not marry up, but with an equal. Superiority at the affinal level of the wife-taker over the wife-giver is limited to the relationship between the two families; it cannot be passed on from one generation to the next because repetition of the same marriage between these two units is not allowed. Furthermore, the children of the two brothers-in-law, *behnoï/sālā* are *bhāī* to each other and, from this standpoint, are equals. Lastly, this superiority does not entail a ban on commensality between the two sides. To be sure, the boy's father does not go with the *barāt* and does not eat at his future in-laws' at the time of the wedding, but his stand-in, the eldest member of the *barāt*, and the groom are supposed to be given a ceremonial meal at the home of the girl's parents. To be sure, the two sides of the marriage do not eat together, but the superior side receives in this case food from the inferior side. And once the ceremonies are over, there will be no fundamental distinction between the two sides, which belong to equal groups.

The position conferred by and in the rite to certain kin ties subordinates separation to interdependence. Superiority here is limited to the relative position of the ritual roles. Which is the same as saying that the marriage rites institute—and not reaffirm or reinforce—a hierarchical superiority between wife-takers and wife-givers, and between the married sister and her brother. In this context, it would be more accurate to compare Meo kinship systems, not with the caste system, but with the varna system of relations: in both cases, the differentiation and interdependence are defined between those who occupy ritual functions and not different social statuses.

The comparison between the Brahmin and the married sister can be approached from yet another angle. I have said that the married sister does not officiate in the funeral rites. This is because her role is not to take charge of transforming the dead but to provide a new lease of life for the generation of her brother's children. In the funeral rites, it is the fakir who officiates as priest, taking upon himself the pollution occasioned by death. Throughout the year-long mourning period following a death, he acts as an intermediary between the deceased's close agnates and the deceased. He receives the offering of *khir* (rice pudding) made to the deceased and, by consuming it, nourishes the deceased and keeps him from coming back to trouble the living. When the mourning period is over and the deceased has reached the afterworld, no particular care is taken of his tomb. The exact spot is soon forgotten. He disappears into the host of anonymous dead who have gone before. The only personal trace remaining is his name in the genealogical notebooks of the Jagga Brahmins. This will be added to the list of the names of the dead and the more remote ancestors. It is thus the men of knowledge who keep the memory of the past, what remains of men once they have completed their journey. Ancestrality—to designate what connects the Meo with their past, their territory, their agnatic group, their status as Rājpūt descendants of the Hindu gods—is not restricted to kinship; it is also a relevant social fact of caste relations. The Jagga Brahmin here ensures that the Meo are located in time and in the regional space, just as they are in the caste system. The married sister as chief officiant in the rites does not deal with the dead or with death, but with the life force which animates the Meo community. She intervenes in the present only to prepare the way for the future, to inscribe Meo identity in the succession of generations. In life as after death, the members of this community are not perceived as individuals but as an integral part of the world of kin ties.

Kinship, rites, and 'secular' life

The effects of the rites do not stop when the rites themselves are over. They go on and give 'direction' and shape to 'secular' relations. It is significant that, until her marriage, the sister is not the recipient of any specific treatment. She has only to marry and all this changes. The ceremonial fees and ritual services will make their appearance not only in life-cycle rituals but also in the course of other ceremonies. A man building a house must send for his married sister so that she will tie a yellow thread around the door frame. For this service he gives her *neg*. It is considered that the foundations of the house are now secured and that the brother's family will prosper.

But these ties between a brother and a sister can also be seen on non-ritual occasions. When a brother visits his married sister, he is made welcome and fed, and before leaving, he must give presents to her as well as to her children, to his second *bahin*, his sister's husband's sister, to the various households in his brother-in-law's lineage and to the nine members of the village council.[64] When the married sister comes home for a visit, she runs her brother's house and can order around her sisters-in-law, her *bhābī* when rites are performed. When she leaves to return to her husband's village, she receives gifts from her brothers.[65]

The standards concerning kin ties are laid out in the rites which define the meaning of these same relationships in 'daily' or 'secular' life. There is no kin tie which for the Meo is not in someway ritual or ritualized. Once more we find the idea already mentioned in conjunction with the *jajmānī* system, namely that the economic aspects of this system must be understood in the context of ritual caste relations.[66]

But we can go further and stress that not all ritual services and fees, which constitute the encompassing point of view in the rites, find expression in secular life. Only the ceremonial prestations, that is the subordinate viewpoint, continue outside the ritual context. In other words, 'secular' life is not a simple extension of ritual life. It is only a partial and incomplete expression of it.

In short, the raison d'être of the Meo life-cycle rites does not lie somewhere outside the rites themselves; they are not responses or attempts at responding to questions posed by conflictual or economic or political relations outside the ritual setting. It is in the movement which drives them that the specific forms of social relations arise and develop, and this is particularly true of Meo kinship relations.

Notes

1. According to Aggarwal (1971: 180), the term can be translated as 'female companion'. Certain informants have confirmed this sense. One of the definitions of the Sanskrit term *sahvāsanī* is 'the one who lives with'. This gives us an indication as to the status of this woman, the sister, who has married out of the village and who comes home to officiate in her brother's house.
2. *Gaunā* means 'departure'.
3. The girl's paternal aunt will try to find for her niece a husband in the village where she herself lives.
4. As a rule, the agnatic kinsmen harass the delegation and demand more and more money. They also try to intimidate and even somewhat belittle the visitors to show them that the boy's side is superior to the girl's.
5. This date must always be set by the lunar calendar (for instance fifteen days after the new moon).
6. The *sehrā* crown is reserved for the groom.
7. In their analysis of the marriage rituals in the Hindu villages of Shanti Nagar, not far from Delhi, and those of the Mewat region, Freed and Freed reported similar details concerning the ritual bath: 'The groom was bathed ritually by seven married women of his lineage who were his real or classificatory sisters. They were assisted by the female Naï barber who served the family' (1980: 426). They pointed out that these sisters must be married (but not pregnant at the time of the ceremony). Many other similarities in the performances of these life-cycle rites can be seen. That said, it should be noted that, among the Meo, the ritual role of the married sister is more visible than in Shanti Nagar. There is probably a reason for this: among the Meo, the Brahmin priest is absent, and the married sister, the *sahvāsanī* ensures the role that he plays elsewhere, and notably in Shanti Nagar.

8. This term can be translated literally as 'who goes to the forest'.
9. The Meo do not pronounce it *neota* like most groups. The two terms nevertheless have identical meanings.
10. Customarily all cash gifts are odd amounts: Rs 11, 21, 51, 101. For a detailed analysis of the 'plus one' in India, see Malamoud 1989.
11. Today the *sehrā* crown is replaced by a rolled towel.
12. The sugarcane juice is boiled down until all the water has evaporated; the remaining paste, called *gur*, is given out at rituals.
13. During their stay in the village, the members of the *barāt* are lodged in the *tharu*, the lineage house.
14. It is not unusual, as a favour to the bride's mother, for the maternal uncle and his group to be fed inside the house rather than in the tent.
15. During this ceremonial meal, the guests often seem uncomfortable eating together and are eager to get it over as quickly as possible.
16. In principle, payment of the dowry at the time of the wedding is imperative. In reality, however, if the girl's father has been unable to assemble the full amount of the *dahej*, he can give only part of it, promising to pay the balance at the earliest.
17. Afterwards, when she is settled in her new home, she will return to her natal village for shorter or longer visits. Each time she leaves to go back to her husband's village, she will again weep and wail in the same manner.
18. It sometimes happens that the bride refuses to leave or that the groom 'forgets' to come for her (generally speaking, a woman does not leave for her husband's village unless he comes for her and does not return to her home village unless her brother comes to fetch her). If one of the spouses decides to separate, negotiations are undertaken to decide whether or not the dowry must be returned. In any event, a woman can leave her husband and remarry without a divorce. Here is how it is done: the woman sends her brother a message to come and take her home. Her brother waits outside his brother-in-law's village. Under cover of night, the woman slips out of her husband's village and joins her brother, who takes her back home. This means that, barring an exceptional occurrence, she will never go back to her husband's house. If she is still young, she can remarry and go to live with her new husband. The first husband has a right to demand a compensation, called *jhagra*, 'quarrel', from the second husband. Payment of this compensation regularizes the situation; but we know of cases where it has never been demanded or paid, without this calling the woman's new marriage into question. When asked if they do not see any contradiction between this custom and the Islamic rule which stipulates that an act of divorce must be delivered before remarriage, the Meo express surprise at our question and reply: 'That's the way we do things, that is our custom.'
19. To reply to the invitation is in a way to accept to officiate, to play a role in the ceremony, as Malamoud emphasizes (personal communication).
20. The affines related as *sālā* also bring a gift for the *fatiya* which will not be repaid, will not be the object of any counter-gift.
21. Someone who does not want to continue the relationship with a particular agnatic kinsman will, when giving *nota*, simply repay his debt. This will give rise to friction, acts of violence between the two parties, with sometimes very serious consequences.

22. We can analyse in the same manner the *munh dekhna*, the ceremony in which the women of the groom's lineage pay a small cash fee to raise the bride's veil and see her face.
23. These gifts are made directly to the *bahin* or to one of the boy's agnates, who will redistribute them among these women.
24. Several particularly significant events deserve mention here: the paternal aunt, who receives a gift, no longer lives in the village and is not present at the ceremony. This gift that is given her underscores the fact that the important role she played at the time of her nephew's birth and circumcision has been taken into account, as that which she will play at the time of his marriage.

    How are we to interpret the fact that the paternal uncle and his wife each receive a gift while only the paternal aunt, and not her husband, is the recipient of a cash gift? The Meo explain that to give to a married sister is to give to her husband as well. They recognize the paternal aunt and her husband as one, whereas they separate the paternal uncle and his wife. If we adopt the viewpoint of ego's father, we have in one case a brother–sister tie plus marriage and, in the other, a brother–brother tie plus marriage. It is as though, through their gifts, the bride's people recognize, on the groom's side, the differences between the two kinds of chains: an unbreakable one formed of opposite-sex metasiblings, and the other which distinguishes between consanguines and affines.
25. Unlike at the *sagāī*, no gifts are made to the boy's village council because this ceremony is held in the girl's village. His council receives gifts only when the wife's brother or one of his agnatic kinsmen comes to see her.
26. Vatuk reports analogous findings for Meerut (1975: 165–6).
27. The importance of the unidirectional gifts has been pointed out in numerous works, beginning with Dumont's monograph on the Pramalai Kallar, *Une sous-caste de l'Inde du Sud* (1957). In this group, asymmetry does not express any superiority of one side over the other. We are in an isogamous setting. Parry's work on Kangra (1979), Vatuk's on the Gaur Brahmins of Meerut (1969, 1975), and Madan's on the Brahmins of Kashmir (1975) resemble the Meo case.
28. For a detailed description of the rites performed for a birth, see Aggarwal (1971: 171–5). I will simply remark that the maternal uncle does not bring his gifts until the principal rites are over (in order: the purificatory bath, the first suckling, the naming, and the cutting of the first lock of hair). Analogous rites can be found in the village of Shanti Nagar, described by Freed and Freed (1980, esp. 399–401).
29. The steps of the circumcision rites are patterned after the marriage ceremony. Moreover, in addition to the part played by the maternal uncle, the presence of the paternal aunt as *sahvāsanī* is also required.
30. The meaning or meanings of the term *cūcak* are not known.
31. Parry stresses the analogy between the gift and the sacrifice: 'As the victim is a surrogate for the sacrifier, so the gift is a surrogate for the donor' (1986: 461). We will return to this aspect later.
32. The woman leaving for her husband's house is adorned like the statues of goddesses carried in procession. And for the Meo, she is a queen analogous to those essentially divine mythological figures.
33. Gray, who has analysed the specific problem of the *kanyādān* (1980: 1–33), tries to make it into a sort of divine, pure gift on which is founded the asymmetry

of the two sides of the marriage. It is difficult to accept this search for a substance which might explain the relationship, as though it were enough to say that the gift of the cow is what makes the Brahmin superior. One could just as easily say the opposite, and show that the divine gift makes the giver superior. The problem is this desire to make the substance the essential element, whereas the gift and the asymmetric relationship go hand in hand, without our having to seek a relationship of cause and effect.

34. Marcel Mauss's *Essai sur le don*, to which Parry refers, should have encouraged him not to separate the gift and its giver in so radical a manner.
35. A digression by way of Vatuk's study on the Gaur Brahmin of the Meerut region will shed some light on this problem. The author emphasizes that marriage entails the complete transfer of a woman from her own natal group to that of her husband: 'While there is in practice considerable ambiguity in the position of a married woman vis-à-vis her natal and conjugal families—in an important sense, she belongs to both—it is nevertheless clear that the formal allegiance is transferred on marriage to her husband's extended family and that rights to her services, to the products of her labour, and to her person and possessions are for most purposes also transferred to them along with her potential fertility. Thus it is not surprising that the key category in this indigenous conceptualization of the nature of affinity should classify a woman together with her conjugal affines rather than with her natal kin or separately as a "link" between the two' (1975: 178–9). Vatuk maintains that the woman belongs both to her natal and to her conjugal family, but she deals solely with her transfer to her husband's group and not with her ties to her natal group. Her demonstration is based primarily on the analysis of the term *dhyānē*, which designates, for the wife-givers, the different members of the wife-taker group; in addition, *dhyānī* designates the girl who has been given. It is as though the woman were assimilated to her husband's group. But, as Dumont (1975b: 212–13) showed, things are not that simple: the married sister will follow her brother in designating as *dhyānī* the women of her natal group younger than she and given in marriage. This term thus indicates that, while she is assimilated in a certain sense to her husband's family, the woman nevertheless remains connected with her natal family. Dumont (ibid.: 213) writes: 'This is the decisive juncture: the category here is not univocal, exclusive and permanent, as if *dhyānī* was classed once and for all with affines: assimilated to affines in one regard, the woman remains kin in another, the category is oriented from the past to the future and in the past it fades out partly into consanguinity long before disappearing altogether with its bearer.' Furthermore, the husband of this married sister will do as she does and will also call *dhyānī* his wife's younger sister given in marriage.

What does this mean if not that the sister is changed by marriage—hence the importance of the reference to the husband—yet without ceasing to be a sister or a daughter? Would anything be gained by maintaining that the married sister becomes an affinal kinswoman while remaining an agnatic kinswoman? The problem of *dhyānē* and *dhyānī* exceeds the limiting framework of unilineal descent and affinity, since, contrary to Vatuk's conclusion, it leads us to a field which transcends the distinction, in other words, to what I have called metasiblingship.

36. Unlike, for example, the Pramalai Kallar, for whom he is the father's brother-in-law (see Dumont 1957: 258–64).
37. Vatuk has produced a very fine analysis of this problem. After having emphasized that the 'wife-giver'–'wife-taker' relationship supposes a 'perpetual' string of gifts, she goes on to say: 'This relationship is mediated through the person of the "bride" herself, who not only serves (qua bride) as the supreme gift in and of herself, but also serves (qua daughter or sister) as the key recipient of gifts' (1975: 174).
38. Only married sisters with children can officiate.
39. The future mother must stand on a board so as not to touch the ground. The midwife helping her is low-caste. The amniotic fluid must fall onto the ashes, which will be buried in the *jañgle*. The placenta is buried under the threshold of the entrance to the house, if it is a boy, and at the back of a bedroom, if it is a girl. The umbilical cord is wrapped in a piece of cloth and, like the foreskin, placed in the thatching.
40. It is interesting to note that *guṛ* is distributed to the children especially before the start of an important rite. This is regarded as auspicious for the performance of the ceremonies. It will be remembered too that one of the last rituals of the wedding ceremonies is that in which a small boy sits on the lap of the bride and the groom and says: 'a boy for you and *guṛ* for me'. To feed a child *guṛ* is therefore, to place one's future under an auspicious sign.
41. This rite, called *chuchi dhona*, is described for the village of Shanti Nagar by Freed and Freed (1980: 369), and is interpreted as a rite protecting the child after the period of pollution following its birth.
42. Traditionally, the Brahmin priest used to be consulted, who, owing to his astrological knowledge, could tell the family what name would be auspicious for the child. Today a divination rite, called *akika*, has replaced this consultation: the fakir, funeral priests, sacrifice two young goats less than a year old and read the child's name in the entrails (see Aggarwal 1971: 174).
43. For a description of a similar ceremony in Shanti Nagar, see Freed and Freed (1980: 372).
44. During these forty days, the mother cannot do any cooking because she is unclean. At the end of this time she takes a purificatory bath, discards the clothes she has worn and puts on a new set. The lifespan of the *hamzad* must, therefore, be associated with the mother's impure state. The other forty-day period of impurity is the time of mourning, which ends with the *fatiya* ceremony in which the agnatic kin (but also the *sālā*-type affines) bring gifts to the eldest son of the deceased and receive a meal at the same time as the other guests.
45. For a similar use in south India, see Dumont 1957: 224; the term used is *alatti*.
46. Aggarwal reports that, in the Meo village of Chavandi Kalan, the husband of the bride's paternal aunt, the *phūphā*, performs the *arti* on the eldest member of the *barāt*, who brings the *tokri-ka-neg* for the young bride. This takes place in front of the entrance to the house following the mocking ritual of the *barothī*, performed by the paternal aunt, the bride's *phūphī* (1971: 188).
47. It is as though, by demanding her son's head, the mother had turned him into a *bhūṭ*. Her action contrasts with that of the old woman who performs the *arti*.

One can wonder whether the mother's deed does not have something to do with what happens after the birth of a child. The *hamzad* survives only if the mother unwittingly nourishes it. The mother who gives birth to the child can also be responsible for turning it into a *bhūt*, whereas the paternal aunt is the one who protects it from evil spirits and keeps it alive. This is another way of saying that, in the brother's house, his married sister outranks his wife.

48. The presence of the rice on the tray and the pitcher of water into which silver coins are dropped are also signs of the couple's future prosperity. The tray, with which the *sahvāsanī* circles the head of her nephew or her niece, carries a lighted candle. The Meo consider that fire keeps these wandering spirits at bay and prevents them from attacking. For instance, when a house is being built, a light must be left burning every night so that the *bhūt* will not move in. Likewise, during the three days following the birth of a child, a candle is kept burning all the time in the room occupied by the mother and the newborn child.

49. Unlike the case of the Pramalai Kallar, one cannot say that the 'prestations are the most important aspect ... of these ceremonies' (Dumont 1957: 217). Without the presence of the *sahvāsanī* and her ritual services, the ceremonies cannot take place.

50. For an interpretation of caste initiations, see Biardeau 1981: 40–2.

51. It should be remembered that, when the married sister receives the *bhāt* from her brother's hands, she bears the pitcher on her head while her husband holds the tray. In the *arti* the pitcher features once again, but this time it is placed on the tray (along with the lighted candle).

52. It is hard to explain the gesture of placing the blackened hand on the back of the *samdhī*.

53. In both *samdhī* pūjā rites, the prestations and counter-prestations mark the two aspects of this relationship: the reciprocity and the direction of the gift. At the time of the wedding, it appears clearly in the gifts from the *samdhī* (male side) to his *samdhan* (female side) and in the counter-gift of twice the amount from the *samdhī* (female side) to the *samdhī* (male side). At the time of a birth, the *samdhī* (female side) pretends to give a large cash gift but it is ultimately he who receives a small gift.

54. This ideal pattern is not always respected. Sometimes, one of the husband's married sisters acts as the *sahvāsanī* when there is no paternal aunt or when she is not available and, conversely, a paternal aunt can sometimes officiate not only for her brother's children, but also for the children of his son.

55. Figure 5.8N is at first sight analogous to the 'rows' studied by Pauwels (1990) on the island of Selaru in the Tanimbar Archipelago, East Indonesia. But the Meo do not have an ideological formula for relating households on a diachronic scale. In Selaru, gifts can and must flow back up the row and, in the ritual order, not all households occupy the same position. Among the Meo, prestations flow downwards, and there is an awareness that a uterine nephew takes over from the maternal uncle, but it goes no further. The latter does not look two generations below, and there is no ritual for actualizing such a relationship.

56. This section is inspired by Malamoud's work on the interpretation of the rites found in the Sanskrit texts, notably those from the Vedic period. I intend to outline a comparison between the interpretation of Meo marriage rites and that

proposed by the Vedic authors and the analysts of rituals in Brahmanic India. But this does not mean a term-for-term comparison or confronting a present-day fact with a past norm, or even less, reducing the modern rites under study to those of the Vedic sacrifice which are known only from the exegesis they have inspired. Malamoud (following, it seems to me, Dumont's approach) gives us the rule for comparing these two kinds of material: first of all look for consistencies in each of these bodies and then compare their structure (1974–5: 123). It seems to me that, beyond the undeniably important differences, it is possible to compare certain points (as the following notes will show).

57. One finds in the Sanskrit texts, but obviously in a different formulation, both ways of looking at the marriage rites: one focused on the individual subjects who are transformed and the other taking into account a whole set of relationships. Malamoud remarks that 'the wedding ceremony can be viewed either as a *saṃskāra* or as a *yajña*' (1974–5: 123). 'As a *saṃskāra*, "a bringing to perfection", marriage is an event—among others—in the sacramental life of each of the two spouses' (ibid.: 123–4). From this standpoint, marriage is a rite of passage which permits the transformation of the young man as well as the girl. 'As a sacrifice, *yajña*, marriage no longer concerns only the personal biography of each of the two spouses but the group comprised chiefly of the young man, the girl, the girl's father and the *purohita* of each of the two families' (ibid.). In this context, the girl's father is the sacrifier, the girl is the victim, and the husband, of course, is the god who receives the offering from the priest conducting the sacrificial rituals. Of course, the texts stress the relationship between the two sides of the marriage, while we add the metasibling relations.

58. Each of the different life-cycle rites has its specificity. Those performed for a birth emphasize the ritual work needed to deliver the mother and the child from the impure state resulting from childbirth. In the circumcision rites, on the other hand, as in marriage, the main protagonists must be purified and elevated above their 'secular' condition in order to carry out their ritual task in the circumcision proper and in the wedding. Furthermore, if the marriage rites mark the passage from metasiblingship to affinity, and those performed for a birth—especially for the first boy—manifest the passage from affinity to metasiblingship, circumcision involves only metasiblingship. We will come back to the absence of the funeral rites from this cycle. In effect, the metasibling chain is not involved in this setting. We will see in the conclusion how this fact is to be understood.

59. For the Vedic authors interpreting the rite, 'the beginning is a formidable threshold, a violent opening: symbolisms need to be invented, points of view discovered which deliver the first instant from its singularity and remove its cutting edge' (Malamoud 1987–8: 121). 'To be sure a rite has a beginning. But this beginning is made up of or preceded by, no one knows, a series of preliminaries, preludes, preparations, introductions during which the rite gradually acquires consistency, but in which the beginning as such is fragmented and dissolves' (ibid.). The solemn sacrifice is preceded by a consecration, the *dīkṣā*, itself preceded by the declaration of intention to offer the sacrifice, by the invitation extended by the sacrifier, by the offering, etc. But above all: 'The idea of a beginning is made all the more confused by the fact that, in some regards, the preliminary *dīkṣā* is actually the crucial point of the sacrifice itself' (ibid.: 122).

60. In the different context of the Vedic sacrifice, a similar idea is expressed. In his article, 'Cuire le monde', Malamoud writes: 'In order to be fit to celebrate the sacrifice, the sacrifier must put off his secular body and put on a sacrificial body. This is accomplished through the *dīksā*, "consecration"' (1987–8: 60). This action, which transforms the sacrifier supposes sexual abstinence or a reduction of secular activities. The sacrificial body looms like a metaphorical cooking, before the real cooking of the sacrifice. 'The body of the sacrifier is the genuine sacrifice, and the animal or vegetable offering, the cooking and their destruction of which constitutes the sacrifice proper, is only a substitute for the true sacrifice. The whole strategy of the sacrifice consists in giving the only offering which counts, one's own person, then in taking it back afer having created a surrogate. In a certain fashion, the *dīksā* is a preparatory phase of the sacrifice. In another, it is the essential phase: the sacrifice proper consists in going through with the offering of a surrogate victim, while the *dīksā* consists in hinting at (but only hinting) the offering of the true victim' (ibid.: 61).
61. For more on this important subject, see Malamoud's article on ritual fees in Brahmanism (1976).
62. The first can thus initiate the second in her future role and through her keep up a relationship with her natal village even though she no longer officiates there.
63. From the standpoint of caste endogamy, isogamy is an attribute of caste (status is inherited from the father and the mother, so that the two parents must have the same status, or the difference between them must be neutralized, which means that hypergamy operates against a backdrop of isogamy). If, on the other hand, isogamy is viewed from inside the kinship system, there is discontinuity because the relationship between the marriage units is based on equality and not on hierarchy, as is the case of inter-caste relations. We are talking about the latter aspect here.
64. Hershman indicates analogous findings in Punjab. He tells how a Brahmin, visiting his classificatory sister in her husband's village, failed in his obligations and did not give her anything as he was leaving. A poor leather-worker who was with him and who came from the same natal village as the woman tried to give her two rupees because she was also a *bahin*, a 'sister' for him, even though she belonged to a different caste. It is common in north India for all members of a village to regard each other as *bhāī* and *bahin*. The woman took one rupee because to refuse would have been tantamount to denying her 'village kinship' with the tanner, and gave him back the other to shame her Brahmin 'brother' (1981: 204–5).
65. We find the same practice in relations between agnatic or consanguineous *bhāī*. In everyday life, prestations between these kin take a form analogous to that of the *nota* ceremony. And when a Meo contracts a *bhāī* relationship, with a non-Meo, he gives him a turban and receives one in return. This exchange indicates that this is a relationship built on the model of a consanguineous tie.
66. In her work on the *jajmānī* system, Reiniche develops this idea, remarking: 'Every secular activity (set of acts) directed to a material end is implicitly modeled on a rite, carries the implications of a rite. This is also why any technical skill has a religious dimension, is a ritual skill' (1877: 95).

The Meo kinship system: A comparative view

We have now completed our analysis of the Meo kinship system from the standpoint of its various aspects: terminology, kinship and territory, marriage alliance and rituals. In so doing, we have followed a presentation analogous to Dumont's (1957) analysis of the Pramalai Kallar subcaste in south India. In effect, the same questions arise concerning the two communities, even if the answers differ slightly. In this concluding chapter, we would like to compare the kinship systems of the two communities. However, it is not individual features or sets of features that we will be comparing or contrasting, but whole structural configurations.

COMPARISON WITH THE PRAMALAI KALLAR KINSHIP SYSTEM

Kinship and territory

If territory is only a partial fact in the two communities, the same is not true of its connection with the headmen and kinship systems.

There is a series of similarities between the Meo and the P. Kallar. Both communities are part of larger entities: the Rājpūt in one case and the Kallar in the other; each has a territory described by a formula expressing the articulation of two kinds of unit: the thirteen *pal* and the fifty-two *got* for the Meo, and the eight *nad*, or provinces, and the twenty-four *upagraman*, or secondary villages, for the P. Kallar. But some differences can be seen:

• If we regard the entire Rājpūt group as a caste, the Meo form a subcaste within this vast entity. Inclusion in the overall group is established through reference to the five great agnatic groups—the *vamsh*—from which all Rājpūt claim to descend. The Meo are set apart from the other Rājpūt by the organization of the Mewat region into *pal* (territories connected with a patrilineal clan) and *got* (patrilineal clans), and by their being members of the Muslim faith. The Kallar caste calls for a different analysis: the relationship between the two endogamous subcastes, the Ambalakkarrar and the P. Kallar, is conceptualized in terms of an elder and a younger branch, the latter having broken away from the former.[1] The Meo have no such opposition with regard to the other Rājpūt. The clans belong to one of the five Rājpūt groups and to nothing else. The absence in one case and the presence in the other of an elder/younger opposition at this level of segmentation is the first difference between the two communities.

- We have stressed the Meo's rejection of a supreme headman over the whole Mewat region and their refusal to be subjects of a Rājpūt king or a Mughul emperor. But there is a headman, a *tevar*, over all the P. Kallar. This man is a member of a particular patriline which has supremacy over all the others. To be sure, the *tevar*'s authority is not much different from that of the *caudri*, but his presence at this level and above all the legitimization of his authority by a royal charter granted from outside establish the headman as a royal institution.[2]
- The difference between the two communities becomes more clear-cut if we consider the two kinds of units found on either side. In the case of the Meo, the *pal* territorial units and the *got* agnatic kin units are not of the same nature. Alternatively, in the case of the P. Kallar, the eight *nad*, or provinces, and the twenty-four *upagraman*, or secondary villages, both designate territorial units, each of which contains a certain number of agnatic lines (Dumont 1957: 141–65). The line which constitutes the largest agnatic unit 'is always contained entirely within a territorial unit, it never overspills the boundaries: if agnates belong to two different units, they constitute two separate lines' (ibid.: 168). There is no equivalent of the Meo clans, which may or may not be connected with a territory that neither encloses nor in any way limits the agnatic group.

But this analysis is still incomplete. Dumont indicates that 'each territorial unit also contains by definition either a *tevar*, the head of the main or eldest line, or as many *tevar* as there are lines' (ibid.: 143). We have already seen a similar connection between territorial sections and headmen. Furthermore, the difference between the two kinds of unit is connected with the existence of headmen in yet another way, since the inferiority of the secondary village 'has to do with the inferior status of their founders, "younger" sons, actually bastard sons of headmen' (ibid.: 146). This distinction relates to the opposition between elder and younger and to that between the principal union (or marriage proper) and secondary unions (notably with lower-status concubines).[3] I do not intend to review Dumont's entire analysis, in which he articulates the two kinds of opposition, but I do want to point out that children born of a secondary marriage or a union with a concubine are in a position of younger children and that only the first-born son of a principal marriage is regarded as the eldest son (who perpetuates his father's marital union) (ibid.: 188–96, 256–71). It is through the institution of headmen, through the elder/younger opposition combined with the marriage types, that agnatic kin ties assert their supremacy over territoriality. We will see that, at this particular level of segmentation, the same principles operate at the broader level in the Kellar territory.

By contrast, for the Meo, the institution of headmen is not an intermediary order linking agnatic groups and territory. Not all kin units are related to the territory in the same way, and most of them do not have a headman. Certain clans, the *got* and their subdivisions, the subclans, give their name to the corresponding territorial units, *pal* and *thamba*, which have headmen. But this does not give them a higher status or rank than the others. As has been shown, the headman's authority does not extend beyond the boundaries of the territory; it is closely associated with it, and both institutions are subordinated to the agnatic kin group. In the formula, the thirteen *got-pal* and the fifty-two *got*, it is the agnatic principle which defines the dominant framework.

This first comparison between the two communities of south and north India enables us to understand some of the variations found in the relationship between agnatic kin groups, territory, and the institution of headmen. But this level of analysis is also insufficient, for among both the P. Kallar and the Meo, marriage introduces yet another dimension, which relativizes the territory in a different manner.

The marriage alliance

In both communities, the marriage alliance is significant from a global and from a local point of view.[4] Let us bear in mind a few points concerning marriage among the P. Kallar. Dumont speaks of 'the archetypal alliance' between lines (the largest agnatic kin group in a province) or between a province and a secondary village (1957: 170ff). Theirs is an asymmetric marriage tie initiated with the foundation of a line or a territorial unit and subsequently continued over several generations. These original units are not necessarily carried on. However, the archetypal ally manifests himself at the time of the lineal cult, when the maternal uncle of this agnatic group or of the province is charged with sacrificing the ram.

The contemporary marriage alliance takes place between families. This applies to the principal marriage, which has a beginning and generally an end. The alliance can be inaugurated in one generation, when two families decide to unite their son and their daughter, and can be discontinued a few generations later. Between these two points, the alliance, once established, must be 'maintained generation after generation' (ibid.: 189). If one wishes, 'every marriage must be repeated at least once in the following generation' (ibid.). 'The obligation is in principle to provide a spouse for every eldest son of all the sisters and for every eldest daughter of all the brothers' (ibid.). Marriage with the first-degree matrilateral cross-cousin is the rule, and Dumont adds:

On the one hand the matrilateral obligation does not extend to classificatory kin, which would result in linking broader units. And on the other hand, the patrilateral link is not absolutely excluded. In fact it is less vigorously excluded than the double formula. Wherever the matrilateral tie proves to be impossible, its inversion is generally preferred to its extension, which is understandable in the light of what goes before: the ideal being a unidirectional link between two individual families, direction will be sacrificed to preservation of a tie between the two families when preservation of the direction would turn it into a tie between more extended groups. (Ibid.: 195)

These details on the two levels of the marriage alliance among the P. Kallar are sufficient to create a striking contrast with the Meo case. Among the latter, marriage between groups is not a form of archetypal alliance as the P. Kallar understand it. It is rooted in the distant past, probably at the time the subclan and the village lineages were founded, and it is projected into the future. As a consequence, it is both a link with the origins as well as a contemporary phenomenon and a movement implicating the generations to come. At the local level, a man is forbidden to marry his first-degree matrilateral cross-cousin or any of his patrilateral cross-cousins. It is thus impossible to reverse the direction of the marriage in order to preserve the alliance, as the P. Kallar do. The Meo need at least three families to set up the preferential marriage: two on the side of the wife-takers and at least one on the side of the wife-givers.

But another essential difference appears, which is the fact of a hierarchical relationship between the two viewpoints on the marriage alliance among the Meo: the alliance between same-status groups serves as a reference and encompasses the alliance between families, which supposes ritual superiority of the groom's side over that of the bride. By contrast, for the P. Kallar, the local viewpoint is the principal form of marriage alliance, and the global point of view appears only in a ritual relationship between groups: the two levels of the alliance are homologous and both entail an 'equistatutory' relationship between the units involved.

Marriage alliance and terminology

Writing on Dravidian groups, and on the P. Kallar in particular, Dumont emphasized the structural homology between the marriage alliance, which reveals the distinction between the agnatic principle and the marriage principle, and the kinship terminology, which divides all kin into two classes: consanguines and affines (1975a: 85–100; 1957: 273–81). In both these dimensions of kinship, the distinctive opposition implies complementarity between the two sides without the possibility of establishing superiority of one over the other. For the Meo, the structural homology we found between marriage alliance and kinship vocabulary is that of a hierarchical opposition: isogamy at the group level encompassing the superiority of the wife-taker's family over that of the wife-giver and metasiblingship encompassing the relative distinction between consanguines and affines.[5]

Two comments are needed here:
• First, the P. Kallar marriage establishes an affinal tie between brothers-in-law (or sisters-in-law), the wife (or husband) being the means of bringing

this about. This kind of relationship exists for the Meo, but it is subordinated to the more essential relationship between two brother–sister pairs linked by a marriage. In one case, marriage conceals or overshadows the brother–sister tie so as to mark the primacy of transgenerational affinity; in the other, the chain of brother–sister ties is asserted through marriage and through the succession of generations, while affinity becomes a subordinate aspect since it is not passed on through these generations.

• Second, in the Dravidian terminology used by the P. Kallar, the terms divide kin into two distinct categories with no overlap between consanguines and affines. This is not the case with the Meo: here some of the main terms used by ego partially overlap and above all have different meanings depending on the chain of relatives in which they appear. This terminology is thus not characterized so much by the terms themselves as by their place in the chains of relatives. In other words, if, for the P. Kallar, the logic of the terms is also that of the kinship relations, for the Meo, the logic of the kinship relations dominates and subordinates the terminological order. Given this context, I felt it necessary to relativize the distinctive opposition between consanguinity and affinity, and to invent the term 'metasiblingship' to designate the relationship which transcends this opposition.

The marriage rites

Here again we find analogies between the two communities: the life-cycle rites follow one after the other, not by virtue of any biological rule or because they are rites of passage, stages in the life of a man or a woman, but because they perpetuate a series of social ties and give them a transgenerational character. That said, the differences are important.

The affinal relationship, among the P. Kallar, is transgenerational not only in the case of the marriage alliance, but also when it comes to the rites. In the case of the modern-day marriage 'to use the simplified formula', and in other life-cycle rites, the 'prestations are the most important aspect ... of these ceremonies' (Dumont 1957: 217).[6] 'The allies' prestations, whether these be gifts or ceremonial functions, are ultimately the core of the family ceremonies' (ibid.: 258). The unidirectional 'wife-giver'-'wife-taker', 'uncle-'uterine nephew' or niece relationship has pride of place. The prestations which began with the marriage continue when the couple has children. In this context: 'The relationship between father-in-law and son-in-law is transmitted to the following generation in the form of a relationship between maternal uncle and uterine nephew' (ibid.: 259). In the first generation, the father-in-law may or may not be his son-in-law's maternal uncle, and in the second generation the maternal uncle may or may not give his daughter to his nephew in marriage. That in no way alters the situation. In Tamil, 'the term "father-in-law" and the term "maternal uncle" are in part the same' (ibid.). And 'when it comes to the gifts, the maternal uncle is not different in nature from the father-in-law' (ibid.: 260). The affinal ties which began or which were continued in one generation are passed on to the next. Here the paternal aunt has virtually no ritual existence. She appears, Dumont tells us, only in the matrilineal communities of south India, where she competes with or replaces the maternal uncle (ibid.: 264).

The contrast with the Meo is striking. The affinal relationship between father-in-law and son-in-law does have certain analogies with that of the P. Kellar. But it can be established only by stepping outside the two opposite-sex metasibling chains. And when the maternal uncle of the new couple's children takes over from his father, he does not take over the affinal relationship, but rather takes his place in a new opposite-sex metasibling chain.

The ceremonial gifts made by the maternal uncle are only one aspect of the facts; one must also take into account the ritual services performed by the paternal aunt; it is the complementary relationship between the two, and, to be more accurate, the hierarchical superiority of the latter over the former, which is the primary characteristic of Meo rituals.

This comparison leads to an important conclusion: ceremonial prestations among the P. Kallar perpetuate the affinal ties central to the marriage alliance, and the rites present no notable difference, and therefore, no specificity, with respect to the alliance.[7] In this sense, the isogamy in the choice of the spouses is continued by the unidirectional prestations. The hierarchical principle of caste does not come into the marriage alliance.[8]

On the contrary, among the Meo, the marriage rite has its own specificity which manifests itself in the ritual services provided by the married sister. These subordinate and colour the ceremonial gifts, which become no longer simply the expression of affinal ties but also and above all of the opposite-sex metasibling chain. In this setting, the isogamy characteristic of the marriage alliance gives way to a status difference, conferred by and in the rite, between the married sister and her brother, between the paternal aunt and the maternal uncle, which introduces the 'hierarchical principle' of caste into ritual kinship.

To sum up, what differentiates the Meo from the P. Kallar is not the ceremonial role of the maternal uncle, but the presence of the ritual action of the paternal aunt in one case and its absence in the other. More specifically, the Meo stress these services and give the ritual action its full value, while the P. Kallar subordinate this action to the demands of the marriage alliance.[9]

Table 6.1 summarizes the analogies and differences between the two communities from the standpoint of kinship. The P. Kallar kinship system is characterized by opposition between consanguinity and affinity, and unidirectional marriage alliance and ceremonial prestations. Alternatively, among the Meo, where these facts exist but occupy a secondary position, metasiblingship—expressed particularly by the two brother–sister pairs linked by a marriage—and the ritual services of the married sister occupy a preponderant place. While among the P. Kallar, marriage, as it appears in its various manifestations, is independent of caste, among the Meo, it is the institution which ensures the continuity as well as the discontinuity between caste and kinship.

In the light of this analysis, we can now formulate a working hypothesis and ask ourselves if the other Indian communities might not stand somewhere between these two kinds of kin ties: between the predominance of the brother–sister tie and that between brothers-in-law, between metasiblingship and the consanguinity/affinity opposition, between preference given to ritual services or to ceremonial gifts.

Thus we see the importance of marriage in India either in the form of affinity (south India) or in the form of opposite-sex metasiblingship (north India). Dumont has laid the way for the search for an overarching formula of kinship for the whole of India through marriage. I believe I have contributed to his effort by the study of this Meo community.

Table 6.1: Comparison between the P. Kallar and the Meo kinship system

Pramali Kallar	Meo
1. *Headman (Tevar)* encompasses Agnatic kin groups and territory (agnatic kinship and elder/younger distinction inseparable)	*Agnatic kin groups* encompasses Territory and headman (agnatic kinship not a function of elder/ younger distinction)
2. *Asymmetrical marriage alliance* Global standpoint: archetypal alliance (alliance original but not contemporary) Local standpoint: predominant form of marriage alliance Isogamy in both viewpoints	*Asymmetrical marriage alliance* Global standpoint: obligatory alliance (alliance repetitive and contemporary) Local standpoint: preferential form of asymmetrical alliance between families Isogamy between groups Superiority of taker-family over giver-family
3. *Rituals* Unidirectional ceremonial prestations (father-in-law → son-in-law maternal uncle → uterine nephew)	*Rituals* Unidirectional ceremonial prestations (father-in-law → son-in-law brother → married sister including maternal uncle → uterine nephew) Ritual services (married sister → brother including paternal aunt → agnatic nephew)

(Table contd.)

(Table contd.)

Pramali Kallar	Meo
Dominant tie affinal tie between brothers-in-law	Dominant tie metasibling chain: two brother–sister pairs united by a marriage
4. Terminology Distinctive opposition consanguinity/affinity	Terminology Hierarchical opposition metasiblingship encompassing consanguinity/affinity
Logic of terms = logic of ties	Logic of ties encompassing relative order of terms

THE BROTHER–SISTER TIE: TOWARDS AN OPEN MODEL OF KINSHIP

In conclusion, I will position the view presented here with regard to the perspective developed by Héritier. This anthropologist proposes a general model of marriage alliance, whereas I have dealt with a single case. The question is whether this case fits into the proposed model and, if not, what other avenue of inquiry is indicated by our analysis.

There are some convergences between Héritier's analysis and mine which should be noted: in both cases we have emphasized that the brother–sister tie is essential to the construction of the kinship models; then that the marriage alliance is expressed not only in the elementary structures of kinship, but also in specific forms in the semi-complex structures (into which category the Meo preferential marriage would seem to fit).[10]

That said, for the sake of clarity, we need to look at the divergences between the two perspectives. The brother–sister relationship with which Héritier is concerned is considered in terms of its universal aspect and is situated before the marriage, or more accurately, before the marriage alliance: this relationship is, in conjunction with the same-sex sibling tie, at the 'origin of the fundamental mechanisms of this alliance' (1981: 12). Among the Meo, on the other hand, the brother–sister relationship manifests itself in its entirety and takes on its full meaning only after the marriage, which reveals the entire extent of its potentialities.

What are these potentialities? For Héritier, who stresses the point throughout her book, one must see in the asymmetric brother–sister relationship: '... the no doubt universal principle of the dominance of male over female' (ibid.: 11), the 'massive bias of male domination ... in the different kinds of social structures, including those where the kinship system is built around a formal equivalence between brother and sister, or on their unmarked difference, or even on the sister's virtual supremacy over the brother' (ibid.: 49).

This formula is in agreement with Lévi-Strauss's assertion that it is men who exchange women. The concept of dominance poses a problem: does it refer to an empirically defined balance of power or to some legitimization of a dependency relationship, and how can this be assessed? In all events, it has the drawback of expressing kinship relations uniquely in the language of political relations, of flattening and ascribing a univocal sense to the brother–sister relationship. Dumont's analysis of the Indian caste system taught us to distinguish between hierarchy and stratification, status and power, religion and politics. In the present context, can we still speak of 'the sister's virtual supremacy', which in this case would be incomplete or unachieved (ibid.: 171)?

For the Meo, the priestly function of the married sister in the rites places her in a superior position, equivalent to that of a Brahmin and not merely that of a warrior or a powerful man. By reducing the brother–sister relationship to the univocal principle of male domination of all things female, Héritier is looking only at the realization of this tie in the marriage alliance and not at its expression in the rites. Yet it is in the rites that this relationship attains its greatest amplitude, quite precisely after the marriage and not simply before, as a social fact and a major ritual, and not as the biological fact of siblingship.

This is not to deny the importance of the immense task accomplished by Lévi-Strauss, followed by Héritier. But the study of the way kinship is deployed, particularly in the brother–sister relationship, in the vocabulary and especially in the rites, seems to open a new approach to the understanding of the social facts that the structuralist perspective has not yet considered.

Finally, I would like to indicate some of the trails we have followed and which deserve further exploration in other examples.

The anthropological analysis of kinship retains the two categories of consanguinity and affinity, with emphasis on the first (in descent theory and in the componential analysis of kinship vocabularies) or on the link between the two (in alliance theory). We have shown that these two categories do not represent the whole domain of kinship. The notion of metasiblingship is made necessary by the need to designate a social reality which cannot be reduced to either of the two categories. One wonders whether there are not other examples of kinship systems in which the relativization of both consanguinity and affinity might be called for.

The literature on kinship terminology has reasoned as though the logic of the relationships and the logic of the terms were identical. Our study has led us to distinguish the two and to privilege the logic of the relationships and therefore, to relativize the logic of the terms.[11] One wonders whether the phenomenon is peculiar to north India or whether other terminologies may not in their own way display similar features.

In the marriage alliance and unilineal-descent theories, one exclusive principle (sister-exchange in the first case and the univocal rule of succession in the second) is considered to be sufficient to define the shape of a structure, the other aspects of kinship being regarded as residual or being ignored altogether. The synchronic and diachronic dimensions have the same characteristics: the model makes sense only if the principle of descent or of alliance appears down through successive generations.

In the Meo kinship system, it is difficult to function with a univocal principle, whether we are dealing with the vocabulary, marriage alliance, or the rites. The different kinds of relationships always refer back to two hierarchically ranked principles: on the one hand, metasiblingship in its 'non-differentiated' form or in the form of two brother–sister pairs linked by a marriage and, on the other, the opposition between consanguinity and affinity. When it comes to the marriage alliance, the diachronic movement is captured in the linkage between 'non-differentiated' metasiblingship and affinity.[12] At the overarching level, which associates marriage alliance and rites, the diachronic movement supposes reference to this fixed 'non-differentiated' metasiblingship—which forms the backdrop for this endogamous community—and the movement of ritual transformation: the opposite-sex metasibling chains preparing the way for affinal ties, which in turn result in new opposite-sex metasibling chains, and so on. Affirmation of the supreme principle can come only through the mediation of the subordinate principle. Repetition of sameness is possible only by way of difference.

The brother–sister tie has the major characteristic at the level of kinship of being at once a relationship of sameness and one of absolute difference, whereas the tie between same-sex siblings has only the first characteristic and that between husband and wife only the second. Héritier indeed saw this aspect when she noted that the brother–sister relationship 'is one in which sibling sameness suddenly turns into difference' (1981: 171). This movement, which is expressed in marriage but also in the rites, retains both features. The brother–sister tie appears as the only relationship which, on the one hand, partakes of a sterile redundancy, of an impossible marriage and, on the other, produces life, more specifically a new lease of life which lends meaning to the principle of generation. This context helps us grasp the meaning of the double movement entailed in this marriage which separates the sister from her brother and then returns her to his family to ensure, by ritual means, the continuation of the generations.

But this last point exceeds the boundaries of kinship proper. Whereas the principle and the outcome of the marriage alliance is to outline a model of kinship, the brother–sister tie with its two characteristics opens up or extends

The Meo kinship system: A comparative view   187

the field of relationships beyond kinship proper. Furthermore, its interest is that it is a site which articulates different dimensions of social life. In the Meo case, we have seen that the brother–sister relationship is as significant for defining the specificity of the domain of kinship as an expression of sameness as it is for translating on the level of difference the caste values involved in kinship, notably through the priestly role of the married sister.

NOTES

1. Dumont adds: 'The presence has been observed in the square in Tengalapati [a provincial agglomeration] of a stone bench called *amballakkalu* "ambalam stone" which is interpreted as marking the symbolic presence of the eldest man, the Amballam, without whom the village meeting could not be held' (1957: 132–3).
2. Ibid.: 136–41, esp. p. 139, where Dumont writes: 'Headmen are a royal institution. Failing this, apparently nothing in the Kallar community itself would have been of a nature to justify the pre-eminence of one particular line over the others.'
3. '[T]he distinction of the largest territorial units into *nad*s and *upagraman*s rests on the distinction between the principal sons, who have full status, and the secondary sons, born of irregular unions and having a diminished status' (ibid.: 150).
4. It is not L. Dumont but I who point to the presence of the marriage alliance from the global point of view among the Kallar. The author merely speaks of archetypal alliance.
5. The same significance can, therefore, not be attributed to isogamy in the south and in the north.
6. Dumont goes on to stress: 'If one considers marriage ... from the standpoint of the rites proper, excluding the prestations, the first thing that strikes one is their relative poverty compared to the plethoric abundance of the orthodox Hindu ritual' (1957: 220–1). All that is left is the circumambulation and the *tali* rite. 'Their ceremony is much more a social affair—a formal contract between two families, if you will—than a religious affair' (ibid.: 221).
7. At least insofar as kinship is concerned.
8. What Dumont says of the kinship vocabulary also applies to the Dravidian marriage alliance: 'In the southern vocabulary ... the (main) categories show no overlap inclusion; they stand in neat distinctive opposition, an opposition in which the two poles or terms have the same status and which we may call, to distinguish it from the former, equistatutory opposition. This goes to show, to my mind, that the hierarchical principle of caste, which is quite in keeping with the *bhāī* disposition, on the contrary does not enter the basic framework of south Indian categories' (1981: 166–7).
9. 'The Kallar maternal uncle performs "ritual" services, even if these are fewer in number. During the marriage preparations, in the course of a short ceremony, he solemnly leads his nephew or his niece by the hand three times around the

dais' (Dumont 1957: 218). 'The point of this circumambulation is not for the young couple to call the fire to witness, but for the maternal uncle to formally introduce the bride or the groom' (ibid.: 221). This ceremony is a matter of prestige, Dumont underlines, and does not add anything essential with regard to the prestations, the most important of which are brought by this same maternal uncle. Among the Meo, on the contrary, gifts and ritual services are not only very clearly distinguished, they are, in addition, the privilege of two persons occupying different ritual statuses: the maternal uncle and the paternal aunt.

10. See Chapter 4, 'The marriage alliance'.
11. Dumont had sensed this need for the north Indian terminology when he made a distinction between kin type and kin name, between that which defines a kin category distinct from other equivalent categories and that which can vary in meaning and use depending on the context (1975b: 199).
12. Are there no equivalent processes in the semi-complex structures studied by Héritier? The span of the prohibitions makes it necessary to skip one or several generations before reproducing the same union or returning a girl given between the exchange units, or to shift the union to one of the alternative lines. In these different scenarios, the affines in one generation become consanguines in the following generation; repetition of the marriage with the closest relative results, on the contrary, in the transformation of consanguines into affines. This process cannot be reduced to that of the elementary structures in which the consanguines/ affines opposition is transgenerational. In these semi-complex structures, it is clear that consanguineous kin are at the same time those with whom one does not marry and those among whom one chooses one's wife. This figure of consanguinity is analogous to that of Meo metasiblingship, and one wonders whether the analysis of the rites in these cases might not enable us to understand this movement which establishes a diachronic connection between consanguinity and affinity.

Bibliography

Abdulaziz n.d. *The Meo of Mewat,* Ph.D. dissertation, New Delhi: Jawaharlal Nehru University (manuscript).
_____ n.d. A tentative attempt at the study of the interaction of the social and geographical dimension of the Mewat region (manuscript).
Aggarwal, P. (1971). *Caste, Religion, and Power: An Indian Case Study,* New Delhi: Shri Ram Centre for Industrial Relations.
Ahmad, I. (ed.) (1978) (first edition 1973). *Caste and Social Stratification among Muslims in India,* New Delhi: South Asia Books.
Amir-Ali, H. (1970). *The Meo of Mewat: Old Neighbours of New Delhi,* New Delhi: Oxford & IBH Publishing Co.
Barth, F. (1959). *Political Leadership among the Swat Pathans,* London: The Athlone Press.
Biardeau, M. (1971–2). 'Brahmanes et potiers', *Annuaire de l'EPHE,* section 5, Tome 70, pp. 31–55.
Biardeau, M. and C. Malamoud (1976). *Le sacrifice dans l'Inde ancienne,* Paris: Presses Universitaires de France.
Biardeau, M. (1981). *L'hindouisme, Anthropologie d'une civilisation,* Paris: Champs Flammarion.
Bouglé, C. (1969). (first edition 1908). *Essai sur le régime des castes,* Paris: Presses Universitaires de France.
Carter, A. (1974). A comparative analysis of systems of kinship and marriage in south Asia. Proceedings of the Royal Anthropological Institute for 1973, pp. 29–54.
Dumont, L. (1957). *Une Sous-Caste de l'Inde du Sud. Organisation sociale et Religion des Pramalai Kallar,* Paris, La Haye, Mouton.
_____ (1962). 'Le vocabulaire de parenté dans l'Inde du nord', *L'Homme* 2, pp. 5–48
_____ (1964). (second edition U Prisme 1975). *La civilisation indienne et nous. Esquisse de sociologie comparée,* Paris: A. Colin.
_____ (1966a). (Edition Tel 1979). *Homo Hierarchicus, le système des castes et ses implications,* Paris: Gallimard.
_____ (1966b). 'Marriage in India. The present state of the question: North India in relation to South India', *Contributions to Indian Sociology,* 9, pp. 90–114.
_____ (1971a). *Introduction à deux théories d'anthropologie sociale,* Paris-La Haye: Mouton.
_____ (1971b). 'On putative hierarchy and some allergies to it', *Contributions to Indian Sociology,* 5, pp. 58–78.
_____ (1975a). *Dravidien et Kariera,* Paris-La Haye: Mouton.
_____ (1975b). 'Terminology and prestations revisited', *Contributions to Indian Sociology* (n.s) 9, pp. 197–215.
_____ (1981). *Affinity as a value,* Chicago: University of Chicago Press.
_____ (1983). *Essais sur l'individualisme,* Paris (ed.), Seuil.

Evans-Pritchard, E.E. (1940). *The Nuer*, Oxford: Clarendon Press.
Freed, R. and S. Freed. (1980). *Rites of passages in Shanti Nagar*, New York: Anthropological Papers of The American Museum of Natural History.
Fruzzetti, L. and A. Östor (1984). *Kinship and Ritual in Bengal: Anthropological Essays*, New Delhi: South Asian Publishers.
Gaborieau, M. (1977). *Minorités musulmanes dans le royaume hindou du Népal.* Nanterre, Laboratoire d'Ethnologie.
Gray, J. (1980). 'Hypergamy, kinship and caste among the Chetris of Nepal', *Contributions to Indian Sociology* (n.s.), 14(1), pp.1–33.
Héritier, F. (1981). *L'exercice de la parenté*, Paris: Hautes Etudes, Gallimard-Seuil.
Hershman, P. (1981). *Punjabi Kinship and Marriage*, Delhi: Hindustan Publishing Corporation.
Hocart, A.M. (1952). (second edition 1970). *The life-giving myth and other essays*, London: Tavistock Publications Limited.
Jamous, R. (1981). *Honneur et Baraka, Les structures sociales traditionnelles dans le Rif*, Paris: Cambridge University Press—Maison des Sciences de l'Homme.
Kepel, G. (1987). *Les Banlieues de l'Islam. Naissance d'une religion en France*, Paris, (ed.), Seuil.
Leach, E. (1954). *Political System of Highland Burma*, London (French translation 1972, [ed.], F. Maspero).
Lévi-Strauss, C. (1967). (first edition 1949). *Les structures élémentaires de la parenté*, Paris: Presses Universitaires de France.
Lounsbury, F.G. (1964a). 'A formal account of the Crow- and Omaha-type kinship terminologies', in W. Goodenough (ed.), *Exploration in cultural anthropology*, New York: McGraw-Hill, pp. 351–93.
—————— (1964b). 'The structural analysis of kinship semantics', in H.G. Hunt (ed.). Proceedings of the Ninth International Congress of Linguistics. The Hague: Mouton, pp. 1073–92.
Madan, T.N. (1975). 'Structural implication of marriage in north India: Wife-givers and wife-takers among the Pandit of Kashmir', *Contributions to Indian Sociology*, 9(2), pp. 217–43.
Malamoud, C. (1974–5). 'Résumés des conférences et travaux'. *Annuaire de l'EPHE*, sections, pp. 122–7.
—————— (1976). 'Terminer le sacrifice. Remarques sur les honoraires rituels dans le brahmanisme,' in M. Biardeau and C. Malamoud : *Le sacrifice dans l'Inde ancienne*, pp. 155–204.
—————— (1987–8). 'Résumé des conférences et travaux', *Annuaire de l'EPHE*, sections, 118–24.
—————— (1989). *Cuire le monde, rite et pensée dans l'Inde ancienne*, Paris, (ed.) La Découverte.
Mauss, M. (1968). *Sociologie et anthropologie*, Paris: Presses Universitaires de France. second edition.
Mauss, M. and H. Hubert (1899). 'Essai sur la nature et la fonction du sacrifice'. *Année sociologique* 2, quoted in M. Mauss *Oeuvres*. Paris, (ed.) de Minuit, 1968, tome. 1, pp. 193–307.
Mayer, A. (1960). *Caste and Kinship in Central India: A Village and its Region*, Berkeley: University of California Press.

Parry, J. (1979). *Caste and Kinship in Kangra*, New Delhi: Vikas Publishing House.
_____ (1986). 'The Gift, the Indian Gift and the "Indian Gift"', *Man* (n.s.), 21, pp. 453–73.
Pauwels, S. (1990). 'La relation frère-soeur et la temporalité dans une société d'Indonésie de l'est'. *L'homme*, 116, pp. 7–29.
Pouillon, J. (1979). 'Remarques sur le verbe "croire"', in M. Izard and P. Smith: *La fonction symbolique*, Paris: Gallimard, pp. 43–51.
Reiniche, M.L. (1977). 'La notion de 'Jajmâni' qualification abusive ou principe d'intégration', *Purusârtha*, vol. 3, pp. 71–107.
Scheffler, H.W. (1980). 'Kin classification and social structure in north India', *Contributions to Indian Sociology*, 14, pp. 131–69.
Schneider, D. (1968). *American kinship: A cultural account*, New Jersey: Prentice-Hall.
Sharma, S.L. (1982). 'Conversion, continuity and change: A study of the Meo community', *The Journal of Sociological Studies* (Jodhpur), 1(1).
Vatuk, S. (1969). 'A structural analysis of the Hindi kinship terminology', *Contributions to Indian Sociology*, (n.s.) 3, pp. 94–115.
_____ (1975). 'Gifts and affines in North India', *Contributions to Indian Sociology* (n.s.) 9: 155–96.

Glossary

arti	:	presentation of a lamp in a circular movement, performed before a god or before the bride and the groom
ashraf	:	prestigious Muslim groups (*saiyid, sheikh, pathan, mughal*)
badhar	:	prestation to the service castes of the bride's people
bahaura	:	ceremony with gift to the bride's paternal aunt when the couple leaves
baniyā	:	merchant caste
banglā	:	male part of the house
banvarā	:	ritual procession to the forest
barāt	:	party of the groom's agnates who goes with him to fetch the bride
barothī	:	mocking rite bringing together the eldest man in the *barāt* and the bride's paternal aunt
batnā	:	ritual bath
bhangī	:	sweeper caste
bhaṭ	:	genealogist
bhāt	:	gifts presented by the mother's brother at the time of a circumcision or a marriage
bhublā	:	earthenware vessels used in ceremonies
bhūṭ	:	evil spirits, a bad death
biāh	:	wedding
butā	:	a steel cane carried by the groom-king
camār	:	leather-worker caste
caudri	:	headman of a clan or subclan associated with a territory
cak pūjā	:	'ritual worship of the potter's wheel', performed during the marriage ceremonies
chatiko	:	literally. 'the sixth day', ceremony in which the first locks of the newborn child are cut and the name given
cūcak	:	gifts made by the mother's brother for the birth of the first boy
dahej	:	dowry
dakṣiṇa (Sanskrit)	:	ritual fees
dān	:	a unidirectional gift
dargah	:	mausoleum of a Muslim saint
dharma (Sanskrit)	:	socio-cosmological order
dhobī	:	washerman caste
dhyānī	:	the maiden given in marriage
dīkṣā (Sanskrit)	:	consecration of the sacrifier
dub	:	herb used in certain rites
fakir	:	Muslim caste of funeral priests

Glossary 193

fatiya	:	end of mourning rite
gaon	:	village
gaunā	:	the bride's definitive 'departure' for her husband's home
ghar	:	house
gorva	:	gift to the eldest man of the *barāt*
got	:	exogamous partrilineal clan; *–palya* or *–nepalya*: with or without a territory
guṛ	:	a small, flat cake made of sugarcane
hamzad	:	literally 'born with', the bodiless double of the newborn child
hookah	:	water tobacco-pipe
jahiliya	:	time of ignorance preceding Islam
jajman	:	master
jajmānī (system)	:	division of ritual labour
jañgle	:	forest
jat	:	agricultural caste
jhagra	:	literally 'quarrel'; compensation paid by a second husband to the first
kabristan	:	graveyard, cemetery
kaccā	:	ordinary food (without butter); house made of dried-mud bricks
kamin jāti	:	service caste
kangnā	:	sacred thread tied around the wrist
kanyādān	:	'gift of the maiden'
kasaī	:	slaughterer caste
kazi (or *saiyad*)	:	descendant of the Prophet
khandan	:	lineage or line
khir	:	rice pudding made during mourning
khitam (Arabic)	:	circumcision
Kshatriya (Sanskrit)	:	second varna, the warriors
kuan pūjā	:	ritual worship of the well
kumba	:	family
kumhar	:	potter caste
lagan	:	wedding announcement
lohar	:	blacksmith caste
lotā	:	copper pitcher used in particular in rites
mirasī	:	singer caste
Moharram	:	Muslim festival evoking the battle of Kerbala in which the son of Ali, the Prophet's son-in-law, was killed
musulmani	:	Meo term for the circumcision rite
nad	:	Pramalai Kallar territorial unit (province)
namaj	:	Muslim prayer
naï	:	barber caste
nausā, (fem.) *nausī*	:	groom, bride
neg	:	ritual fee
nikah	:	Muslim marriage contract

nota	:	literally 'invitation', prestation between consanguineous kin, implying a return gift
paink	:	'soldiers' of Hussain, Ali's son, in the battle of Kerbala
pakkā	:	ceremonial food (cooked with butter; a cinderblock house)
pal	:	territory of an exogamous patrilineal clan
pallakra	:	little *pal*
panchayat	:	clan, subclan, village or lineage meeting
pir	:	Muslim saint
purohit	:	household priest
Rājpūt	:	warrior caste
rath	:	ceremonial cart
roza	:	Muslim fast
sadhi	:	first harvest of the year (March–April)
sagāī	:	betrothal
saiyad, see *kazi*		
sahvāsanī	:	literally 'female companion', the paternal aunt as officiant
sakkā	:	water-carrier caste
salam	:	'departure' of the groom or the couple
samdhī pūjā	:	'ritual worship of the co-father-in-law'
saṃskāra (Sanskrit)	:	'bringing to a state of perfection'
savani	:	second harvest of the year (September–October)
sehrā	:	crown worn by the groom
sheikh	:	prestigious Muslim group
sonar	:	goldsmith caste
śuddhi	:	'purification'
śudra (Sanskrit)	:	fourth varna: the servants
tajiā	:	cenotaph constructed for the feast of Moharram
talwar	:	sword carried by the groom
tevar	:	Pramalai Kallar headman
thamba	:	subclan associated with a territory
tharu	:	patriline group house
thakar	:	high-caste Hindu
thok or *mohalla*	:	patrilineal lineage
tokri-ka-neg	:	literally 'fee for the basket', gift made to the bride by the groom's family
umma	:	'Community of the believers', in Islam
uncī jāti	:	'high caste'
vaishiya (Sanskrit)	:	third varna: the producers
vamsh	:	Rājpūt caste agnatic group
varna (Sanskrit)	:	colour, category, class
yajaman	:	'sacrifier'
yajña	:	'sacrifice'

Index

Abdul Aziz 1–2, 4–5, 7, 12, 82, 100, 102, 103n–104n
adoption 11–12
affine, affinity 6–10, 14, 39–42, 48–57, 60–4, 66, 68–9, 71, 73–4, 77–78n, 108, 111, 114, 119–21, 123n, 124, 129, 141–3, 146, 148, 153, 170n–173n, 180–1, 188n
Aggarwal, P. 27, 31, 33n, 36, 80–2, 103n, 126, 169n, 171n, 173
agnate, agnatic relations 7–8, 10, 13, 19, 35n, 65, 85–6, 89, 95–7, 101, 111, 115–16, 119, 124–5, 128, 134, 140, 142–4, 159, 167, 171n
Ahmad, I. 17
Amir-Alih 27–8, 36n
ancestor 5, 17–18, 25, 26–7, 30, 39, 47, 80, 84, 86–91, 102, 103n–105n, 111, 168
arti 126–7, 149–52, 173n
Arya Samaj 36n
ashraf 17

backward castes 14, 18, 20, 22–4, 34n
badhar 135, 145
bahaura 139, 145
baniyā 2, 18–22, 34n, 125
banglā 2
banvarā 126–7,149,151
barāt 129, 133–7, 139, 144–6, 158–9, 167, 170n, 173n
barothī 135,144–5, 157–9, 169, 173n
Barth, F. 103n
batnā 126–7, 151–2
bhangi 18, 20, 22, 137
bhat 31
bhāṭ 26, 127, 130, 136, 144, 147–8, 153–5, 157, 159–61, 174n
bhubla 137

bhuṭ 19, 34n–35n, 127, 149–52, 173n–174n
biāh 124
Biardeau, M. 25, 35n, 174n
Bougle, C. 18
Brahmin 14–15, 18, 20, 22–3, 25–6, 28, 34n–35n, 39, 41, 80, 104n, 118–19,125, 147, 150, 153, 164, 166–8, 169n,171n–173n,176n, 185
brother–sister, *see* metasibling
butā 127, 129

camār 18, 20, 22
Carter, A. 75–6, 79
cak pūjā 128
caudri 19, 85, 87–8, 94, 99–100, 104n–105n,178
chatiko 149
clan, sub-clan 6, 8, 10, 17, 19, 25, 27–9, 81–2, 84–9, 93–4, 98–102, 103n–104n, 110–12, 121–2, 129, 177–80
conflict 20, 29, 85, 89–91, 94–6, 122n, 169
consanguine, consanguinity 6–8, 11–14, 38–42, 48–57, 60, 62–4, 68, 70–4, 78n–79n, 106–9, 111, 116, 119–20, 122n–123n, 129, 142–3, 146, 148, 155, 171n–172n, 176n, 180–6, 188n
cūcak 146, 148, 153, 155, 159–60, 171n

dahej 137–8, 144–5, 147–8, 157–9, 170n
daksina 26, 150, 164
dān 144, 147
dargah 29
dharma 36n
dhobi 18, 20
dhyānī 172n
diksa 175n–176n

divorce 170n
Dravidian 38–9, 47, 73–5, 180–1,187
dub 126, 128
Dumont, L. 14, 17, 22–3, 26, 30, 33n, 34, 37n, 38–9, 41–2, 49, 56–7, 73–4, 75n, 77n–79n, 104n, 106–10, 118, 121n–122n, 147, 171n–175n, 177–83, 185, 187, 188n
endogamy (caste) 19, 160, 167, 176
exchange, *see* marriage alliance
exogamy, exogamous unit 107, 110, 113, 121
Evans-Pritchard, E.E. 77n, 84, 104n

fakir 18, 22, 35n, 99, 104n, 167, 173n
family 2–3, 5, 7, 10–12, 14–15, 20, 23–5, 29, 35, 42, 52, 68, 72–3, 78–79n, 90, 93, 96, 105, 115, 118, 125–6, 134, 142–8, 158, 160, 163, 165, 168, 169n, 172n–173n, 180–1, 183, 186
fatiya 8, 142, 170n, 172n
Freed, R. and Freed, S. 169n, 171n, 173n
Fruzetti, L. and Ostor, A. 75n

Gaborieau, M. 36n
gaon 19, 89, 93
gauna 124, 140–1, 169n
genealogist (Jagga) 25–6
ghar 93
gift 6, 8–14, 24–5, 31, 35n, 90, 101, 105, 118, 120, 124–5, 127–9, 132–7, 139–48, 153–7, 159–60, 163–6, 170n, 171–4, 181–3, 188n
gorva 134–5, 145
got 19, 27–30, 80–2, 84–5, 87–91, 93, 95–6, 98–101, 103, 104n, 105n, 177–9
Gray, J. 171n
gur 128, 131,140,149,170n, 173n

hamzad 150–1, 173n–174n
Heritier, F. 117, 184–5, 188n
Hershman, P. 122n–123n, 176n
hierarchy, hierarchical opposition, 18, 23, 39, 42, 53–8, 63–4, 68, 70–3, 75n, 77n, 109, 119–21, 122n–123n, 164–7, 176, 180, 182, 184–5, 17–87n
Hocart, A. M. 76n
holism 107
hookah 34n, 88, 97
hypergamy 108, 117–18, 122n–123n
incest 107

Islam, Islamic religion 1, 15, 17, 27–31, 33, 170

jahiliya 30
jajmān 23
jajmani (system) 23–6, 104n, 141, 169, 176
jañgle 19, 126–7, 151, 173n
jat 34n, 82, 84, 94
jhagra 170n

kabristan 19, 27, 99
kacca 2, 20
Kallar 74, 171n–174n, 177–84, 187n
kamin jati 18
kangna 2, 126
kanyadan 25, 144, 147–8, 171n
kasai 18, 20, 24
kazi (or *saiya*d) 20, 33, 34n, 37n
Kepel, G. 36n
khandan 93, 104n
khir 35, 167
khitam 31
Kshatriya 18, 23, 26, 150
kuan pūjā 28–9, 36
kumba 93
kumhar 18, 20, 128

lagan 125
Leach, E. 108, 122n
Levi-Strauss, C. 106–8, 121n, 185
lohar 18, 20
lotā 126, 128, 159

Madan, T.N. 171n
Mahabharata 17, 35n, 134
Malamoud, C. 26, 75n, 86, 103n, 150, 170n, 174n–176n

Index

marriage alliance 12–14, 74, 88, 107 and *passim*, 124, 161, 164–6, 177, 179–86, 187n–188n
maternal uncle 6, 31, 124, 127, 136–7, 141, 146, 148, 154–5, 159–61, 163, 170n–171n, 174n, 179, 181–3, 187n–188n
Maulvi Maulana Ilyas 28
Mauss, M. 172n
Mayer, A. 23
metasibling, metasiblinghip 42, 48, 64, 66–8, 70–4, 77n–78n, 109, 119–21, 124, 146, 148, 150, 153–7, 159–66, 171n–172n, 175n, 180–6, 188n
mirasī 18, 20, 26, 143
Moharram 31–2, 90
mosque 27–9
Mughal 18, 19, 27, 36, 81, 85, 98, 105n
musulmani 31

nad 177, 178, 187n
naï 18, 20, 143, 169n
namaj 28
*naus*a, (fem.) *nausi* 124
Needham, R. 108
neg 2, 14, 35, 129, 136, 144–5, 149–50, 153, 157, 168, 173n
nikah 135
nota 129, 142, 170n
Nuer 84, 103

paink 32
pakka 2, 20, 22, 24, 34n, 125, 149
pal 80–2, 84–5, 88–9, 91, 93–5, 97–103, 110–11, 113, 115, 122n, 177–9
pallakra 80–1, 84
panchayat 24, 90–1, 97–8, 100–1, 143–5
Parry, J. 23, 33n, 76n, 122n–123n, 147, 172n
paternal aunt 115–16, 124, 127, 135, 141, 143–4, 146, 154, 157, 160–1, 163–4, 169n, 171n, 174n, 182–3, 188

Pathan 18, 27
Pauwels, S. 174n
pir 34n
Pocock, D. 23
Pouillon, J. 30
power relations 23, 78n, 100, 152, 185
purity, impurity 22, 24, 33, 34n–35n, 127, 149, 150, 173n
purohit 25, 33n, 175n

Rajput 1, 14–15, 18, 23, 25–7, 33, 81, 87, 103n, 168, 177–8
rath 134, 137
Reiniche, M.L. 24, 26, 34n–35n, 176n
Rif (Moroccan) 1, 10, 15
roza 28

sacrifice, sacrifier, sacrificer 26, 35, 150, 164, 171n, 175n–176n, 179–80
sadhi 17
sagāī 124–5, 143–6, 171n
sahvasani 124, 126–7, 136, 139–40, 145–6, 148–51, 160–1, 164–6, 169, 171n, 174n
*saiya*d, *see kazi*
sakka 20, 143
salam 129, 132–3, 137, 140, 142, 144, 195
samdhi pūjā 136, 144–5, 157, 159–60, 174n
samskara 175n
savani 17
Scheffler, H.W. 75n–76n, 79n
Schneider, D. 79
sehrā 126–7, 169n, 170n
Sharma, S.L. 80–1
sheikh 17
sonar 18, 20
status 18, 20, 22–3, 25–6, 33, 34n–35n, 37n, 49, 51, 55–6, 73, 75n, 78n, 82, 84, 86, 90, 99, 103n, 108, 114, 118, 123, 127, 150, 152–3, 155, 157, 160, 165–8, 169n, 178–80, 185, 187n–188n
śuddhi 36n
śudra 33n

Tablighi Jama'at 28–30, 33, 36n
tajīā 32, 90
talwar 127, 183
tevar 178
thakar 34n, 82, 84
thamba 85–9, 91, 93–101, 104n–105n, 179
tharu 88, 90, 92
thok or *mohalla* 90, 93
tokri-ka-neg 136, 144–5, 157, 173n

umma 28

uncī jati 18
unilineal descent group 13–14, 115, 161, 172n, 186

vaishiya 32
vamsh 27, 177
varna 18, 23, 26, 33n
Vatuk, S. 38–41, 51, 61, 74n, 76n, 78n

yajamān 26
yajña 175n